THE ANALYTIC EXPERIENCE

THE
ANALYTIC
EXPERIENCE

NEVILLE SYMINGTON

ST. MARTIN'S PRESS
New York

First published in the United States of America in 1986

Printed in Great Britain

Library of Congress Cataloging-in-Publication Data

Symington, Neville.
  The analytic experience.
  Based on lectures delivered at the Tavistock
  Clinic, London, England.
  Bibliography: p.
  Includes index.
  1. Psychoanalysis.   I. Title.
BF173.S886   1986   150.19'5   86-15533

ISBN 0-312-03288-9

For Joan

Who gave me Encouragement

CONTENTS

ACKNOWLEDGEMENTS

This book was forged between myself and successive audiences at the Tavistock Clinic. It is to them that I owe the existence of this book. They questioned me, they challenged me and demonstrated their appreciation so, from one year to the next, the lectures improved. I have to thank the committee in charge of inter-departmental studies for first inviting me to give these lectures and in particular Dr John Padel who showed enough confidence in my abilities to recommend that I take his place and give the lectures when he retired. I have to thank Peter Hildebrand and all the psychologists of the Adult Department at the Tavistock who, in my last year of lecturing, gave me two sessions a week to devote to writing up the lectures in a form suitable for publication. They agreed to this when they were under considerable pressure and my withdrawal from supervising and administrative work meant that even more fell on the shoulders of others. I would also like to thank the trainees who instantly agreed to my request despite the fact that they knew they would be deprived of even more senior staff time. I would also like to thank numerous colleagues at the Tavistock who helped me to formulate clinical and theoretical matters more precisely through their willingness to discuss issues with which I was having diffficulty. I would also like to thank Beattie

Gellert who looked up references and had lectures and papers photocopied for me at lightning speed. It was very heartening to find such a weight of support on all sides.

I would like to thank Bob Young of Free Association Books, without whose enthusiasm this book would never have been born, and also Karl Figlio for reading the manuscript and drawing my attention to passages which were obscure. In particular I would like to thank Ann Scott, who did weeks of hard, painstaking editorial work to turn the original manuscript, a savage beast, into a more civilized creature.

Last but not least I should like to thank my family who willingly suffered an absence when my emotional attention was being enticed away both by the demands of the lectures and then the book.

PREFACE

Psychoanalysis is an experience that occurs between two people. It is a deep experience and can only be very inadequately communicated to another person. It is as impossible to convey the sense of it to another person as it is to explain to an eight-year-old child what it is like to be in love. However, much of the world's literature is a record of the attempts to express the experience of being in love with all its attendant joys and agonies. The state of being in love cannot be described with mathematical accuracy in the way an architect can precisely describe a building through an ordered set of drawings. The author uses imagery and analogy that spark off an emotional sense in the reader who has had some cognate experience. He can lead his reader into that arena of feelings provided that the latter has made a similar journey.

When I was asked by the Dean of Studies at the Tavistock Clinic in London if I would undertake a series of lectures entitled 'Psychoanalytic Theory', to be given to all those professionals working in mental health seconded to the Tavistock for in-service training, I was faced with something of a problem. The theories within psychoanalytic discourse have as much relation to psychoanalysis as a manual of sexual techniques has to the emotion of being in love. So I decided that I would try to convey the *atmosphere* of the analytic experience. I managed to achieve this, though of course imperfectly. I did so principally by trying to give the audience some glimpse into what was happening inside me, and also by the tone in which I spoke to my audience. The audience was on the whole pleased with these lectures and felt they had learned a lot from them. Several members of the audience asked if they could have transcripts. It was because a growing number of people began to demand that these lectures be transferred to the printed page that I decided to seek their publication. I cannot say whether the reader will feel as satisfied with the result as my audience at the Tavistock seemed to be but I made a decision to leave the lectures as they were given, notwithstanding very considerable editorial work.

So the central aim of this book is to impart some flavour of the analytic experience. The subject matter considered here is less important than the way it is treated. In fact the topics are less important than the areas of experience which become illuminated through their discussion. It is for this reason that subjects that a reader might expect to find in a book about psychoanalysis are hardly mentioned at all, such as the different theories of anxiety, Freud's theory of symptom formation, or the work of Anna Freud and the ego psychologists. For many years I have believed in Thomas Aquinas' intuition that too much information blocks the act of understanding. I would personally feel very satisfied if, from reading this book, the reader came away with just one new emotional insight; so, following Aquinas, I have been sparing on information. If the reader had been hoping that he would learn all that Freud had to say on dreams, or find a comprehensive survey of Fairbairn's, Klein's or Balint's views, he will come away disappointed. I have described their views only in so far as I have felt it necessary to convey some particular aspect of analytic experience. The same applies to the lectures on Freud's early contemporaries. It is also clear therefore that this account is exceedingly personal.

As I say, I have treated only those aspects of theory or technique which have a personal resonance for me. This does not mean that I have tried to transmit only certain aspects of the analytic experience. My intention has been the exact opposite. The upheavals of subjectivity that occur in psychoanalysis are deep and pervasive, but extremely difficult to describe. Therefore what I have tried to do is to come at the matter from one angle and then another, and hope that the reader may catch a glimpse of the extraordinary occurrences that go on in the analytic process.

Throughout the book, I am talking of a single reality but coming at it from different perspectives. This is the Hebrew rather than the Greek way of treating a human phenomenon. The Hebrew way is to go round and round a subject, each time using different images to illuminate what is most profound. The Greek way of arguing by logical stages can never, in my opinion, do justice to any deep human experience. My intention throughout has been to convey the spirit and not the letter of the psychoanalytic process, and therefore the reader will find contradictions. I can only hope that these will not so irritate the reader that he or she will abandon the book altogether.

The method of the book is idiosyncratic because there is no doubt that the psychoanalytic process occurs within an interpersonal interaction, and in the absence of the latter there is substituted an empty ritual. This book is therefore an expression of the author's own understanding of psychoanalysis as an emotional, interpersonal relationship. I hope the reader will check at various points his understanding with my own. One's own self-understanding is enormously enhanced by coming up against the personal understanding of another. It is my hope that at the end of an analysis the patient will get a clear enough silhouette of his or her analyst to be able to separate out his or her own experience. Only in this way will the patient's own individual subjective development be fostered. I hope that the reader may have a similar, though necessarily less intense experience.

This series of lectures is the record of the seventh year that I gave them. Each year they changed considerably and, if there had been an eighth year, they would have been different from what is here. If I had waited another year then perhaps there would have been a better book but, on the other hand, there might not have been one at all so I decided to publish the lectures as they stand.

There is a growing disenchantment with theory which I share. I hope that something of the analytic experience instead will be taken away by the reader. This is the book's purpose.

Neville Symington
November 1985

SETTING
THE SCENE

I PSYCHOANALYSIS: A SERVANT OF TRUTH

'Upon my word, I think the
truth is the hardest missile
one can be pelted with.'

George Eliot, *Middlemarch*

There is an inherent contradiction in this series of lectures. Psychoanalysis cannot be taught. I can tell you about Freud, who was the first psychoanalyst and who gave us its name. I can tell you about the topographical model of the mind, the concepts of resistance, repression or transference. I can tell you what is meant by the pleasure principle or the death instinct, but you will not be an inch nearer knowing what psychoanalysis *is*. Psychoanalysis is a phenomenon which occurs at the centre of the individual. So when I say you cannot be taught psychoanalysis it is because it can occur only through a personal act of understanding.

Psychoanalysis is not a thing; it is a complex reality which is both intrapsychic and interpersonal, both individual and social. I can try to describe it, I can lead you to it, but you have to experience the reality of it. It occurs at the centre of your personality which is the source of all our actions and also the locus of all that happens to us. Patient and analyst can come together five times a week, forty-two weeks a year for one year, two years, three years or fifteen years. As people pass the door of the consulting-room they whisper 'Hush' in anguished tones: on the door a notice announces 'Analysis in progress'. Do not for a moment be deceived: this is no guarantee that there is any analysis going on. How can it be since analysis is an act at the centre of your being? I do not mean that it stays at the centre, that it does not reverberate, that others will not perceive it. Of course this will happen. However, the word psychoanalysis is unfortunately usually taken to mean the formal ritual procedure of visiting someone called an analyst five days a week, forty-two weeks a year, and I shall not be discussing psychoanalysis again in this sense.

Psychoanalysis has two other senses, and these will concern us for the rest of the series. One refers to the external ritual, but now accompanied by the internal activities and passivities at the centre that I have already mentioned. The two are interlocked to form a single reality, which is what I mean by psychoanalysis. Psychoanalysis in this sense often does take a very long time, but eventually the procedure comes to an end, ideally by mutual agreement. However, the day that the analysis finishes is the day that psychoanalysis in my third sense starts. Those activities and passivities at the centre of the individual's being now continue without the formal ritual. This is the really long analysis because it lasts, or can last, until you die. In these lectures I shall call the purely internal process self-analysis. I regard it as the goal of all we do and will devote much attention to it; I see psychoanalysis as the agent which helps self-analysis to occur.

Psychoanalysis is a method of investigating the unconscious mind, and its particular focus is on the inner world. There are other ways of understanding the individual's manifest or *external* behaviour. A sociologist would account for it in terms of the social system of which the individual is a part. An economist would understand it in terms of the economic structure in which the person is situated. A theologian would stress the person's values, ideals and so on. The psychoanalyst attempts to understand manifest behaviour and communications, too, but in terms of the individual's inner conflicts and phantasies. Yet psychoanalysis does not have possession of the whole truth, so now let me dwell a little on the nature of truth.

Truth is real; it exists. Positivistic thinking has had such a strong influence on our basic assumptions that we tend to identify the real with what we can touch, taste, feel, see or hear. We need to ditch this preconception if we are to think psychologically. Most psychological realities do not have the property of extension or tangibility: a dream, a hallucination, a belief, a thought, a relationship, love, hatred or desire. But it is not true that these realities exist in some non-material sphere *only*. They are inextricably linked with the physical – this is so even of a thought. Truth is a reality of this nature. It cannot be measured but it does exist; the fact that it is difficult to define does not detract from this. Truth does not exist though as some eternal idea, as Plato thought, but as a reality that exists *in between*: in between two persons seeking it, in between psychoanalysis, sociology, psychology, economics and religion. It will not be possessed by any one person or group. Someone who proclaims 'I *have* the truth' has lost it. For truth can be seen or glimpsed, not possessed. When I see the truth some change occurs in me. I can never be the same again. Something in my personality has altered; a previous preconception gives way to truth, but it is in the very nature of truth that each glimpse only emphasizes the degree to which truth still lies outside or beyond. This means that the individual is always in relation to truth and is in a state of *potentia*. By *potentia* I mean a state of *movement towards*.

I said that the state before the truth is glimpsed is one where a preconception exists, and I will give you a clinical example of this. For some time I had been treating a man whose elder brother had been killed in an accident when my patient was aged three. There was initially enormous denial of my importance to him. He used to say at the beginning of the therapy that it was nice 'to pop in for a chat' every week, yet when I went away on holiday he collapsed. Now he had reached a stage where he recognized that what I did or did not do had a great effect on him. On one occasion his train was delayed so badly that he rang from the station and told my secretary that he would not be coming. He had tried to get through to me but I had wandered out of my room and was chatting to someone.

I thought he was probably angry at not getting through to me on the telephone, and also that he would deny his anger about it. This was the preconception in my mind when he came for his session the following week. When he started by saying that he had felt like not coming that morning my preconception ground into action and I said, 'Perhaps because you were angry that I was not in my room when you telephoned last week.' 'No, I felt quite all right once I had got through to your secretary.' Now, I momentarily thought this was a denial; then I pondered and puzzled, wondering why on earth he was relieved once he had got through to my secretary. Then the truth struck me, 'Ah, of course, he was relieved that I was not dead.' I communicated this to him and he immediately assented. We both realized how great was his anxiety that I would suffer the fate of his elder brother. My preconception gave way in the face of the truth, and a new understanding took its place.

What had occurred to me intrapsychically at that moment of truth? My preconception was based on some understanding of my own past combined with an analytic theory about anxiety. All this was in that part of my personality which categorizes, forms theories and gives an orientation to my way of thinking and acting. At the moment of truth *I* glimpsed something new. A minute later this had been categorized and became part of my habitual way of thinking. Two minutes later the truth would be a different one and I would have to be ready to abandon that preconception.

From my description so far I know it may sound as if truth is grasped in a moment of insight within the individual. Yet I am actually saying that truth is grasped in dialogue with another or others: it emerges *in between*. It may seem as if an intellectual truth may be grasped just by the individual in relation to data of the physical universe: even here the truth arises between the thinker and the data, and has the effect of reconfiguring the data in the thinker's mind. This new schema orientates the thinker to his world afterwards. Although this kind of intellectual truth can occur without a dialogue with another person, the thinker is still inwardly in dialogue with his own teachers, the masters of his own science, and it is these which form his preconceptions.

Truth in psychoanalysis emerges between the analyst and the patient, and in the moment of understanding there is a change in both. The glimpse of truth demands that a preconception is abandoned in both, for both have come to the encounter with their own preconceptions. Apart from his own personal ones the analyst has his psychoanalytic ones: these are his theories, and it is these that I shall be telling you about in the course of these lectures. The paradox is that these theories have, by their very nature, to be abandoned, just as the emerging butterfly has to relinquish its chrysalis if it is to take flight. The patient also comes with preconceptions, which may be closer to or more distant from the truth than the analyst's theories. But we should not assume that the analyst's preconceptions are closer to the truth, especially as our concern is to find out the truth about this patient – what the world is for him or her.

Research into language has revealed the extent to which a person's world is structured by his or her language. The analyst's task is largely to see the world as the patient does – to understand *his* world, why this patient is frightened of spiders, why this man cannot form relationships, why this woman cannot concentrate for her exams. The moment of understanding occurs in both – it cannot occur in just one. You may contradict this, and say that the analyst may understand, but needs to couch his interpretation more sensitively so that the patient understands. If that is the case then I would still say that the analyst has understood only when he realizes that he *needs* to be more sensitive.

I will give you an example of what I mean. I was treating a highly sensitive woman who had never managed to engage sexually with a man of her own age group. She was talking one day about a new boyfriend but complaining about him that he just sat most of the time: she had to do all the talking, he never told her about himself, and when she displayed sexual feelings towards him he did not respond. I interpreted that she was talking about her frustrations with me; she flew into a panic. I think she *was* talking of her frustrations with me, but the point was that I had not understood her. When I later said to her that she did not feel safe enough with me to discuss how she felt about me, she acknowledged this to be true. I was then able to say that I thought some of the feelings she was expressing about her boyfriend were feelings she could not express about me because she did not feel safe to do so. She was also able to acknowledge this. I was then able to point out to her how even the thought of expressing her feelings about me *to* me caused her extreme anxiety. What I now understood was something different from what I thought I understood in my first interpretation, indeed the truth we arrived at was a very simple one. A central difficulty in her life was an inability to say directly to people what she felt; it was not that she could not show her sexual feelings. My experience is that most of the truths arrived at in psychoanalysis are simple, in this sense, yet paradoxically the simplest truths are also the deepest.

I want now to come back to the point that the truth exists between the analyst and the patient, and is arrived at by mutual discovery. A patient may come for analysis with the idea that I have the truth, and if he is nice enough to me I will impart it to him. When this does not occur the patient may begin to feel I am being perverse. If he stays long enough he may give up that preconception and come to some idea that the truth lies between us, and that this strange psychoanalytic process edges bit by bit towards it. I will give you an example of what I mean from an experience I had with a patient who frequently rebuked me for not 'moving', and complained that she could not move until I moved first. At other times she complained that I needed to change my approach; she felt that I was deliberately withholding responses in order to control her. I was really in a bemused daze with her: I frequently did not know what she was talking about or alluding to, and I found myself annoyed that she blamed me for deliberately not helping her.

At the same time I was having certain experiences – internal changes of feeling – connected with her. For instance, early on in her analysis I had been linking together the hallucinated elements as best I could, and therefore weaving together with her some kind of integrated pattern that was the product of our joint activity. Then one day I had a strong feeling – one of the 'internal changes' – that I did not want to go on with this; so I made an interpretation about her desire that I link these discrete elements. Each of these inner experiences of mine led to a different interpretative schema and a change in the direction of the analysis.

Later on in the analysis, the patient would often say that she could not change until I changed my approach first. For ages I did not understand what she meant, thinking for the most part that she wanted me to change my technical approach towards her. Then suddenly it hit me that she was saying she could not change until I had changed inwardly first, and that she had perceived these inner changes. Nevertheless she had the illusion that I could turn them on at will. So I said that she seemed to think I had the power to effect these changes within me; she retorted hastily that the power certainly did not lie in her. I pointed out that she seemed to think that if the power of change did not lie in me, and did not lie in her, then it did not exist at all. Of course, the power of change lay in a process that existed between us and incorporated us, and yet was not within our control.

This process, which we call psychoanalysis, does have access to truth in one of its forms, but which? To answer this we need to consider the question of psychological development for a moment.

The most basic truth about psychological development is that it does not necessarily accompany anatomical development: for various reasons it gets held up or arrested in one of its aspects, while anatomical development continues. Actually it would be wrong to suppose that anatomical development remains the same, as if the psyche ran along some parallel track but never met up with the anatomical happenings, for a psychological stoppage usually manifests itself in the somatic sphere. (This is most obviously the case with impotence, for example.) Nevertheless, however much someone may be in a state of psychological arrest, bodily development will continue. A person will grow old even if he or she does not mature emotionally, and Freud called those blocks to psychological development 'fixations'. Psychoanalysis does address itself to an understanding of this process, but to put it this way makes psychoanalysis out to be more cognitive than in fact it is. I will elaborate on this point in the next lecture.

The sphere of psychoanalysis is not quite coterminous with the sphere of psychological development. Its focus is on those factors which have impeded the psychological process of development, and therefore it tends to be oriented towards pathology. Yet to understand pathology it is necessary to have a notion of psychological health, and it is here that we again see the place of truth, for psychological health is insured through the person's individual relationship to truth. The truth of my or your failure to develop psychologically is the sphere with which psychoanalysis is concerned.

Psychoanalysis, as I have said, is a method of investigating the truth. It is not necessarily the case that the same truths cannot be arrived at in other ways, but psychoanalysis comes to the fore when insightful understanding has broken down. Insightful understanding is necessary for our passage through life –

there may even be disasters in our lives if we lack it – and people come to psychoanalysis when there is some awareness, however dim, that it is defective. On one occasion, for instance, I had a patient in analysis whose father managed a small hotel outside London. He came back after a weekend visit to his father, very surprised that his father had had the insight that it was better to write off a bad debt early rather than pursue it relentlessly year in year out: 'He had this insight and has never had analysis', he said. He went on to point out other ways in which his father had come to develop a philosophy of life via insightful understanding – all this without analysis. I made the observation that it seemed a somewhat shocking truth that it was those people who lacked this capacity who found their way to the analyst's couch. Psychoanalysis does not have the truth, but rather tries to repair the capacity to arrive at truth.

Also rather shocking is the fact that the truths which we arrive at in psychoanalysis are frequently quite straightforward ones, a point which I made earlier. Let me give you some examples. It was only after three years of analysis that it became clear to a male patient that he had no sympathetic understanding at all of the values that are important to a woman. This blindness caused him and others considerable suffering. An intelligent woman did not know what she really felt when she read the latest academic book on a subject. She would therefore read all the reviews by the critics and make a good synthesis of all that was said, but felt an aching pain that she did not know what she herself felt. A musician played the violin beautifully but had no perception of this, with the result that he did a boring office job instead of joining an orchestra. When he finally did the latter he felt fulfilled through the whole breadth of his life, including his marriage. In all these cases these truths about themselves were hidden, yet in each case when the patient and I arrived at these understandings they told me – each in a different way – that these had been told them before.

The points I am making are very obvious, but I have become

convinced over the last two or three years that they are worth making. I am struck by the fact that so many of us share an illusion that we possess the truth. But the truth lies in between the analyst and the patient, between the Kleinian and Classical Freudian, between Freudian and Jungian, between psychoanalysis and sociology. That which is in-between can never be possessed. If we remember that psychoanalysis is a servant of the truth, we rub shoulders closely with all those who seek truth in other disciplines and walks of life.

2   INSIGHT AND EMOTION IN PSYCHOANALYSIS

The analytic process incorporates change as a conscious goal. Patients leave behind aspects of themselves and achieve new ones; they integrate aspects of themselves which were disowned, relations between the internal structures alter in their balance. We hope that the patient changes for the better, though Freud, in order to caution some of his over-enthusiastic disciples, used to have two photographs on his desk. One was of a patient before he started his analysis and the other of the patient after it was over. In the former the patient looked well, hopeful and healthy and in the latter dejected, depressed and beaten by life. In this lecture I want to address myself to the task of understanding *how* change occurs. I want to start with a little parody, but I think it contains an uncomfortable measure of truth.

> *Enquirer:* Could you tell me how psychoanalysis works?
> *Analyst:* Well you see it's like this, well, er, the patient freely associates, that is, he says whatever is in his mind and then the analyst gives an interpretation. . .
> *Enquirer:* Yes, what then?
> *Analyst:* Well, the patient sees the truth of the interpretation. Of course it might be quite a shock to the patient so he goes away with it and works at it. . .

Enquirer: Yes?

Analyst: Well, then the patient slowly changes as he realizes the truth of what the analyst has said and allows it to 'work through'. . . .

Enquirer: What does that mean?

Analyst: Well, it takes time for a new truth to permeate the whole personality. The period between the initial insight and the acceptance of it throughout the whole personality we call the period of 'working through'. It works its way through the system. What has been received in the intellect is slowly fed through into the feelings and emotions.

Enquirer: Is there any difference between counselling and psychoanalysis, because what you have just described seems to fit counselling just as well?

Analyst: Well, in psychoanalysis the patient comes five times a week and the whole process becomes deeper and more intense.

Enquirer: Oh, I see.

Now this sort of explanation is defective on several counts. It is a case of culture-lag. It presupposes that the rational-intellectual part of man rules the rest, a philosophical inheritance from Plato and Aristotle which really reigned supreme until the last century. Darwin made us uncomfortably aware of the degree to which we share our life force with the animals, and Freud exposed the extent to which we are ruled by the irrational. Yet paradoxically, for it was 'the analyst' speaking, the Freudian understanding has not permeated our philosophical anthropology.

This type of explanation also gives too much weight to the act of insight, and assumes that change originates from that act. But if so, then it is not immediately clear why, for instance, change could not occur just as well through reading a book, coupled with introspection. After all we all gain enormous insight through reading. Although insight is an integral part of psychoanalysis I believe it is a misconception to view it as the foremost agent of change, as Hanna Segal seems to do:

> Insight is a precondition of any lasting personality change achieved in the analysis and all other factors are related to it. I mean here specifically psychoanalytic insight, that is: the acquiring of knowledge about one's own unconscious through experiencing consciously, and, in most cases, being able to acknowledge explicitly and verbally, previously unconscious processes. To be of therapeutic value, it must be correct and it must be deep enough. It must reach to the deep layers of the unconscious and illuminate those early processes in which the pattern of internal and external relationships is laid down and in which the ego is structured. The deeper the layers of the unconscious reached, the richer and the more stable will be the therapeutic result. (1962, p. 70)

Change starts from insight (received at the conscious level) and works its way down to the deepest layers of the personality. As I have already implied, this view is rooted in the Greek philosophical tradition, rather than in Freud's revolutionary notion that we are governed by irrational forces.

The other danger of Segal's position is that it places the centre of truth in the analyst who gives the interpretation. Yes, insight can be arrived at jointly, but the danger of a one-sided situation occurring is greater when the explanatory schema of change is weighted in favour of an intellectual cause; or where insight is placed at the head of a hierarchy of causes. The further danger of arrogance and omnipotence on the analyst's part is not far off once this form of explanation of change is accepted unchallenged. Too much that is also of crucial importance is left out.

I want now to approach this subject from a different angle. In the psychoanalytic endeavour two people meet: a meeting between two people can generate an enormous explosion of emo-

tion with lasting effects. Let me quote a passage from Bertrand
Russell's autobiography in which Russell describes his first
meeting with the novelist Joseph Conrad:

> An event of importance to me in 1913 was the beginning of
> my friendship with Joseph Conrad, which I owed to our
> common friendship with Ottoline [Morrell]. I had been for
> many years an admirer of his books, but should not have
> ventured to seek acquaintance without an introduction. I
> travelled down to his house near Ashford in Kent in a state of
> somewhat anxious expectation. My first impression was one
> of surprise. He spoke English with a very strong foreign
> accent, and nothing in his demeanour in any way suggested
> the sea. He was an aristocratic Polish gentleman to his
> fingertips. His feeling for the sea, and for England, was one
> of romantic love – love from a certain distance, sufficient to
> leave the romance untarnished. His love for the sea began at
> a very early age. When he told his parents that he wished for
> a career as a sailor, they urged him to go into the Austrian
> navy, but he wanted adventure and tropical seas and strange
> rivers surrounded by dark forests; and the Austrian navy
> offered him no scope for these desires. His family were hor-
> rified at his seeking a career in the English merchant marine,
> but his determination was inflexible.
>
> He was, as anyone may see from his books, a very rigid
> moralist and by no means politically sympathetic with
> revolutionaries. He and I were in most of our opinions by no
> means in agreement, but in something very fundamental we
> were extraordinarily at one.
>
> My relation to Joseph Conrad was unlike any other that I
> have ever had. I saw him seldom, and not over a long period
> of years. In the out-works of our lives, we were almost
> strangers, but we shared a certain outlook on human life and
> human destiny, which, from the very first, made a bond of
> extreme strength . . .

At our very first meeting, we talked with continually increasing intimacy. We seemed to sink through layer after layer of what was superficial, till gradually both reached the central fire. We looked into each other's eyes, half appalled and half intoxicated to find ourselves in such a region. The emotion was as intense as passionate love, and at the same time all-embracing. I came away bewildered, and hardly able to find my way among ordinary affairs. (1967, pp. 207-209)

This is a particularly moving description of what an encounter between two human beings can be. The passage clearly stresses the ecstasy and union between the two men. It affected Russell for the rest of his life, and led him to call his first son Conrad. It does not speak of the pain, distress, hatred, rage and disappointment that also occur in most human encounters of any depth, but it is not this that I want to draw your attention to. I want rather to stress the emotional turbulence that is aroused by such an encounter. Dr Bion drew attention to this at the beginning of his last public lecture to the British Psycho-Analytical Society:

When two characters or personalities meet, an emotional storm is created. If they make a sufficient contact to be aware of each other, or even sufficient to be unaware of each other, an emotional state is produced by the conjunction of these two individuals, these two personalities, and the resulting disturbance is hardly likely to be something which could be regarded as necessarily an improvement on the state of affairs had they never met at all. (Bion, 1979)

John Klauber also stressed the intense anxiety that is caused by the beginning of an analysis:

Psychoanalysis has both traumatic and therapeutic elements. The clearest indication of its traumatic quality lies in the fact that it regularly induces a flight from reality. This is the most dramatic feature of analysis, and we describe it as the development of transference. It is due to the disruption of the stimulus barrier against the unconscious and therefore accords well with Freud's definition of trauma (1926) in 'Inhibitions, Symptoms and Anxiety' as an experience of helplessness of the ego in the face of accumulation of excitation whether of external or internal origin. I am sure that many psychoanalysts remember the experience of their ego being partially put out of action quite vividly from their own analysis. The traumatic power of analysis may be inferred from the patient's attempts to defend himself against the transference by projecting it into the outside world and trying to solve it there. A not infrequent example is by starting a sexual relationship at the beginning of analysis which may end as marriage as a defence against ending the analysis – that is, against the full power of the transference at all stages. (1979, p. 112)

Therefore the emotional upheaval of the very first encounter changes the two participants, who will never be the same people again. I also believe that a new entity is forged; a new reality emerges. The two people do not remain independent entities. A joint existence which was not there before, a corporate reality, appears. In the psychoanalytic process this is the first change that occurs, and we might ask why it is that such a change takes place. In the analytic encounter I think that whenever two people meet there is an instant fusing so that a new being emerges. This fusion does not take place at the centre of the personality but around the edges: a true self, to use Winnicott's phrase, remains untouched but the object part of the psychic entity becomes fused with that of the other person. Large parts of the analyst's personality are sucked into the personality of the patient and vice versa.

I am aware that my way of looking at the situation is rather different from the picture of the detached analyst who observes his patient and on to whom the patient projects his archaic images. This latter view suggests that the transference takes place despite what the analyst does or who the analyst is; yet Freud himself says that at the beginning of treatment the analyst needs to allow the transference to develop (1913a, *se* 12, p. 139). If you will provisionally accept my notion that transference is the process whereby the analyst is sucked into the patient's outer personality structure, then Freud is recommending that the analyst allows this process to occur. The countertransference too is a similar process; the analyst allows the patient to be sucked into his outer personality structure. If this were not the case the feelings which an analyst experiences – which is what, among other things, we call countertransference – would not occur. This statement may need some further justification.

Here I am following a position taken by the philosopher Martin Heidegger, the psychologist Maurice Merleau-Ponty, and by those who have followed their existentialist line of approach. They all want to repair the damage which has been done to Western thinking by the dichotomy which Descartes codified and made characteristic of European attitudes to human knowledge of the world. Descartes cut man off from his surrounding environment so that man only had certain knowledge of his inner world. Hence his famous dictum 'I think therefore I am', but underlying this is the conviction that thinking is an entirely inner activity capable of being divorced from the so-called 'outer world'. Descartes put a great cleavage between man and the outside world so that it began to sound quite normal to talk of an inner world and an outer one. These two worlds were quite separate from one another – so much so, Descartes said, that it is not possible to know this outer world or even know whether it existed at all. (His argument for the existence of a world outside is that God would not deceive us into thinking that there was an outside world if there weren't.) Kant subsequently addressed himself to the problem of proving

that we have real knowledge of the world outside, but it still
meant that he accepted the underlying Cartesian assumption:
that there is a divorce between man and the world. This split is
so deeply rooted in Western thought that it pervades all our
thinking.

The existentialist endeavour has been to repair this split. Man
and the world are not two separate entities but a single reality,
man-in-the-world. Therefore the question of how man is to get
across the gulf between inner knowing and the outer world
does not arise because it is based upon a false assumption. In
addition the existentialists do not accept the split between the
cognitive and the sphere of sensation. Man is part of the world
and knows it through his senses, in his feelings and in his acts of
judgement. The faculty for awareness of this state of being in
the world resides in man in a special way: he is not bounded by
the bodily contours that a tailor would need to take note of. (A
captive trying to escape from a prisoner-of-war camp would
need to remember that the sentry's awareness is much wider
than that which is available to him by touch.) The whole world
that is within his field of vision and his hearing is within the
man, and the man is within that world.

The idea that what is outside his physical skin is psychically
outside is quite false. The act of knowledge, even more than the
visual or the auditory act, is a psychic registration of an interaction between the subject and the environment that has already
occurred. It is an inner co-ordination which registers the man-
in-the-world, the totality; not the so-called outer world alone;
or the inner instincts, stimuli, wishes or desires alone.

I want now to return to where I was when I said that analyst
and patient are sucked into each other's worlds. When two
people meet there is a new world-being. This is because the
other person is not just an object like a stone, a plant or an animal, but because the knowingness of one is in the world of the
other's knowingness. This allows a special knowledge between
human beings. But the creation of a new world to be known

occurs first, and first there is a stage of upheaval, which I described at the beginning. Although this occurs in any human encounter, something is added in the analytic encounter: the *threat* in the analyst's knowing and understanding, which human beings defend against. So a double activity gets into operation: on the one hand the thrust to reveal, and the reverse, the urge to conceal.

In the analytic situation, then, we have a state of turbulence indicative of a new system. Now to be in a state of chaos with not a clue as to what is going on is disturbing in the extreme; therefore both participants attempt to understand the situation. The analyst has usually been through the situation several times; even the trainee analyst with his first training case has undergone the experience himself or herself as patient, and has also read papers and listened to discussions and case presentations, and so has a body of experience. The patient, on the other hand, is usually experiencing the situation for the first time. However, since the focus of the endeavour is on the patient's world, he has the great advantage that it is his and that he knows it rather well. If there is then a moment of real understanding it is a great joy to both, although it may of course also be very painful. These moments of insight are unique to a particular system: this patient and this analyst. Quite how these occur is obscure but we can try to approach some avenues that lead in the right direction by drawing some basic distinctions.

I divide interpretations up into three classes: expressions of insight, of a unique moment of understanding; guesses necessary to keep the conversation going or moving in the right direction; and interpretations that have partial understanding, and are midway between an insight and a guess interpretation. My experience is that in an analysis creative moments of individual understanding are rather rare. When such moments do occur they cause a therapeutic shift, but a welter of preparatory work has to occur first. Also the analyst cannot just sit in silence session after session: he has to keep the conversation going but at the same time try not to say anything that will block the moment of insight from occurring.

I remember a case that might illustrate the point. When I was more of a novice than I am now, a girl was referred to me whom I saw three times a week. She came absolutely regularly, but I had no idea why she came. For quite some time I tried interpretations of all kinds but they were no good at all; I gave up 'making interpretations' and instead followed the themes, making comments from time to time. After two years the thought occurred to me that it was important to her to know that I existed. I made this interpretation, she instantly responded, and then other interpretations became possible. Now in those two years I think it was important that I gave up 'making interpretations' but just kept the conversation going with reasonably civil and innocuous comments, particularly since that girl did not take kindly to guesses.

Guesses are made when the analyst's state of mind is one of not being sure yet feeling that some expression of effort is probably required. I experience this quite frequently, and know that it is a quite different state of mind from one where I suddenly 'see' something; I also think that an analysis cannot operate without both. So, not being sure what is being said yet not necessarily being confused – simply lacking inner certainty – I make a guess. I like to think it is an educated guess: one whose origins – its breeding, one might say – are impeccable. It may come from Klein, Winnicott, Balint, Anna Freud or Sigmund Freud; or from my own analyst; or from some principle that I have formulated from past experience. When I make one of these educated guesses I am conscious of my own uncertainty, and I watch the patient's response rather carefully to see whether it is confirmed, denied or qualified in some way.

I want now to turn to some simple examples of insight in analysis. I was treating a borderline patient with obsessional features who told me again and again about her feelings for her quasi-boyfriend, and her extreme anxiety when she had a burst of feeling for another man who appeared on the scene. I tried many 'guess' interpretations, but her behaviour remained unmodified for about two and a half years. My patient was the younger of two daughters and when she was born her mother became very ill; one day I suddenly saw that in her behaviour she was re-enacting her mother's conflict when her mother gave birth to her: an eruption of feeling for the new baby, after which she turned back to her first child. She seemed to have been unable to encompass two children within her love, and became severely asthmatic at the time of my patient's birth. I interpreted this – that is, the idea of her behaviour as a re-enact-ment – to the patient and it clicked immediately; over the fol-lowing weeks it became possible to relate both the experience and her behaviour to the transference. In its acute form her par-ticular anxiety cleared up.

Another example. A patient had told me in the initial inter-view that he needed simple things to be said to him. After sev-eral months of variegated dreams and diverse associations, the thought suddenly struck me that the man was unable to grieve. Grief was simply too painful to bear. I said just this to him and it had a great impact. There was noticeable change in his behaviour.

I would add that the moment of insight often coincides for analyst and patient. A female patient who was extremely aggressive in sessions from time to time saw that this was a defence against loving feelings at the same time as I saw it. A hail-fellow-well-met kind of man, who was liked by everyone and always greeted me cheerily, became aware that he was dis-passionately callous in his love relationships. It was clear to me that at the moment that he was able to see this, the callousness was already less intense. Similarly, a female patient became aware how driven by jealousy she was, just as I sensed intuit-ively that the jealousy was already within manageable propor-tions. I think all analysts frequently meet examples of this pro-cess, and it points to the fact that insight is the *product* of a process and not its cause. Actually I think the truth is that the moment of insight is a product of previous change, and also that change is a product of insight. Emotional change and insight are manifestations of changes going on at a deeper level of the psyche.

I have said that, at the beginning of treatment, there is a great storm and then, some time later, a moment of insight such as I have described occurs (I am leaving on one side those people who manage to make brilliant deep interpretations in the first interview). What has happened between this first upheaval and the moment of insight? I think one obvious point is that insight is accompanied by relative calm: the psychosomatic entity is in a quiescent state. Such is the state of affairs on the surface but how do we hypothesize about the inner happenings? When I start trying to formulate something I always remember the admission interview of a new inmate at a psychiatric prison where I once worked. When asked what he hoped for from his stay at the prison he said,

> Well, it's like this, Doctor, I feel at the moment as if you had taken all the pieces of a jigsaw puzzle and thrown them up in the air and now they are all scattered higgledy-piggledy on the floor. I hope while I am here to start putting some of these pieces together again.

Quite simply, the process of analysis starts off identifying these pieces; which is why Freud uses the term 'analysis': analysing the different elements. Using the jigsaw analogy the first thing to do is to turn all the pieces up the same way so that they can be clearly seen, then group together the blue pieces that seem to be sky, then those that seem to be parts of a house, then those which seem to belong to some type of meadow, and then those that seem to be a river. Freud said that the synthetic process then occurs of its own accord:

> . . . the neurotic patient presents us with a torn mind, divided by resistances. As we analyse it and remove the resis-

tances, it grows together; the great unity which we call his ego fits into itself all the instinctual impulses which before had been split off and held apart from it. The psycho-synthesis is thus achieved during analytic treatment without our intervention, automatically and inevitably. (1919, *SE* 17, p. 161)

I think that turbulence occurs when there is a jostling of the pieces – bits in our psychic structure are being jostled around. Calm occurs as the bits move together. Insight and emotional satisfaction accompany the joining of the pieces. It is not one of those jigsaws with a picture of the final form on the outside of the box, and as several blue pieces of the jigsaw come together it suddenly becomes obvious that the shape is that of a lady's blue dress and not blue sky. At the same time we begin to re-adjust our notions about the picture in general. (I might say in an aside that an important aspect of psychoanalytic technique is that the emotions accompanying synthesis should be carefully tended and nurtured.)

What I have said about an initial turbulence and a synthetic process needs to be joined together with the psychic adjustment that is necessary when someone moves from emotional isola-tion or hostility to intimacy. That emotional intimacy requires a different inner psychic structure from one of emotional dis-tance. It is not that emotional isolation or distance from others is necessarily wrong, but it causes a particular kind of pain within the social structures that are dominant in the twentieth century. However, to examine this would take us too far from the confines of our subject. For the moment, the point that I am trying to stress is that the knowledge that is arrived at in psychoanalysis *through insight* occurs through a new kind of being-in-the-world for analyst and patient together. Our knowledge as analysts is a manifestation of this new mode of being.

3 PSYCHOANALYSIS:
THE SCIENCE
OF MEANING

I want now to introduce the issue of meaning, and the role that it plays in the psychoanalytic process. In a postscript to his paper 'The Question of Lay Analysis' Freud says,

> After forty-one years of medical activity, my self-knowledge tells me that I have never really been a doctor in the proper sense. I became a doctor through being compelled to deviate from my original purpose; and the triumph of my life lies in my having, after a long and roundabout journey, found my way back to my earliest path. I have no knowledge of having had any craving in my early childhood to help suffering humanity. My innate sadistic disposition was not a very strong one, so that I had no need to develop this one of its derivatives. Nor did I ever play the 'doctor game'; my infantile curiosity evidently chose other paths. In my youth I felt an *overpowering need to understand something of the riddles of the world in which we live* and perhaps even to contribute something to their solution. (*SE* 22, p. 253, my italics)

And Ernest Jones says of him:

> When . . . it fell to his lot to treat neurotic patients he soon abandoned the method – customary then and recently

revived in another form – of stimulating them by means of electricity. And it was not long before he gave up the use of hypnosis, which he found a 'coarsely interfering method'. He chose instead to look and listen, confident that *if he could perceive the structure of a neurosis he would truly understand and have power over the forces that had brought it about.* (Jones, 1953, p. 58, my italics)

Freud describes what made him give hypnosis up in his *Autobiographical Study*:

> One day I had an experience which showed me in the crudest light what I had long suspected. It related to one of my most acquiescent patients, with whom hypnotism had enabled me to bring about the most marvellous results, and whom I was engaged in relieving of her suffering by tracing back her attacks of pain to their origins. As she woke up on one occasion, she threw her arms round my neck. The unexpected entrance of a servant relieved us from a painful discussion, but from that time onwards there was a tacit understanding between us that the hypnotic treatment should be discontinued. I was modest enough not to attribute the event to my own irresistible personal attraction, and I felt that *I had now grasped the nature of the mysterious element that was at work behind hypnotism.* In order to exclude it, or at all events to isolate it, it was necessary to abandon hypnotism. (*SE* 20, p. 27, my italics)

His researches now led him into the field of the unconscious and there, at this stage, he found infantile sexuality. It was this, still operative though unconscious, that lay behind the experience described above. Tearing off the veil of hypnotism had opened up a rich field to explore and tabulate. The unconscious itself was not a new descriptive entity; ideas about it had been aired by philosophers and writers for over two hundred years, but it was Freud who explored the laws and principles which governed it. He was therefore concerned to discover meaning.

Meaning is achieved when one isolated phenomenon is located in relation to others and thus brought within the structure of a system, an organization. A patient screams when she sees a mouse, a man marries though he knows his wife despises him and will maltreat him, or a patient has no close friends and yet wants them. Meaning occurs when these discrete events are connected up to other psychical factors in the personality and grasped as a whole. As Freud put it, 'It was discovered one day that the pathological symptoms of certain neurotic patients have a sense. On this discovery the psychoanalytic method of treatment was founded' (*SE* 15, p. 83).

Our adult world is so suffused with meaning that it is very difficult for us to imagine a world where this does not exist, to imagine the primitive state where the world is just a chaos of disconnected sensations. It is a difficult sense to convey, but one of the writers who has perhaps done it best is Kafka in *The Trial*:

His landlady's cook, who always brought him his breakfast at eight o'clock, failed to appear on this occasion. That had never happened before. K. waited for a little while longer, watching from his pillow the old lady opposite, who seemed to be peering at him with a curiosity unusual even for her, but then, feeling both put out and hungry, he rang the bell. At once there was a knock at the door and a man entered whom he had never seen before in the house. He was slim and yet well knit, he wore a closely fitting black suit, which was furnished with all sorts of pleats, pockets, buckles, and buttons, as well as a belt, like a tourist's outfit, and in consequence looked eminently practical, though one could not quite tell what actual purpose it served. 'Who are you?' asked K., half raising himself in bed. But the man ignored the question, as though his appearance needed no explanation, and merely said: 'Did you ring?' 'Anna is to bring me my breakfast,' said K., and then with silent intensity studied the fellow, trying to make out who he could be. The man did not submit to this scrutiny for very long, but turned to the door and opened it slightly so as to report to someone who was evidently standing just behind it: 'He says Anna is to bring him his breakfast.' A short guffaw from the next room came in answer; one could not tell from the sound whether it was produced by several individuals or merely by one. Although the strange man could not have learned anything from it that he did not know already he now said to K., as if passing on a statement: 'It can't be done.' 'This is news indeed,' cried K., springing out of bed and quickly pulling on his trousers. 'I must see what people these are next door, and how Frau Grubach can account to me for such behaviour.' Yet it occurred to him at once that he should not have said this aloud and that by doing so he had in a way admitted the stranger's right to an interest in his actions; still, that did not seem important to him at the moment. The stranger, however, took his words in some such sense, for he asked: 'Hadn't you better stay here?' 'I shall neither stay here nor let you address me until you have introduced yourself.' 'I meant well enough,' said the stranger, and then of his own accord threw the door open. In the next room, which K. entered more slowly than he had intended, everything looked at first glance almost as it had done the evening before. It was Frau Grubach's living-room: perhaps among the furniture, rugs, china, and photographs with which it was crammed there was a little more free space than usual, yet one did not perceive that at first, especially as the main change consisted in the presence of a man who was sitting at the open window reading a book, from which he now glanced up . . . (1927, pp. 7–8)

In fact K. had been arrested but throughout the whole book he never knows why. He lives in a world of no meaning, and cannot make sense of what has occurred.

We cannot imagine what the world is like for a baby, and

should remember that our ideas are always adultomorphic, even though Anna Freud has taught us things, as have Melanie Klein, Piaget, and Winnicott. We know that the infant has an ever changing field of perception in which there is no object constancy, such that when a piece of paper goes out of sight it 'ceases to exist'. An infant has tactile and olfactory sensations but they do not cohere. Memory is not developed enough for recognition of the object to occur. There is no consciousness of being separate from mother. There is no sense of personal agency; things just happen; the infant is bombarded. Now follows a purely imaginary attempt to get inside an infant's perception:

> There's that lovely purple. It came yesterday and those wet sponges sucked it. It hit the wood with a clack-clack-clack. It trembled all over – even down into far away. Those white flesh puddings kicked. Then it went. The front flabbies went towards it but it would not come. It wouldn't make those nice sponges wet. And purple. No tremors. The flabbies waved but no purple. They waved and a huge pain like a tiger eat flesh and water came streaming from those dark-and-lights and the purple, no it's not purple, there's white-and-purple. A huge hole and noise pouring out. A black cave and a booming noise like sea waves smashing rocks. No tremors, no purple, just blank. It is a plastic capsule under the sea, waters beating upon it: just darkness and flashes of light and a murmur . . .

> Mmm – there there; mmm – there. Cave and sea goes away, purple, purple but empty cave and terrible fire. Hard brown rods with yellow and white ball. Ball on rods, ball in flabbies, clacky clacky. Great big spongies touch little spongies, then dark to light, lovely tremors all through flabbies, dark-and-lights and down far cool spring of water. Big hole, spongies full of lovely lovely. All lovely lovely, Mmm-there-there-Mmm. Sweet honey, bouquet of vintage claret.

Pink rods to skin-skin, soft music. A blue summer's day. No noise, no purple, no flabbies. A lovely white cloud, beautiful light . . . burning, burning, just burning. No yellow, no purple, no 'Mmm, there-there', but just burning, burning. Huge crackling flames. Joan of Arc at stake . . .

There-there, Mmm, Mmm – great pink balloon, gulpy gulpy. Oasis and light and smell of jasmine. Strokey, strokey, pink balloon. Lying on cloud of cotton-wool. No darkness, all light . . .

Discrete, chaotic, unlinked elements. I think Samuel Beckett may be trying to convey such an idea in his short play *Not I*, where he is describing an old woman, but my inference is that she is flashing back to a very early experience:

> ... sudden flash... even more awful if possible... that feeling was coming back... imagine... feeling coming back!... starting at the top... then working down... the whole machine... but no... spared that... the mouth alone... so far... ha!... so far... then thinking... oh long after... sudden flash... it can't go on... all this... all that... steady stream... straining to hear... make something of it... and her own thoughts... make something of them... all... what?... the buzzing?... yes... all the time the buzzing... so-called... all that together ... imagine!... whole body like gone... just the mouth... lips... cheeks... jaws... never... what?... tongue?... yes... lips... cheeks... jaws... tongue... never still a second... mouth on fire... stream of words... in her ear... practically in her ear... not catching the half... not the quarter... no idea what she's saying... imagine!... no idea what she's saying!... and can't stop... no stoppping it... (1973, p. 11)

So we have looked at a baby. In *The Future of an Illusion* (1927b) Freud spoke of the same terror in man, with the accent on primitive man, faced with meaningless nature:

No one is under the illusion that nature has already been vanquished; and few dare hope that she will ever be entirely subjected to man. There are the elements, which seem to mock at all human control: the earth, which quakes and is torn apart and buries all human life and its works; water, which deluges and drowns everything in a turmoil; storms, which blow everything before them; there are diseases, which we have only recently recognized as attacks by other organisms; and finally there is the painful riddle of death, against which no medicine has yet been found, nor probably will be. With these forces nature rises up against us, majestic, cruel and inexorable . . . Impersonal forces and destinies cannot be approached; they remain eternally remote. But if the elements have passions that rage as they do in our own souls, if death itself is not something spontaneous but the violent act of an evil Will, if everywhere in nature there are Beings around us of a kind that we know in our own society, then we can breathe freely, can feel at home in the uncanny and can deal by psychical means with our senseless anxiety. (*SE* 21, pp. 15–17)

The world is in bits and we are in bits. The binding of these bits into a coherent whole is the science of meaning. The personality is a mass of bits, and psychoanalysis is concerned with binding them together. The external world as a chaos mirrors the inner abyss. Teilhard de Chardin, the modern religious mystic, has expressed this point poetically:

I took the lamp and, leaving the zone of everyday occupations and relationships where everything seems clear, I went down into my inmost self, to the deep abyss whence I feel dimly that my power of action emanates. But as I moved further and further away from the conventional certainties by which social life is superficially illuminated, I became aware that I was losing contact with myself. At each step of the descent a new person was disclosed within me of whose name I was no longer sure, and who no longer obeyed me.

And when I had to stop my exploration because the path faded from beneath my steps, I found a bottomless abyss at my feet. (1957, pp. 76–77)

Lastly I want to give you some communications from a psychotic patient, a man of forty, subsequent to a psychotic breakdown:

Circles that are blue...a yellow giraffe...and a devil.

You feel encircled by my cold presence and though you would like to stroke me with my yellow tie on yet you hate me.

Bits of carpet...chair leg...a face looking over the door.

You have to play all on your own and I don't come down to your level.

The Boy of Aveyron...a man in pigtails...an empty house.

You feel happy playing, using your hands and smelling and looking and here you have to make the transition to language and although you understand it with your intellect it has no emotional meaning so life is like an empty house. When you come up to my level with language you feel in an emotional abyss.

Interpretations in analysis are concerned with making meaning. Psychoanalysis is a search for meaning, but does it cure?

The reason for my speaking of a chaos of bits is that the human entity appears to be of a single piece but *is* in fact a mass of bits. The psyche is not a unity. Jung has this to say: 'In the psychology of our unconscious there are typical figures that have a definite life of their own. All this is explained by the fact that the so-called unity of consciousness is an illusion. It is really a wish-dream. We like to think that we are one; but we are not, most decidedly not' (1935, pp. 72–73).

What I have described above as the world around all split up, means that the psyche, in its dual nature made up of subject and object, is all split up. The psyche is a reality though not like the material reality of a table, an elephant or a table lamp; Freud speaks of psychic reality. Now all the evidence seems to point to the fact that it is split up and that each bit acts as a little personality of its own. Jung called these psychic personalities 'complexes' and he says: 'Complexes are autonomous groups of associations that have a tendency to move by themselves, to live their own life apart from our intentions. I hold that our personal unconscious, as well as the collective unconscious, consists of an indefinite, because unknown, number of complexes or fragmentary personalities' (1935, p. 73).

So whatever this reality is we know that it is broken up and, under stress, it causes suffering. Sometimes people can get along quite well with contradictions and crazy ideas and irritating symptoms, but sometimes they experience pain in one of its many forms. Then they go to a psychiatrist, a psychoanalyst or perhaps a faith healer or hypnotist.

Nevertheless man wants to feel that he is a unity. He strives for it and usually consciously vigorously defends the notion that he is. He likes to feel of a piece. Contradictions of this notion are visible to others but usually hidden from him, a topic on which Somerset Maugham speaks with enlightenment:

> What has chiefly struck me in human beings is their lack of consistency. I have never seen people all of a piece. It has amazed me that the most incongruous traits should exist in the same person and for all that yield a plausible harmony. I have often asked myself how characteristics, seemingly irreconcilable, can exist in the same person. I have known crooks who were capable of self-sacrifice, sneak-thieves who were sweet-natured, and harlots for whom it was a point of honour to give good value for money. (1938, p. 40)

Now there are two ways in which man can feel a unity. Either he clings to a unified system outside himself or he tries to unite something inside himself. In the first case the disunity within remains, but he protects himself from nameless dread by hanging on to a religion, a political ideology, a cultural value system, or national, tribal or familial traditions. This method can work well in a traditional society or one with a single value system, but given the pluralistic value system of the modern large conurbation it does not work as well, or it is more likely to fail.

The other way is for man to go into himself and forge his many different complexes into a cohesive whole. A person may achieve this without professional help, as Freud and Jung did, and as a certain number of people still do, but he may need to approach a psychoanalyst. In the giving of meaning to the patient's utterances the psychic bits come together, slowly and hesitatingly, and form a cohesive unity. Asking how this comes about produces a complex answer.

Firstly, we can recognize an inner thrust to form a unity, and this is by far the most important element in the psychoanalytic process. I have not yet encountered a patient in whom this process was not already under way, but it needed the help of an analyst to get it unblocked. The process has come up against a resistance and it needs help to overcome it. This is why Freud said that the work of analysis was not the uncovering of memories, but the overcoming of resistances. The analyst meets the resistant personality, the resistant complex, and it is this that makes his job difficult, for to do so requires insight and skill.

Secondly, unity comes about through the analyst's capacity to bear the patient's anxiety. The affect of a disunited personality is anxiety and it is anxiety that keeps the different bits disconnected from each other. Do not ask which causes which: it is a chicken-or-egg dilemma. But we know that if some of the anxiety can be removed from the situation then the bits come together more easily. The analyst makes an unwritten contract with the patient: 'You may hand some of this excess anxiety over to me and this will help us in our work.' The resistant, anxious part of the personality which the patient wants to be rid of is then projected on to the analyst. This is the phenomenon which we know as transference.

Thirdly, unity comes about through interpretation. The analyst makes interpretations to relieve anxiety, and to link the patient's contradictory thoughts and feelings. Non-material words enter a non-material psyche and bind the different bits together: of all forms of expression the spoken word is the most psychic, the least tangibly material.

The person of the analyst bears the anxiety, then, the interpretative words bind the psychic parts together; at the analyst's disposal are the communications of the patient and his own psychoanalytic theories. Every interpretation reflects a theory, every interpretation is embedded in a meaning structure; the more theories, meaning systems that he has available the better. In order to interpret he gives himself over to 'reverie' or 'free-floating attention'. His imaginative processes are stimulated by the patient, otherwise he is victim of his own preconceptions. Ultimately, however, the patient has to construct his own individual, personal world-view.

FREUD'S DISCOVERIES

4 FREUD AS A DISCIPLE OF DARWIN AND THE FOUNDERS OF THE PHYSICALIST TRADITION

Freud was born in 1856, three years before Darwin was finally persuaded to publish *On the Origin of Species*. This book, which sold out in half a day, caused a revolution in the scientific world – biology, ethnology, anthropology, psychology, sociology, economics and theology were all profoundly affected by Darwin's evolutionary theory. Freud, like all his contemporaries, was deeply influenced by Darwin. As a young man his microscopical research was largely motivated by a desire to test certain hypotheses that flowed naturally from Darwin's position. At the same time Freud was trained in the most rigorous manner at Ernst Brücke's Institute of Physiology in Vienna, and Brücke was one of the four founders of the Physicalist Society, the ideas of which dominated most of the medical schools of Europe at the time. We do not understand Freud's scientific attitude unless we have some grasp of these two traditions of thought.

The central tenets of Darwin's theory are quite easy to state. His first observation is that if unchecked, all organisms increase their number in geometrical ratio. The principle is that, starting from one, and increasing by geometrical ratio, a great multitude is soon arrived at; and it can be illustrated by the following story. An Ethiopian traveller was staying with a wealthy

Chinese landowner and during his stay saved his host's son from being drowned. In gratitude the Chinaman asked his guest to choose any gift that he would like, however expensive it might be. So the Ethiopian fetched a chess board and said to his host, 'Would you please put one grain of rice on this bottom corner square of the chess board and then put double the amount on the next square, and then double the amount on the following square, and double on the next and so on, until the whole board is filled.' The Chinaman protested, saying he was thinking of a much more magnificent gift than that and also a much more expensive one. However, the Ethiopian insisted that he just wanted what he had asked for.

I think you will have guessed the end of the story but I will just tell you what the Chinaman had let himself in for. He placed one grain of rice on the first square and then two on the second, four on the third, eight on the fourth, sixteen on the fifth, thirty-two on the sixth, sixty-four on the seventh, and 128 on the eighth and last square of the first line. I will not bore you by going on square by square, but on the basis of there being 1,024 grains of rice in a pound the Chinaman had to put down 65,536 pounds of rice at the end of the second line. By the end of the third line he had to put down 16,777,216 pounds of rice. By the end of the fourth line 113 tons of rice. By the end of the fifth line 28,000 tons, by the end of the sixth 7,168,000 tons, by the end of the seventh four billion tons, and by the end of the chess board he had to put down one million billion tons of rice!

Until I had read Darwin it had not come home to me what increase by geometrical ratio really means. In *Origin of Species*, Darwin states the matter quite clearly:

> There is no exception to the rule that every organic being naturally increases at so high a rate, that if not destroyed, the earth would soon be covered by the progeny of a single pair. Even slow-breeding man has doubled in twenty-five years, and at this rate, in a few thousand years, there would literally

not be standing room for his progeny. Linnaeus has calculated that if an annual plant produced only two seeds – and there is no plant so unproductive as this – and their seedlings next year produced two, and so on, then in twenty years there would be a million plants. The elephant is reckoned to be the slowest breeder of all known animals, and I have taken some pains to estimate its probable minimum rate of natural increase: it will be under the mark to assume that it breeds when thirty years old, and goes on breeding till ninety years old, bringing forth three pairs of young in this interval; if this be so, at the end of the fifth century there would be alive fifteen million elephants, descended from the first pair. (1859, p. 117)

This constantly exploding population of all living things presses for life and pushes into every available ecological niche.

Darwin's second proposition is that a massive level of destruction is going on all the time. He says:

Seedlings also are destroyed in vast numbers by various enemies; for instance, on a piece of ground three feet long and two wide, dug and cleared, and where there could be no choking from other plants, I marked all the seedlings of our native weeds as they came up, and out of the 357 no less than 295 were destroyed, chiefly by slugs and insects. (1859, p. 120)

The question, then, is which individuals perish and which is the minority that survives. Minute observation shows the existence of variations between one individual and another, and the colour or shape of one individual will have a slight advantage over another (Popham, 1941). Overall it can be seen that the better survivors are selected out.

As a species pushes into a new ecological niche those minute variations that are better adapted survive better. The variations at birth are random, but statistically one type of variation will do better than another over long periods of time. We are talking in thousands and millions of years, and as the structure of the earth has changed living forms have been forced into new environments. The minute variations that improve the chances of survival of one against another have been continually at work.

In this way one species has developed into a new form, starting from fish and working up through amphibians, reptiles, mammals and then through primates to *Homo sapiens*. If we are prepared to think in millions of years instead of centuries or millennia, then some fifteen million years ago we shared an ancestor with the apes. If we go back a further fifteen million years then we can count all mammals as our cousins. If we go back further we must include reptiles and eventually fish.

Ernst Haeckel was one of Darwin's followers and he formulated the notion that ontogeny recapitulates phylogeny, that is, that in the development of the individual he or she traces through the stages of our prehuman ancestry. So the proportional ratio of brain to body size is the same in the human and gorilla foetus and diverges only in infancy. Again, the human foetus is clothed with a fine hair called lanugo which it sheds before birth, and the human foetus, like all mammals, lives in a watery environment like our fishy ancestors. I am aware that Haeckel's principle is not unconditionally accepted by biologists, but Freud was undoubtedly influenced by Haeckel, and regression to a more primitive mode of functioning was and remains a keypoint in analytic theory. We usually think of this regression just to an earlier stage in the human life cycle but we rob psychoanalysis of some of its explanatory power if we do not include the possibility – at least as a hypothesis – that in certain states there is a regression to prehuman modes of mental functioning. For instance, a lady had powerful desires to devour her husband after intercourse – a regression to those arachnids that do this.

I will now describe as briefly as possible the scientific stance of the Physicalist Society, which was the creation of a group of four eminent physicians: Hermann Helmholtz, Ernst Brücke, Carl Ludwig and Emil du Bois-Reymond. These four men were passionately opposed to any form of vitalism, the belief that living organisms are animated by a soul, or at least a special principle not reducible to physics and chemistry, and together they formed the *Berliner Physicalische Gesellschaft*. Its creed was formulated in the following oath, known as the anti-vitalist pact:

> No other forces than the common physical and chemical ones are active within the organism. In those cases which cannot at the time be explained by those forces one has either to find the specific way or form of their action by means of the physical-mathematical method or to assume new forces equal in dignity to the chemical-physical forces inherent in matter, reducible to the force of attraction and repulsion. (Jones, 1953, p. 45)

Within twenty-five years this scientific attitude dominated most of the medical schools of Europe. The philosopher Franz Brentano, for instance, who took a different viewpoint, was ridiculed by the scientific establishment as 'that antiquated old Aristotelian', despite the fact that his lectures drew great crowds and Freud himself attended them at Vienna University for two years. However, it is, I think, significant that Freud never once acknowledged influence by Brentano in his written works.

The physicalist tradition was one of many offshoots of the spirit of the Enlightenment, and before coming to Freud I want to give just passing consideration both to that spirit, and to the philosopher whose thinking dominated the previous age, namely René Descartes. Until the Enlightenment Christendom was the sacred order according to which all phenomena were explained. In the Christian schema a hierarchy of explanations was subordinated to a single centre of meaning. Even the natural world, as part of creation, was the stage and sets necessary for divine action in human history. The Enlightenment violently repudiated this order of explanation and put in its stead rational, scientific principles according to which the whole universe could be understood. Yet the Enlightenment was also thoroughly intolerant of any other principles of explanation, and the anti-vitalist pact is an eloquent example of its dogmatism, if not fanaticism.

Descartes preceded the Enlightenment and died a pious Christian, but his philosophy, as I said in my second lecture, had codified a cleavage between God and the observable world, between the soul and the body, between man the knower and his environment. His philosophy broke up the meaningful coherence of all these and we might think of him as the philosopher who exemplified the psychological phenomenon of splitting into philosophical and theological thinking. God became the object of faith, the human person became located in the soul, and the body became a sensational machine through which the soul became imprinted, so effecting knowledge. With this came the notion of man as the detached observer of the universe, though he could not prove its existence. Feelings became highly suspect and were not to be trusted. It was through feelings that men 'knew' there was an external world. Once feelings became invalid agents of knowledge, how could man be certain that there was any existence outside himself? With this attitude went the ideal of the scientist as the man who deduced phenomena from first principles and sometimes had to check his deductions by scientific observations. Literature, art and poetry could contribute nothing because they were the fantasy productions of their creators and as such had no place in the scientific endeavour.

I will now return to the Physicalist Society. It was formed in 1845, so that by the time Freud entered medical school in 1873 the scientific temper it represented was well established, but by this time too Darwin's discoveries had burst upon the scientific world and devoted followers immediately set about proving various aspects of his theory. Freud became a pupil of Brücke's in 1876, and a great admirer of all the great figures in the society; on one occasion, when Helmholtz made a brief visit to Vienna but Freud missed seeing him, he said that Helmholtz was one of his heroes.

Early on in his research Freud was one of a few students chosen to go to a zoological experimental station at Trieste, where he was to work on the gonadic structure of eels. No one had ever found a mature eel with its testicles: the difficulty was evidently bound up with their extraordinary migration before the mating period. The year before Freud went to Trieste, a zoologist, Syrski, had found a small lobed organ which he considered was the undiscovered testes; the finding had to be checked and this was the task given to Freud. He dissected about four hundred eels and in many of them found the organ which Syrski had described. On examination in a microscope he thought that the organ might well be an immature testicle but that the evidence was not sufficient for certainty.

Brücke set him to work again on the histology of nerve cells, in particular a large cell in the spinal cord of the Amoectes (Petromyzon), a genus of fish belonging to the primitive Cyclostomata. Brücke was trying to determine whether the cell structure of these primitive organisms – specifically of these Reissner cells – was essentially the same as that in the human body.

Freud discovered a new technique for staining the tissue, and so was able to come to some conclusion about the Reissner cells. He stated that they were 'nothing else than spinal ganglion cells which, in those low vertebrates, where the migration of the embryonic neural tube to the periphery is not yet completed, remain within the spinal cord. These scattered cells mark the way which the spinal ganglion cells have made through their evolution' (Jones, 1953, pp. 52–53). Ernest Jones comments that this was a triumph of precise observation, and one of the thousands of small achievements which finally convinced scientists of the evolutionary unity of all organisms.

It has been claimed for Freud that he conceptualized the nerve cells and fibrils as one morphological and physiological unit – in other words what we now call the neurone. Ernest Jones suggests that if he had had more of his later boldness he might well be known today as the father of modern neurology. Jones also makes the interesting point that Freud excelled as an observer through a microscope, and was much less successful in any projects involving experimentation. He disliked savaging organisms, whether animal or human. Later, as you will remember from the start of the last lecture, he was to eschew therapeutic methods which he considered to be coarsely interfering; he came to believe that he could gain power over a neurosis if he could observe its structure. He was first and foremost an observer.

Freud started up in private practice as a neurologist in April 1886, the year in which he married. To begin with he used the customary methods of the day: electrical therapy, hydrotherapy, and hypnotism. As I have already mentioned, he soon abandoned the first two and concentrated on hypnotism, which I discuss in more detail in my next lecture. He was clearly moving away from the confines of the scientific attitude of his former mentors, and it is one of the most fascinating features of Freud: that he managed to combine into a plausible unity more than one metapsychological standpoint. Although his approach became what one might loosely call more humanist, he never shed either the physicalist stance or the scientific spirit that was inextricably wedded to it. (Indeed throughout his life, despite, as we shall see, his humanistic and artistic interests, Freud was very anxious to be respected in the scientific community.) Freud also remained passionately atheist all his life, and I think it likely that he felt it necessary to hold on to the tenets of the physicalist oath if atheism was to be safeguarded.

The physicalist way of conceptualizing permeates all Freud's writings, but nowhere does one find it in such a pure form as in his early work 'Project for a Scientific Psychology', written in 1895. This was his attempt to explicate the clinical phenomena of hysteria according to a physicalist model. Its opening words are as follows: 'The intention of this project is to furnish us with a psychology which shall be a natural science: its aim, that is, is to represent psychical processes as quantitatively determined states of specifiable material particles and so to make them plain and void of contradiction' (*SE* 1, p. 295).

He then attempts to give an account of memory, sleep, hysterical ideas, consciousness and other inner psychological phenomena according to this model. His colleague Josef Breuer, on the other hand, said that he would only attempt explanation in the language of psychology and would make no reference to the brain or to molecules. Shortly after he had finished the 'Project', as it is known, Freud followed Breuer's example, saying that our knowledge was not sufficiently advanced to be able to tie down psychological states to specifiable organic transactions; and that he would in future confine himself to strictly psychological models and cease trying to harmonize them with physiological knowledge. Nevertheless he still hoped that physiological research would one day catch up with his psychological constructs.

The topographical model was just such a psychological model, but it still bears its physicalist heritage in that all activity in the organism is released by purely blind forces. A physicalist model cannot allow any concept of intentionality. I will just quote to you an example from Freud's metapsychological paper, 'The Unconscious', written in 1915 when he was formulating mental processes according to the interactions of three systems: unconscious, preconscious and conscious.

> Surveying the whole process, we may say that the third phase repeats the work of the second on an ampler scale. The system *Cs.* now protects itself against the activation of the substitutive idea by an anticathexis of its environment, just

as previously it had secured itself against the emergence of the repressed idea by a cathexis of the substitutive idea. In this way the formation of substitutes by displacement has been further continued. We must also add that the system *Cs.* had earlier only one small area at which the repressed instinctual impulse could break through, namely the substitutive idea; but that ultimately this *enclave* of unconscious influence extends to the whole phobic outer structure. (1915b, *SE* 14, p. 184)

Although there is no attempt here to locate these systems organically, yet the origin of actions within the organism lies in impersonal agents. No intentional ego is invoked. Freud only finally adopted a model which could take satisfactory account of intentionality in 1923 when he published *The Ego and the Id*. It became known as the structural model but on its adoption Freud did not abandon the old one, and throughout his later writings there is a blend of his physicalist outlook and one which is really vitalist. One might think that to have different models jostling along next to each other would lead to chaos, but actually these metapsychological views do harmonize and form a unified system. Marie Jahoda, for instance (1977, p. 26), considers that Freud's genius lies in this fact.

Different schools within psychoanalysis have followed one or other of Freud's models. I think the physicalist tradition is best preserved by the Classical Freudians: Anna Freud, Heinz Hartmann and the ego psychologists – that is, the primarily American school, whom I will not be concentrating on in the series. I do not personally feel sympathetic towards the physicalist tradition and the models which it spawned, but it had one great value: it had a deep respect for an attitude which was scientific. If we ditch the physicalist model then we must be careful not to ditch the scientific attitude along with it. Lastly, as human beings we share certain essential features with the inanimate world as a whole, some of which are important for the understanding of aspects of human motivation. Unfortunately it would take me too long to explain this idea adequately. Nevertheless the physicalist tradition was perhaps an exaggerated attempt at encapsulating and conceptualizing these aspects of motivation.

5   Freud and the Mesmer-Hypnotic Movement

It is surprising to find a few years later that our rigorous scientist of the Helmholtz school of medicine was championing the cause of hypnotism. In his preface to Bernheim's book *Suggestion*, which he translated into German, he says,

> The subject of hypnotism has had a most unfavourable reception among the leaders of German medical science (apart from such few exceptions as Krafft-Ebing, Forel, etc.). Yet, in spite of this, one may venture to express a wish that German physicians may turn their attention to this problem and to this therapeutic procedure . . . (1888, *SE* 1, p. 75)

In the last lecture we left Freud devotedly ensconced in Brücke's physiological laboratory, and now we find him advocating the use of hypnotism in the treatment of the neuroses, especially hysteria. How did this change come about?

As we have seen, Freud delayed over qualifying as a doctor for three years; this was the time he spent doing valuable research in Brücke's laboratory. Finally, however, realizing that his career demanded it, he qualified in 1881, nine years after beginning his medical training. He went on with his research in the laboratory for a further eighteen months, and then something occurred which made him change direction. He fell in love with Martha Bernays.

All through his medical training he had been financed by his father, who was anyhow in straitened circumstances. In the laboratory he was paid only a nominal sum. He spoke to Brücke, presumably to sound out whether there was any likelihood in the foreseeable future of promotion to a higher post in the laboratory. Brücke advised him to take up a practice as a doctor because he did not have enough personal financial backing to continue in such poorly remunerative work as research. Freud therefore left the Institute of Physiology and set about getting his clinical experience.

For the next three years he held posts in different hospitals doing the rounds in various specialities of medicine, including psychiatry. During this time he continued his neurological researches, published several important monographs, and was selected, in a very competitive situation, as *Privat-Dozent* to the University of Vienna. To become a *Privat-Dozent* one had to deliver a public lecture before the staff of the university, and Freud chose as his subject 'The Medullary Tracts of the Brain'. It was accepted with unanimous satisfaction. The post was not paid but it was very prestigious, and had financial benefits in that Freud could teach students and receive fees from them, and it would also enhance his reputation as a neurologist in private practice.

The main focus of Freud's attention during these three years, however, was to equip himself sufficiently to set up in private practice. In 1885 he applied for a grant which would enable him, if successful, to take six months off and research in a field of special interest. Again, although it was a much sought-after grant, he got it, and he decided without delay to go to Paris and study under J-M. Charcot. The greatest neurologist of the day, Charcot had turned his attention to hysteria and was demonstrating its symptomatology through the use of hypnotism.

However, we need to pause for a moment to have a look at the bizarre history of this therapeutic technique.

The story starts with the strange discoveries of Franz Anton Mesmer, who was born of humble origins on the shores of Lake Constance in the year 1734, and died in 1815. His earliest academic studies were in philosophy and theology under the auspices of the Jesuits. He completed medical studies in Vienna at the age of thirty-three, on the presentation of a thesis concerning the influence of planets on the course of human diseases, and established himself there as a physician. He lived on a splendid estate and became a patron of the arts. Haydn and Mozart both visited his home on several occasions. At the age of forty he discovered his magnetic powers and after practising for a short while he left Vienna, travelled to Paris and remained there for ten years during which time he became famous and also rich through the huge fees which he charged his wealthy patients. At the end of this time his reputation suffered a harsh reversal, so he left Paris, disappeared from the social scene and retired again to the shores of Lake Constance where he died an old man thirty years later.

Mesmer's discoveries started when he was treating a twenty-seven-year-old patient, Fräulein Oesterlin, who was afflicted with about fifteen severe symptoms. He noticed that her illness was characterized by periodic crises, and he linked these with particular movements of the heavenly bodies. Just as the moon controls the tide, Mesmer thought, some mysterious fluid in the patient was controlled by the movements of the heavenly bodies. It occurred to him that were he able to provoke an artificial tide he might be able to cure her. Consequently he made her swallow a preparation containing iron and then attached magnets to her body. The patient began to experience extraordinary streams of mysterious fluid running downwards through her body, and all her evils were swept away for several hours. Mesmer realized that these effects could not be produced by the metal magnets alone, so he reached the conclusion that they must be produced by a fluid accumulated in his own person. This fluid he named *animal magnetism*, and throughout his life he held that the therapeutic results which he was able to achieve were attributable to its presence.

Mesmer achieved success with this patient and went on to work many remarkable cures; in Vienna he cured a special protégée of the Empress Maria-Theresa, Maria-Theresia Paradis, of hysterical blindness. Viennese medical circles were extremely hostile to him; a medical commission which examined this patient claimed that she could see only when she was in Mesmer's presence. When the patient later returned to her own family home, and then became blind for good, Mesmer said that her blindness had returned because her reputation and the financial support of the Empress depended upon it. If Mesmer was right then this would be a case of what Freud was later to call the *secondary gain* from illness, or a benefit from the symptom.

The type of crisis that Mesmer provoked in his patients was of a violent convulsive type, and they seemed to pass through something akin to an epileptic fit. But what exactly lay behind this magnetic power? Louis XVI, as a result of the agitation around Mesmer, appointed a royal commission to investigate his methods in 1784. Well-known people such as the chemist Antoine Lavoisier and the American ambassador, Benjamin Franklin, served on this commission. The commission's official report to the King did not deny that there were therapeutic results but said there was no evidence for the presence of a magnetic fluid, and ascribed the cures to *imagination*. However, the commission also submitted a clandestine report to the King pointing out the dangers resulting from the erotic attraction of the magnetized female patient to her male magnetizer.

All reports on Mesmer and his followers also paid great attention to the phenomenon of rapport between the magnetizer and his patient. This was the strange attraction that existed between the patient and his or her magnetizer – so much so that patients magnetized by the same person frequently referred to each other as brothers or sisters. (In my first year of training at the Institute of Psycho-Analysis another trainee came up to me and said to me that she and I were 'cousins'. I was surprised to find a new cousin that I had not heard of. She then explained to me that my analyst and hers had had the same analyst.) The rapport was understood to constitute a very important element in the cure of the patient, but one of the reasons why Freud later came to abandon the use of hynotism was precisely that he wished to isolate the erotic phenomenon, and ultimately to try to dissolve it through the analytic process.

One of Mesmer's most important disciples was the Marquis of Puységur (1751–1825), whose early life was divided between army service and looking after his estates at his castle near Soissons. The Marquis became a disciple of Mesmer's and one of his first patients was a young peasant on his estate, Victor Race. Race was suffering from some mild respiratory disease, but when Puységur magnetized him he entered a very peculiar crisis. There were no convulsions, no disorderly movements; instead the young man fell into a strange kind of sleep. Puységur named this the 'perfect crisis' and discovered that when the patient was in this state he, Puységur, was able to make suggestions to him. The patient would carry the instructions out when he was wide awake again, without realizing, however, that what he did was not being done autonomously; he took it that they were his own spontaneous actions. Puységur found that it was possible to suggest to the patient that he no longer had the disease which he complained of, and that when he woke it would be gone.

Puységur was soon so successful that he conducted group cures around a particular tree on his estate, and the special kind of crisis which he was able to induce was later named 'hypnotism' by an Englishman, James Braid. After his death, however, Puységur was almost forgotten and the therapy which he had initiated fell into decline. Hypnotism began to be used indiscriminately by charlatans, faith healers and in séances. The subject became a topic of popular fashion in many novels of the time and was no longer regarded as something which any scientist would take seriously until, in the last quarter of the nineteenth century, two schools of hypnotism arose: at Nancy and in Paris.

The founder of the Nancy School was a country doctor, Auguste Liébeault. He came across an early nineteenth century treatise on hypnotism and began to offer such treatment to his patients. On finding that they were not very keen he gave them the alternative of being treated by normal means and paying the usual fee, or being treated by hypnotism free. He found that his hypnotic practice grew enormously. After a time he withdrew and wrote a book on the subject, although it barely sold at all and his medical colleagues called him a quack. In 1882, however, the situation changed after a visit from Hippolyte Bernheim, Professor of Medicine at Nancy University, who began to take an active and admiring interest in Liébault's theory and practice. The latter's book now began to be read by many and its reputation grew enormously. Bernheim himself soon wrote a book on the subject which, as I have already said, Freud later translated into German, having visited Bernheim in 1889. Bernheim's view was that the phenomenon of hypnotism could be entirely explained by suggestion, and was indeed a demonstration of the power over someone that suggestion could have.

I will now turn to Charcot. As I have said, he was the most famous neurologist of his day, and had transformed the old Salpêtrière Hospital in Paris from an old wreck into a place well equipped with laboratories, lecture rooms and other scientific requirements. When he had first gone there it was a place in which no physician hoping for recognition and advancement would stay for a day longer than necessary, but Charcot realized that there was a wealth of clinical diversity within its walls which it would be difficult to find elsewhere, and doctors came from all over Europe to study under him. Freud admired him enormously, and when Charcot died prematurely in 1893 he wrote an appreciation of him. He had been particularly struck by Charcot's methods of working and his manner of scientific observation, and said of him, 'He used to look again and again at the things he did not understand, to deepen his impression of them day by day, till suddenly an understanding of them dawned upon him' (1893, *SE* 3, p. 12). It was the method which Freud used himself, and is also a method which is essential to psychoanalysis to this day. Those who are more experimental in their scientific endeavours will not take kindly to this method, or to psychoanalysis.

Whereas Bernheim used hypnotism principally as a therapeutic tool, Charcot used it, from 1870 onwards, to demonstrate that certain types of hysteria were psychic in origin. Although Charcot believed that all types of hysteria were fundamentally due to factors to be found in heredity, yet there were two main groups of hysteria: those caused by organic lesions in the nervous system, and those caused by a psychogenic factor. In order to prove the latter hypothesis Charcot was able to bring about, through hypnosis, an exactly similar symptomatology.

Again unlike Bernheim, Charcot believed that the hypnotic phenomenon could not be explained purely by suggestion; it was also generated through factors in the nervous system. Freud took this view also and mentions, in his preface to Bernheim's book, the fact that people could go into a hypnotic trance in the absence of any suggestion and instances the case of a patient who became hypnotized when her dentist shone a light on her face. Bernheim, on the other hand, believed that Charcot's results *were* obtained through suggestion and that they had no connection with any particular features within the patient. The two schools were bitterly antagonistic towards each other.

Freud started in private practice on Easter Day 1886. He

made use of the various methods available to a neurologist of the time, in particular electrotherapy, but found that it was absolutely hopeless and after a while used hypnotism almost exclusively. Already by this time Josef Breuer had told him of a patient of his – the famous case of Anna O. – who had suffered from severe symptoms: paralysis of the limbs, disturbances in hearing and vision and inability to eat. Breuer found one day that when the patient told him how a particular symptom had started it cleared up. He then began to hypnotize her each morning, and used the trance to uncover memories that led to the origin of first one symptom and them another. Many of the symptoms turned out to have their origin in the distressing circumstances surrounding her father's last illness, the patient having attended him during it.

Breuer further discovered that a symptom cleared up when the patient spoke about the events which had sparked it off as long as the talking was accompanied with affect, and he named this therapeutic method 'catharsis'. However, he had finally abandoned the treatment of Anna O. when he realized the powerful erotic attachment that she had developed towards him, which his wife had become morose with jealousy about.

When Breuer first told him about this case Freud was most interested in it. In fact he told Charcot about it when he was in Paris, but the famous neurologist did not seem interested. In fact it is easy to see why it intrigued Freud, for here hypnotism was being used in a much more scientific way than hitherto. Instead of giving authoritative instructions, the physician was using hypnotism to discover the origins of a symptom: that is, it was being used to aid serious enquiry. In addition, a scientific discovery was coextensive with a therapeutic result. This last became a feature of psychoanalysis, as I outlined in the first lecture.

To sum up. Freud, in his private practice, was making use of hypnotism in a unique way. The technique of psychoanalysis grew out of the hypnotic method of catharsis between 1892 and

1896, but by 1896 Freud had given up the use of hypnotism entirely. We shall return to this transition in the lecture on transference, but I want now to reflect a little further on the nature of hypnotism and its similarities with psychoanalysis, because these are not sufficiently recognized.

If the therapist is not idealized – that is, if the patient has derogatory thoughts or conscious hostile feelings towards the hypnotist – then the trance cannot occur. The trance disappears if the therapist attempts to interpret what we call the 'negative transference'. This is because in the hypnotic trance the erotic element is converted into an idealization. An important feature of the hysterical condition, shared by someone in a hypnotic trance, is the deep wish to please. The hysteric will, in the subtlest ways, speak about what the therapist wishes to hear, and can pick up, probably unconsciously, the subtle cues that the analyst gives as to what will please him or her. It is this phenomenon that lies behind the cynical comment that a patient in Jungian analysis will produce 'Jungian' dreams and the patient in Freudian analysis will supply 'Freudian' ones. But as psychoanalysis grew out of hypnotism, the question which I think needs to be asked is: 'How many remnants of the hypnotic phenomenon remain in psychoanalysis?' I do not want to give an answer but just to make some observations.

The use of the couch is a relic from hypnotism – a fact that Freud specifically mentions – and could indicate that some of the important elements in hypnosis are also operative in psychoanalysis. Let me give you an example. One reason why certain patients are very frightened of the couch is that they feel they will totally submit themselves to the analyst. I think you could recast this and say that the deep wish to please surfaces when the patient is cut off from the visual cues which are normally available in social intercourse.

A patient who went into a hypnotic trance when she changed from the seated position facing the analyst to the couch comes to mind: the analyst became massively idealized and removed from the sphere of ordinary reality. The patient's greatest wish was to be loved and she felt this had to be won by pleasing; when the negative transference was interpreted she became furious, and quite different. One could therefore say that the hypnotic phenomenon capitalizes upon a denial of negative feelings. I think it would be fair to conjecture that with this patient there was massive hostility towards a mother who did not give love freely and whose love had to be won. In such cases love needs to replace the desire to please if the patient is to get better, and the analyst needs to interpret the negative transference incessantly until he or she is perceived in realistic colours; by which I mean that both the good and the bad are cathected as a unified ensemble.

Nevertheless some elements of the hypnotic phenomenon do remain. I have rarely come across a patient in analysis for whom the analyst is not somewhat idealized. Also I have always sensed that I would not get on very well in the psychoanalytical world if I freely criticized a particular analyst in the company of someone who was being analysed by him or her. This can only mean that analysands tend to hold their analysts in a rather idealized light. It also makes sense of the denigration of particular analysts or their schools, as a displacement of negative feelings from the individual's own analyst. In the Tavistock Clinic, for instance, it is difficult to understand the intensity of feeling for or against Melanie Klein unless one invokes the presence of the hypnotic phenomenon. For although Freud gave up the formal use of hypnotism in 1896, it is still present among us in a variety of disguises. Some elements may even be necessary to achieve cure, although that is not a conclusion I am happy with.

6   FREUD THE ROMANTIC

Although Freud was a scientist whose foremost idol was Helmholtz, yet he was decidedly a Romantic in the spirit of the cultural phenomenon that arose in Europe at the end of the eighteenth century and continued well into the nineteenth. It is not possible to define a cultural phenomenon like Romanticism in a few neat phrases. Romanticism was a spirit or a tendency which is recognizable when we see it, but is difficult to articulate in a way which would satisfy the logician. To convey something of that spirit I have to go back to the Enlightenment and the disillusionment that followed the French Revolution.

Romanticism arose from the ashes of the Enlightenment. The thinkers of this latter movement, as I have already mentioned, looked towards the day when human society would be structured on rational principles, as opposed to the order inspired by Christendom which had governed central Europe since the days of Constantine. All things in heaven and on earth were unified under the Christian schema and could be explained by it. Even creation was understood as being the first step in God's saving purpose which culminated in Christ. Nothing stood outside the central purpose. The thinkers of the Enlightenment, on the other hand, believed that all could now be explained according to the rational principles of science, and the anti-vitalist pact, which I quoted in the lecture before last, was a typical heritage of it. In fact the Enlightenment shared an outlook with Christendom, which had preceded it: that all phenomena could be explained according to a unitary system. Now the political event which was going to overthrow the old order, the *ancien régime*, was the French Revolution. Many pinned all their hopes on this political upheaval and when it failed they were disillusioned. Of course, it is not true to say that the French Revolution failed entirely. Although Napoleon did restore privilege, and a monarchy reappeared after his demise, he had restructured France. There had been a redistribution of land; a completely new legal structure governed social relations and even the monarchy was now an instrument chosen by democratic principles.

But if the *ancien régime* had gone, the old order had not entirely gone. There was still a religious hegemony and anyone could see that the ideals of liberty, equality and fraternity had not been achieved. So disillusion set in. Some became even more frantically determined to opposed anything that smacked of a religious explanation, and held even more fervently to a scientific-materialist explanation of events, whether natural or social. However, disillusion took another group of writers, painters and thinkers in a different direction. These were the Romantics.

The Romantics protested against the submission of all phenomena to a higher purpose, whether it be religious or scientific. A daffodil or a butterfly had a value in its own right. It had a beauty of its own. It did not exist for the glory of God and it did not have to be subjected to a functionalist-scientific explanation. It did not serve some purpose of a higher order, and it was not necessary to find a meaning for it. God, for the Romantic, was in nature and in the soul. In their natural religion the Romantics were pantheistic: even when there is an avowed atheism, as in Shelley, the thrust of the poetry is profoundly pantheistic; the notion of a transcendent God so that there can be a better beyond is foreign to the Romantic's temper. For subjugation to a system of meaning degraded the thing-in-itself. As the philosopher Alfred North Whitehead said: 'The Romantic reaction was a protest on behalf of value' (1925, p. 90).

The inner selves of those who had fervently embraced the ideals of the Enlightenment had been identified with the causes they espoused, but with disillusionment came a detachment of the self from the ideal. In particular, ideals concerning the future betterment of society were held aloof. The Romantics shrank from causes and world-views; they tended to be apolitical and turned from social concerns to the praise of nature. Their paintings typically tend to depict landscapes, rugged mountains or uncouth storms at sea. The Romantic painter deliberately scorned both the subjects and the techniques of neo-classicism, and it is difficult for us today to realize that Constable's *Hay Wain*, when it was first shown in Paris in 1824, caused a turmoil of interest in artistic circles. Its subject was not one which a neo-classical painter would even have considered trying to paint. Turner was violently criticized by contemporaries for his rough paintwork – one critic complained that he had to go right to the other side of the room to be able to see what the subject of the painting was.

We have seen that the Romantics turned their noses up at the quasi-religious values which had been held sacred, but we have still not quite reached the main idea of the movement. What mattered most was not so much the subject matter or technique, whether it be in literature, poetry, painting, music or architecture, but the authenticity of inner feeling. What was represented, in whatever medium, must be an expression of the individual's true inner feeling – nothing was so abhorrent to the Romantic as someone who just copied the technique or style of another. Romanticism could thus be described as the emergence of Protestantism in culture: it was the inner light, the inner spirit that mattered, and Byron's determination to express whatever he was feeling at a particular moment was typical of this temper. Passionate individualists, the Romantics hated all ideals which brought men into amorphous collectivities; to sacrifice oneself for such an ideal was the ultimate horror.

The Romantics wanted the world as it was. They accepted it as they saw it. George Herbert Mead, in *Movements of Thought in the Nineteenth Century*, quotes the story that Margaret Fuller, in Carlyle's hearing, said 'I accept the universe'. Carlyle replied, 'Begad, she'd better'. If it is true to say that the idealist finds it particularly difficult to accept the world as it is, and is always trying to devise schemes that gloss over for him the hard and stubborn facts of the world, then the Romantic is constantly turning his back on the possibilities of betterment that do exist. D.H. Lawrence's statement, 'Art for *my* sake', typifies the Romantic attitude.

The self had supreme value. The Romantic is always suspicious of such higher values. I have often heard discussions about the morality of patient and analyst spending so much time and energy on the life of one person; the Romantic would have no such scruples and would even scorn such a discussion.

Now in fact the self cannot exist in an isolated state; it has to attach itself to something. Whereas idealists turn to the future, Romantics return to the past. Whatever era they turned back to was always better than the present: they mourned a lost epoch. The turning to nature was partly a return to an imagined better state of affairs before the Industrial Revolution, but prototypically the Romantics turned back to eras before or outside the zeal of the Judaeo-Christian tradition. So they turned to ancient Greece and its myths, finding within them expressions of the irrational in man. The Romantics stressed the dark forces and passions in man's soul, praising the irrational, and rejecting the idea that society could be built on rational principles. They distrusted the scientific temper that tried to reduce everything to rational laws. They felt in touch with the mysterious, the unknowable in man. The Romantic favoured introspection and attempted an inner journey into the deepest recesses of his own mind. The Romantic loved wild landscapes partly because they were felt to be symbolic of the inner reaches of man's soul.

The value of man and the truths about man are to be found within: all the excursions of rational science cannot detect what is quintessential in him. To discover man the Romantic looks to the imagination – an instrument that was spurned by the scientist in the physicalist tradition. Therefore he turns to poetry, music, literature, painting: all those media that help him to differentiate the emotions and feelings within. Through imagination man can reach truth, the most important truths about man and his world. The Romantic believes that without imagination there is no truth, only sterile formulae. Imagination, fantasy, intuition and spontaneity are his research instruments.

We must now turn back to Freud. Freud was an extremely cultured man. Culture was in his blood. It seems that most great people who have left an impact on history have been wide readers in their formative years, and Freud was no exception. We should make special mention of his love of England and English literature, and his special interest in seventeenth century history; in particular the revolution that led to the beheading of a king and the reign of Cromwell. Cromwell was one of his heroes, and he named one of his sons Oliver. He also had a particular love of Shakespeare and quotes him quite often in his writings – to Freud Hamlet was one of the greatest literary achievements. He had read Milton, some of the novels of George Eliot, and most of Dickens: one of his first presents to Martha Bernays, his fiancée and later his wife, was *David Copperfield*.

Freud could also read and speak Spanish and his favourite book of all was *Don Quixote*. Over the years he frequently reread parts of it. He also seems to have read the complete works of the Spanish playwright Calderón. (As Calderón wrote about two hundred plays this seems somewhat incredible.) Freud read Latin and quotes in it periodically through his writings. He did not speak French very well but of course he read it, and in fact translated one of Charcot's works into German. Seemingly his other great favourite was Flaubert's *Les Tentations de Saint-Antoine*. In a letter to Martha he says of it:

> I was deeply moved by the splendid panorama [the views on the journey to Gmunden], and now on top of it all came this book which in the most condensed fashion and with unsurpassable vividness throws at one's head all the dross of the world: for it calls up not only the great problems of knowledge, but the real riddles of life, all the conflicts of feelings and impulses; and it confirms the awareness of our perplexity in the mysteriousness that reigns everywhere. These questions, it is true, are always there, and one should always be thinking of them. What one does, however, is to confine oneself to a narrow aim every hour and every day and gets used to the idea that to concern oneself with these enigmas is the task of a special hour, in the belief that they exist only in those special hours. Then they suddenly assail one in the morning and rob one of one's composure and one's spirits. (quoted in Jones, 1953, pp. 191–192)

Of course he was well read in the literature of his native tongue: Goethe was a favourite and so was the poet Heine. Another of his special interests was archaeology. However, the subject in which he was not very well versed was philosophy. He seems to have been a little suspicious of it, also feeling that it could bias observation. He deliberately did not read Nietzsche, he said, because he knew that Nietzsche touched on matters that he himself was trying to observe clinically, and he did not want the purity of scientific observation interfered with. Here was a big difference between himself and Jung, who was considerably influenced by both Nietzsche and Schopenhauer, openly acknowledged it, and criticized Freud for not taking the work of philosophers into account.

So far I have only said that Freud was extremely cultured but not that he was also a Romantic; I want to look at the evidence for the latter assertion. Now the central area of Freud's investigation was the unconscious. As we have seen this was championed by the Romantics: the mysterious, the unknown, the dark areas of the mind denied by scientists was their special province. The concept of an unconscious had been known within religious circles for centuries, but the first philosophical thinker to formulate the concept was Leibnitz, early in the eighteenth century, with *The Monadology*. A growing interest in the concept then developed. J.F. Herbart gave a lengthy exposé on the subject; Mesmer and his followers paid it a lot of attention; as did Schopenhauer and Nietzsche. It was also the cynosure of many nineteenth century novelists.

Scientists, however, scorned the concept as mystical nonsense, and for any scientist to take it seriously was almost unthinkable; when Freud began to be seriously interested in it he was rejected by some of his former mentors, such as the brain anatomist Professor Theodor Meynert. But Freud did not just leave the unconscious as mysterious. His scientific mind would never have been satisfied with that. Just as he could not accept that hypnotism worked without understanding how it worked, so also he could not accept that the unconscious was an area of the mind which must remain mysterious. If there was indeed such an area of the mind then it could be investigated.

Nevertheless, all his investigations centred on something which was of the greatest interest to the Romantics, and his focus on dreams, similarly, brought him into their domain. This interest arose in conjunction with a journey into himself which has become known as his self-analysis, the purpose of which was to discover his inner motivations. Indeed the uncovering of his own dark purposes is a theme running through the whole of *The Interpretation of Dreams*. Many of the dreams in the book are his own, and very revealing of his desires and intentions, although he clearly hides some of what is most intimate and personal. In particular he draws a cloak over conflicts in his sexual life, but he is explicit about his rivalry with colleagues in the sphere of career and ambition.

We do not know everything about Freud's passion for Martha Bernays. Over an engagement of four years he wrote over nine hundred letters, and a four-page letter was a short one. Frequently they were twelve pages long, and Ernest Jones mentions that one of them was twenty-two pages. Freud was passionately in love with her. He was jealously demanding of her love and attention, and during the engagement there were several eruptions of fury on his part. Martha did not submissively give in to him, but stood up for herself when he tried to take possession of her and make her take sides against her family on his behalf. In one letter, where he is expressing his feelings about her possible death, he says:

> There must be a point of view from which even the loss of the loved one would seem a trivial occurrence in the thousands of years of human history. But I must confess I take the extreme opposite one in which the event would be absolutely equivalent to the end of the world, at least the world so far as I am concerned . . . (quoted in Jones, 1953, p. 146)

This declaration is typical of the Romantic, and the soul of the statement is central to the values that surround psychoanalysis. In psychoanalysis the importance and worth of the individual are given concrete expression, where one patient is seen daily over a long period of years.

Such a procedure is a scandal to the idealist, and in this epoch is a stumbling-block to those with strong socialist beliefs. I remember a Labour councillor being asked for his opinion as to whether a grant of £20,000 for a psychotherapy centre should be given for the following year; his view was that the same money could be used for the benefit of a great number of people in other ways, whereas the centre saw only a few. The man was expressing the opposite view to Freud's, and one that is anti-Romantic.

Those cultures which stress the value of the individual's self-surrender to the higher good of the community tend to be against psychoanalysis; this is true of Soviet communism and of those countries dominated by a Roman Catholic culture. Furthermore a psychoanalyst will usually interpret as pathological any sentiment expressed by the patient that he or she intends to sacrifice him- or herself to the demands or views of others. This is because a submissive and self-deprecatory attitude is seen as a sign of pathology which the analyst needs to interpret. As communal cultures function through submission of the individual will, they are generally opposed to psychoanalysis.

Freud was also a Romantic in his disillusionment with the principles of the Enlightenment, which failed to explain the mental phenomena he was trying to understand. He turned to the types of explanation favoured by the Romantics, in particular to the myths of old, those of classical Greece. He believed that in these myths were encapsulated man's deepest conflicts. The most famous, that of Oedipus Rex, he believed expressed man's core neurosis and from it all other mental disturbances flowed.

Indeed when reading Freud one is quite often startled by his sudden flip from a strictly scientific explanation to a mythological one. In *Beyond the Pleasure Principle*, for instance, he is trying to investigate the source of sexual attraction and wondering whether in it there is a principle which already exists in the more primitive organisms. In the midst of this discussion he says:

> . . . science has so little to tell us about the origin of sexuality that we can liken the problem to a darkness into which not so much as a ray of a hypothesis has penetrated. In quite a different region, it is true, we *do* meet with such a hypothesis; but it is so fantastic a kind – a myth rather than a scientific explanation – that I should not venture to produce

it here, were it not that it fulfils precisely the one condition whose fulfilment we desire. For it traces the origin of an instinct to *a need to restore an earlier state of things.*

What I have in mind is, of course, the theory which Plato put into the mouth of Aristophanes in the *Symposium*, and which deals not only with the *origin* of the sexual instinct but also with the most important of its variations in relation to its object. 'The original human nature was not like the present, but different. In the first place, the sexes were originally three in number, not two as they are now; there was man, woman, and the union of the two . . .' Everything about these primaeval men was double: they had four hands and four feet, two faces, two privy parts, and so on. Eventually Zeus decided to cut these men in two, like a sorb-apple which is halved for pickling. After the division had been made, 'the two parts of man, each desiring his other half, came together, and threw their arms about one another eager to grow into one.'

Shall we follow the hint given us by the poet-philosopher, and venture upon the hypothesis that living substance at the time of its coming to life was torn apart into small particles, which have ever since endeavoured to reunite through the sexual instincts? That these instincts, in which the chemical affinity of inanimate matter persisted, gradually succeeded, as they developed through the kingdom of the protista, in overcoming the difficulties put in the way of that endeavour by an environment charged with dangerous stimuli – stimuli which compelled them to form a protective cortical layer? That these splintered fragments of living substance in this way attained a multicellular condition and finally transferred the instinct for reuniting, in the most highly concentrated form, to the germ-cells? – But here I think the moment has come for breaking off. (1920, *SE* 18, pp. 57–58)

We find examples such as this again and again in Freud. He does not give answers but opens up avenues for thought; that which we don't know is always clearly stated. The sense of mystery is preserved, the imagination is stimulated so a doorway for further research is kept open. In all this Freud is a typical Romantic. With a new consciousness he returns to the myths of old and finds in them a source of understanding.

Lastly, we need to turn to the psychoanalytic method itself and see how it is a strange blend of the scientific and the Romantic. Creative imagination finds its basis in a process where the mind roams free of constraint. This mental freedom from social constraint was a virtue in the eyes of the Romantics; that Freud knew about this method of working, if it can be called such, is attested by Ernest Jones, who tells us that Freud had read many of the works of the Romantic writer Ludwig Börne. His reading included Borne's essay 'The Art of Becoming an Original Writer in Three Days', which apparently ends with these words:

> Here follows the practical prescription I promised. Take a few sheets of paper and for three days in succession write down, without any falsification or hypocrisy, everything that comes into your head. Write what you think of yourself, of your women, of the Turkish War, of Goethe, of the Fonk criminal case, of the Last Judgement, of those senior to you in authority – and when the three days are over you will be amazed at what novel and startling thoughts have welled up in you. That is the art of becoming an original writer in three days. (quoted in Jones, 1953, p. 270)

It is very likely that Freud's adoption of the rule of free association for the patient hailed back to Borne's influence. Yet this method, with its Romantic ambience, was also linked for Freud with something that came from his scientific orientation: the belief that a chain of associations would lead to a cause. Here we have Freud's deterministic conviction that a flow is generated by a cause that can be tied down. Freud further prescribed that the appropriate mental attitude for the analyst was one of 'free-floating attention': in other words the analyst needed to day-dream and let his imagination wander. It would help him alight upon the patient's central area of conflict. Therefore his prescription to both parties – analyst and analysand – was to foster imagination and fantasy: meat for the true Romantic and poison for the physicalist scientist.

Yet a new scientific instrument for investigating what we inadequately call the mind was to be found in the method of free association. As time went on this instrument became more finely tuned, but it was Freud who forged the first, crude version. The instrument was a blend of something Romantic and scientific; the object of his research, the unconscious, was the cynosure of the Romantic vision; and yet with this method Freud did something which was abhorrent to the Romantic. He mapped out the unconscious, found out what laws operated within its territory, and systematized it. He applied the logic of scientific enquiry and classification to an area which had never been charted before. His genius was due to his capacity to integrate two traditions, the Romantic and the scientific, which had previously been in antagonism to each other. Science and Romanticism come together in psychoanalysis, but psychoanalysis to this day remains a scandal to the natural scientist as it also is to the Romantic.

7 FREUD'S SELF-ANALYSIS

There came a point in his correspondence with Wilhelm Fliess when Freud began to say that the most important patient whom he was investigating was himself. In 1897 he began to make an inner journey a specific task, seeing the prime focus of psychoanalysis as himself. It is worth quoting at some length from a *New Yorker* article by Bruno Bettelheim:

> In *The Interpretation of Dreams* (1900), which opened to our understanding not just the meaning of dreams but also the nature and power of the unconscious, Freud told about his arduous struggle to achieve ever greater self-awareness. In other books, he told why he felt it necessary for the rest of us to do the same. In a way, all his writings are gentle, persuasive, often brilliantly worded intimations that we, his readers, would benefit from a similar journey of self-discovery . . . For nearly forty years, I have taught courses in psychoanalysis to American graduate students and residents in psychiatry. Almost invariably, I have found that psychoanalytic concepts had become for these students a way of looking only at others, from a safe distance – nothing that had any bearing on them. They observed other people through the spectacles of abstraction, tried to comprehend

them by means of intellectual concepts, never turning their gaze inward to the soul or their own unconscious. This was true even of the students who were in analysis themselves – it made no appreciable difference. Psychoanalysis had helped some of them to be more at peace with themselves and to cope with life, had helped others to free themselves of troublesome neurotic symptoms, but their misconceptions about psychoanalysis remained. Psychoanalysis as these students perceived it was a purely intellectual system – a clever exciting game – rather than the acquisition of insights into oneself and one's own behaviour which were potentially deeply upsetting. It was always *someone else's* unconscious they analysed, hardly ever their own. They did not give enough thought to the fact that Freud, in order to create psychoanalysis and understand the workings of the unconscious, had had to analyse his *own* slips of the tongue and reasons *he* forgot things or made various other mistakes. (Bettelheim, 1982, p. 52)

It seems that through this process of self-analysis Freud arrived at personal insights that led him to give up some of his theories. In the late 1880s and early 1890s he held that hysteria arose because there had been sexual interference with the patient by the father, but a well-known letter to Wilhelm Fliess dated 21 September 1897 made it clear that he no longer believed in this theory. Freud gave four reasons: firstly, he was unable to bring his analyses to a successful conclusion, a source of continual disappointment; secondly, it was hardly credible that each case had to be attributed to the perverse act of a father; thirdly, there is no reality testing in the unconscious and therefore it is not possible to differentiate between truth and emotionally charged fiction; and lastly, the unconscious memory does not break through in psychosis, even when a patient is delirious. 'It seems reasonable to assume,' says Ernst Kris in a footnote to the letter, 'that it was only the self-analysis of this summer that made possible rejection of the seduction hypothesis' (Kris, p. 216).

It is likely that the first inklings of the Oedipus complex were beginning to dawn in his consciousness; he was beginning to become aware of his incestuous wishes towards his mother and aggression towards his father. Then he arrived at a formulation about the child's sexual wishes which he had been resistant to accepting before. On the other hand, it is incorrect to think that Freud was the first to challenge the notion that children are sexually innocent. Stephen Kern has listed over a dozen publications in which Freud's views were clearly presaged, by authors such as Henry Maudsley, Gustaf Adolf Lindner, Albert Moll, Havelock Ellis and Sanford Bell. 'Almost every element of Freud's theory of child sexuality,' Kern concludes, 'was exactly anticipated, or in some way implied or suggested, before him' (Kern, 1973, quoted in Sulloway, p. 279). Havelock Ellis, for instance, had written in 1897:

> The analogy is indeed very close, though I do not know, or cannot recall, that it has been pointed out: the erectile nipple corresponds to the erect penis, the eager watery mouth of the infant to the moist and throbbing vagina, the vitally albuminous milk to the vitally albuminous semen: the complete mutual satisfaction, physical and psychic, of mother and child, in transfer from one to the other of a precious organized fluid, is the one true physiological analogy to the relationship of a man and a woman at the climax of the sexual act. (quoted in Sulloway, p. 309)

Indeed, in his *Freud, Biologist of the Mind*, Sulloway suggests that Freud, rather than being advanced or outrageous in his challenge to the sexual innocence of children, arrived late in the day and in fact had been previously rather prudish. It seems that it was Freud's self-analysis that led him to overcome his resistance to the new conclusion; it was also about this time that he stated that the work of analysis was not the recovery of memories but rather the overcoming of resistances, a point I referred to earlier. It was not the discovery that was significant but its manner.

A piece of knowledge which comes through the overcoming of a resistance is quite different from one which lies in my being as an object that has just been deposited there. If I come out with the bland statement that the core neurosis is centred on the Oedipal conflict it is quite different from a sudden realization that I see portions of the world through my mother's spectacles, that I am attached to her and that I repudiate certain attitudes and values which are associated with my father. In the former the knowledge does not touch my own subjectivity, whereas in the latter I see and understand something from the centre of my being. This is why I said in the first lecture that there is an inherent contradiction in this series because as a teacher I am purveying knowledge of the first kind, whereas psychoanalysis as it is practised clinically is concerned with knowledge of the second. It is knowledge of this second kind which is truly therapeutic. I also believe that only those interpretations which have been gained on the basis of this second kind of knowledge on the analyst's part – from the centre of his or her being – are therapeutic for the patient.

In other words I am saying that a special kind of knowledge, let us provisionally call it *subjective knowledge*, has an effect on the hearer. What is this effect? I think it is that it compels inner assent. Being in the presence of someone expressing subjective knowledge chimes with something within us whereby we are able to know truth and sense authenticity. The Romantic's sense of the authentic is his capacity to register when an expression, in whatever medium, comes from someone's inner light, from his or her *subjective knowledge*.

The reason why Freud as a figure towers over those I have just mentioned like Maudsley, Lindner, Moll, Ellis and Bell is that he arrived at his knowledge subjectively, and it struck a chord in those figures like Ferenczi, Jung, Stekel and Adler who consequently joined him and started the new movement which Freud called psychoanalysis. The knowledge itself is not important in psychoanalysis, but the manner of its attainment is. We might then ask the interesting question why it is therapeutic to gain knowledge subjectively rather than possess it objectively?

In his biography of Freud, Ernest Jones speaks of his self-analysis as being an act of consummate courage, a lone journey. Ellenberger sees the matter differently and invokes the notion of 'creative illness', which he conceptualizes as follows:

> A creative illness succeeds a period of intense preoccupation with an idea and search for a certain truth. It is a polymorphous condition that can take the shape of depression, neurosis, psychosomatic ailments, or even psychosis. Whatever the symptoms, they are felt as painful, if not agonizing, by the subject, with alternating periods of alleviation and worsening. Through the illness the subject never loses the thread of his dominating preoccupation. It is often compatible with normal, professional activity and family life. But even if he keeps to his social activities, he is almost entirely absorbed with himself. He suffers from feelings of utter isolation, even when he has a mentor who guides him through the ordeal (like the shaman apprentice with his master). The termination is often rapid and marked by a phase of exhilaration. The subject emerges from his ordeal with a permanent transformation in his personality and the conviction that he has discovered a great truth or new spiritual world. (pp. 447–448)

Ellenberger does not think that Freud undertook an isolated self-analysis but rather that he had a shaman in the form of Wilhelm Fliess. Nor was it an experience tht Freud alone had passed through in human history: Ellenberger mentions Fechner and also Jung. Indeed it is clear from his autobiographical work *Memories, Dreams, Reflections* (1963) that Jung passed through some similar experience, and he also mentions that to

undertake such an inner journey it is necessary to have supporting figures around. The sociologist Max Weber seems to have
gone through a comparable experience, as also did the
philosopher Ludwig Wittgenstein. However, what Freud saw
was that the attachment to the supporting figure, or shaman,
needed to be analysed. The individual needs to free himself
from his master. Ellenberger's idea that Freud was in the grip of
an illness accords with many of Freud's statements and hints,
especially in his letters to Fliess. It also stresses that there was
the pressure of an inner illness on Freud to undertake his self-
analysis. Thus, Ernest Jones' statements, which suggest a level
of freedom, seem doubtful. The sort of freedom that Jones
attributes to Freud comes possibly as the fruit of analysis; it
does not exist sufficiently when the apprentice comes to his
master. In analysis, to extend Ellenberger's concept, the
analyst becomes the master who helps his apprentice through
this inner journey and finally to overthrow him and become his
own master.

I want to make one last point about Freud's self-analysis,
which is that it was an integrative experience. I suggested at the
end of the last lecture that Freud integrated in himself the scientific and the Romantic traditions. But his self-analysis integrated much more than that. It integrated his physiological
studies with the hypnotic movement. It integrated his inner
wishes towards his mother and father with his wishes towards
his wife and family. He integrated the psychiatric views of the
day with his own inner subjective experiences. He integrated
the psychological views on instinct with those from contem-
porary biology. He integrated a religious view of the world
with childhood wishes and Oedipal conflicts. He integrated his
Jewish identity with his Gentile preoccupations. Nothing
could be in a compartment, not touching other things. His
working life could not be separate from his domestic life. His
writings, which weave in and out of these different areas, give
expression to an inner integration.

8 FREUD'S UNDERSTANDING OF DREAMS

The central notion in Freud's theory of dreams is that a dream is a hallucinatory fulfilment of a wish. This is most clearly seen in the dreams of children because these are not distorted in the same way as those of adults. I will give you two examples: one is from the dream of an eight-year-old girl, quoted in *The Interpretation of Dreams*, and the other is the dream of my elder son when he was aged four. I will start with the dream that Freud tells us of:

> A friend of mine has reported a dream to me which was very much like my son's. The dreamer was an eight-year-old girl. Her father had started off with several children on a walk to Dornbach, with the idea of visiting the Rohrer Hütte. As it was getting late, however, he had turned back, promising the children to make up for the disappointment another time. On their way home they had passed the signpost that marks the path up to the Hameau. The children had then asked to be taken up to the Hameau; but once again for the same reason they had to be consoled with the promise of another day. Next morning the eight-year-old girl came to her father and said in satisfied tones: 'Daddy, I dreamed last night that you went with us to the Rohrer Hütte and the

Hameau.' In her impatience she had anticipated the fulfilment of her father's promises. (1900, *SE* 4, p. 129)

When my son was four he was attending a small nursery school where there was a teacher whom he was very fond of, Mrs Rochester. Mrs Rochester was absent for one whole week of the school term, and on the second day of this absence our son came to us in the morning with a dream. In this dream he arrived at the school and when he arrived in the classroom he was gratified to find that there was Mrs Rochester greeting him and ready to take the class.

In both these dreams the wish-fulfilment is very clear once the life circumstances and recent happenings of the dreamer are known. Another type of dream in which the fulfilment of a wish is also clear is produced by the person who is thirsty or hungry or sexually frustrated. Here the dream satisfies the desire, and Freud mentions that by eating some olives or anchovies before going to bed, he can experimentally produce a dream where he will be drinking cool water. Similarly the hungry person will dream of eating, the sexually starved of sexual intercourse or some sexual activity that discharges the need, and the person with a full bladder will dream of urinating. In all these cases the real need is achieved by means of hallucinatory fulfilment and the wish is not concealed in the dream.

The hallucinated fulfilment in the dream is usually placed in a phantasy context so that, for instance, the person who is thirsty may dream of being in Rome, drinking from one of the fountains on a hot day, or that he is given a drink of Coca-Cola by a red-haired stranger while on a journey. Freud says that this phantasy context leads from the physical need into the psychic sphere. In other words, the drinking in the dream is generated by the real thirst which the dream incorporates, as it were into its pattern, but the psychic meaning of the dream must be sought in the surrounding phantasy structure.

In a similar way the dream incorporates three sorts of stimuli in the real world: external stimuli, internal stimuli and recent happenings that are still in a state of excitation in the memory. I will give examples of each of these. Freud quotes three 'alarm-clock' dreams from the writings of a German named Hildebrandt and I will recount the first of these:

> 'I dreamed, then, that one spring morning I was going for a walk and was strolling through the green fields till I came to a neighbouring village, where I saw the villagers in their best clothes, with hymn-books under their arms, flocking to the church. Of course! It was Sunday, and early morning service would soon be beginning. I decided I would attend it; but first, as I was rather hot from walking, I went into the churchyard which surrounded the church, to cool down. While I was reading some of the tombstones, I heard the bell-ringer climbing up the church tower and at the top of it I now saw the little village bell which would presently give the signal for the beginning of devotions. For quite a while it hung there motionless, then it began to swing, and suddenly its peal began to ring out clear and piercing – sc clear and piercing that it put an end to my sleep. But what was ringing was the alarm-clock.' (*SE* 4, pp. 27–28)

I am sure that we can all think of similar examples from our own experience. Any disturbance to the senses can be incorporated into the dream. Freud quotes L.F.A. Maury, who arranged for an assistant to stimulate him in various ways during sleep and see how these affected his dreams. When his lips and the tip of his nose were tickled with a feather he dreamed of a frightful form of torture: a mask made of pitch was placed on his face and then pulled off, so that it took his skin off with it. On another occasion he was given some eau-de-Cologne to smell and he dreamed that he was in a perfume shop in Cairo. That is, all stimuli are translated into pictorial imagery and even a noise does not seem, upon waking, to be an auditory experience.

The stimuli for dreams can also come from within the

organism. It has been well known since Aristotle that an anxiety dream could be the first premonition of a disease; in a dream the subliminal cues which are not registered in waking life are often picked up. Someone I knew in analysis, for example, dreamed of his analyst's funeral and the analyst interpreted the patient's death wishes towards him, but the next day the analyst died suddenly of a heart attack. I have little doubt that the patient had picked up subtle cues that were probably not available to the analyst's consciousness.

It is well known that recent happenings are registered and become material for the dream. Freud believed that every dream takes up some events of the day preceding the night during which the dream takes place, and referred to this as the dream-day. It is residues from the events of the dream-day which are incorporated into the dream: factors – internal, external and in the memory-store – which have not been digested are worked into the dream and form part of its pattern.

Ella Sharpe (1937) believed that the instigating factors of the dream-day were important in determining the interpretation of a dream. You will notice that dreams incorporating such imagery are not relying solely on wishes, and that dreams are recording something real in all these cases. Freud also says that speeches in dreams are not created as such, but rather originate with some bit of heard speech, often torn viciously out of context. In this way a dream can be seen as a complex pattern of thoughts, but one from which a creating, thinking and judging agent is absent. We shall come back to this in the next lecture and also when we consider Bion's theory of thinking.

Nevertheless, Freud was categorical that the dream was always the hallucinatory fulfilment of a wish and that this was its purpose. As we saw, this is quite clear in the dreams of children and also in those cases where there is powerful physiological need. In most dreams of adults, however, the wish is hidden and it was this which led Freud to distinguish two elements in dreams: the manifest content and the latent content. Freud's idea is that if the wish was to be clearly seen in the dream it would so disturb the dreamer that he or she would wake up; the dream, then, is the guardian of sleep. It is a compromise formation in that it contains wishes which are unacceptable to the conscious ego and so cannot enter consciousness during the waking day and yet, even in sleep, cannot be allowed lucid expression because the dreamer would wake up. The dream therefore expresses the wish, but in a disguise.

I shall try to describe this process because it is quite central not only to Freud's concept of dream formation, but also to his notion of the formation of symptoms and of the significance of jokes, slips of the tongue and, in a wider context, myths and symbols. The dream process is founded on two poles. First there is the forbidden wish struggling to reach consciousness, but unable to make its desired journey unhindered because it meets up with the censorship. The censor's job is to stop the wish reaching consciousness but it cannot do so completely; the wish thrusts for expression and succeeds, but is forced to undergo transformation at the censor's insistence. Like a prisoner who simply must escape from prison, and can do so only by dressing up as a staff member in order to pass by the sentry's eye unnoticed.

Now the wish has to disguise itself in a visual form that has some connection with its own form. This is the principle behind symbol formation: the symbol always bears a perceptual similarity to the thing signified. In dream formation it has to be so, otherwise the forbidden wish would not reach expression. The manifest content, therefore, is a translation of the forbidden wishes into visual images which are related to the wishes, but sufficiently disguised to escape the eye of the censor. To unravel the meaning, and reach the wish, it is necessary to find the common denominators between the manifest content and the latent wish. How is this done? We shall now look at Freud's method of interpreting dreams.

Freud says that a dream can be thought of either as a unit in itself and interpreted accordingly, or as a patchwork of different elements each of which needs to be interpreted separately. To find the meaning of a dream it was necessary to find the symbolic value of each bit, and only by doing so would the hidden meaning emerge. Therefore Freud adopted the method whereby the patient associated to each bit of the dream, and through these associations reached each hidden element, and each precipitating factor. If you want to understand the way that Freud went about this you cannot do better than to read the analysis of his own 'dream of Irma's injection' (*SE* 4, pp. 106–121).

Now, if you go through Freud's dreams you will find that each of them leads to a latent thought, but one which is current and also specific: to the unacknowledged jealousy that a wife feels towards a woman who attracts her husband's attentions, an erotic desire that a man has towards his wife's sister, an undeclared ambition to get high promotion, or a wish that a recent love affair should not lead to a pregnancy. All the instances that Freud gives are of hidden material that is in the preconscious, and though he was aware that dreams tapped deep unconscious wishes he does not give any examples of the latter. Nevertheless he says that dreams always recapitulate memories that pertain to childhood. I myself once had a patient each of whose dreams, when reported in the analysis, opened up a memory from childhood which had until then been sealed in amnesia.

The dimension which is lacking in the wish-fulfilment model, and which has become familiar to us in the dream-interpretation work of later analysts, is that of structural changes within the psyche which are proclaimed through the dream medium. I will give you an example of what I mean. A patient told me that his house was haunted and that all his friends who came into it felt a cold and unwelcome presence in it. I had basically interpreted that the house was in tune with a hostile part of himself which he did not recognize. Some time later he told me that he had a dream in which he walked down the road to his house, but instead of finding the house there was just a gap where it should have been. He interpreted the dream himself by saying that he thought it meant that the hostility was now inside himself, he recognized it, and it had disappeared from the house. This seemed to be quite right to both of us: it enunciated a structural change.

Particular types of distortion are favoured in dreams, and the best known of these is probably condensation. I think we are all familiar with this; most typically we find it in a dream involving someone whom we know and yet it does not look quite like him or her. We realize that it is a combination of two different people, and the meaning of the dream is to be found in the link between these two people. A patient once had a dream of such a figure combining two women whom she knew. At first she could find no connecting link – one lived in America and the other in Greece, one was old and the other young, one was tall and the other short – until it emerged that both were divorced. In the dream they stood for a part of her which was quite divorced from me. In a more general way many dreams are a condensation of a whole range of thoughts and one short dream can have more than one meaning. Because there is often a very artful selection of the symbols, so that they are capable of representing several thoughts, a short dream is frequently full of as much significance as an apparently long one. Then, too, in an analysis it frequently happens that further meanings of a single dream emerge as the analysis proceeds.

Another frequent distortion in dreams is termed displacement. Something of importance is displaced on to something seemingly trivial, and again it is only through associations that it is possible to trace the true location of the affect. Condensation and displacement are the two commonest mechanisms described by Freud, but he does mention others, and still others have been described since his day. Another frequent mechanism, for instance, is that of representing something by its opposite. Since in the unconscious opposites and negatives do not have a separate definition, it always needs to be borne in mind that an opposite may be indicated. A patient of mine had a dream which included a black dog with white spots. I was trying to interpret the dream in its positive sense when she said, 'It's funny – our dog at home is like that, but the other way around – white with black spots.' The dog was there as an indirect clue to the dreamer that the negative of the meaning under discussion was the one to be understood. To represent causation a dream often establishes the main sense in the large part of the dream, and the subordinate part is relegated to a smaller dream that precedes the other. If there is an identity between two things in waking life, then the one will be transformed into the other before the eyes of the dreamer. Similarly, if the dreamer is required in waking life to choose between one thing or another, the dream just has both alongside each other. The dream-maker is like a painter who has a message – an idea or theme – to convey but no words, and his materials are paint, brush and canvas.

As we go through *The Interpretation of Dreams* and pass through the many different aspects of the dream-work, with its representability and the weaving in and out of the unconscious mental processes that are connected with the dream-work, Freud keeps coming back to his central theme: that the dream is the hallucinatory fulfilment of a wish. The decoding of the dream has as its purpose to reach that wish. However, I cannot help feeling, as I read through this seminal work, that there is something dogmatic about the constant repetition of this theme and that it almost has the quality of an *idée fixe*. I do not find it surprising then that with the publication of *Beyond the Pleasure Principle* in 1920 he abandoned the wish-fulfilment theory. I want now to look briefly at this modification.

During the Great War, both directly and through his colleagues, Freud came across the dreams of individuals who had suffered a tremendous shock, like a shell going off and killing or maiming a friend who was close by. Many such victims had a recurring dream of the event exactly as it happened; in no way could Freud attribute this to wish-fulfilment. He explained it in the following way. In all of us, he said, there is a stimulus barrier filtering the stimuli that are continually bombarding the organism. Any massive bombardment that occurs suddenly, however, completely overwhelms the organism, which becomes flooded with a deluge of stimuli with which it cannot deal. The organism then regresses to a primitive way of dealing with such a shock: it repeats the trauma again and again in an attempt to deal with the shock it has sustained. It tries to master actively what was done to it as a passive agent; in such cases dreaming serves the purpose of these repetitive attempts at mastery. This mechanism is well known to us all as the compulsion to repeat, and is something we come across quite frequently with patients.

So, in his sixties, Freud allowed an exception to his wish-fulfilment theory. He allowed the evidence to overrule his previous hypothesis. Next, we shall be considering some of the developments in dream theory since Freud.

9 DEVELOPMENTS IN DREAM RESEARCH SINCE FREUD

The literature on and research into dreams is immense and I am going to outline in the briefest manner just some of this thinking since Freud, and then suggest a common denominator within it.

We shall come to Fairbairn in Lecture 22, but I want to sketch his theory of dreams now. Essentially, he said, a dream does not reveal a concealed wish but is rather a symbolic narrative of the inner 'state of affairs'. To make this idea clear I should put it in its context of Fairbairn's theory that the human psyche is split up and consists of an object part of the personality, split into different little personalities; and an ego part, also split in a way that mirrors the object part of the personality. Libidinal and aggressive thrusts emerge from the ego and go towards the object part of the personality. There is in particular an aggressive part of the personality that attacks the libidinal strivings of the ego which Fairbairn named the internal saboteur – like an internal traitor. The object part of the personality is in identification with external objects from childhood, and continues to be linked to people of the person's present-day environment. This inner state of affairs, or inner world, is in a state of change and development, and governs the real interactive happenings of the individual's social life. The dream, which is a descriptive statement of the inner world at any one moment, brings us into contact with that state.

Jung thought that man in the twentieth century had raced ahead of himself. With all our new technology we might have the impression that the whole of man has kept apace with this advance, but this is not so. What we call consciousness is immersed in the scientific comforts and advantages of modern technology, but the main part of man is rooted in his past. Dreams loom up as constant reminders and become psychic compensators for his advanced state. They therefore record not only the individual's early history from infancy onwards, but also those deep parts of our nature which we share with earliest man and his prehuman ancestors: in this way dream life records elements of ourselves which are genetically transmitted.

Jung therefore disagreed with Freud on several important issues. For Jung, all of us have a collective unconscious as well as a personal unconscious, and our dreams record the former as well as the latter; he therefore opposed Freud's view that the unconscious was created solely through the repression of all the memories and wishes which we personally want to disown. The dream is not primarily a disguise for socially shocking wishes, but rather a symbolic language communicating the place where the psyche is and what it is able to manage: it brings us a message from our soul which we need to heed. Because they are records of more primitive needs and modes of functioning, however, dreams have their own symbolic communicative language and the job of the dream interpreter is to translate from this special communicative form of the unconscious into the language of consciousness. To do this the psychotherapist needs not only to have the patient's associations, but also to know the archetypal symbols and their significance.

Ernest Schachtel, writing in the 1940s, thought that Freud's view of infantile amnesia did not explain why all experience of early childhood is forgotten (quoted in Richard M. Jones, p. 134). In contrast to the specific repression of sexual fantasies and experiences, Schachtel believed that there was something in the general quality of childhood experience which led to the forgetting of that experience. He also thought that the clinical practice of psychoanalysis provided experimental evidence that Freud's view was deficient because, even in long analyses, repressed experiences of childhood were not recalled. Schachtel identified *conventionalization* as a type of repression that suppressed all the experiences of childhood, all its symbolizing forms. The purpose of this kind of repression was to exclude from consciousness the primary process itself.

One point that is closely related to Schachtel's view is that childhood experiences are very intense and are therefore not remembered like later memories. This statement needs some further explanation: extremely intense experiences are not translatable into conscious expression. They have to be enacted, in particular through the process which Melanie Klein has named projective identification (which we will come to in the lectures on her), but also through observable gestural actions. Then there are less intense experiences which are translatable into visual imagery: these are the happenings which are symbolically recorded in dreams. Lastly, those experiences which can be translated into words are the least intense. Now it is my contention that the experiences of childhood are generally much more intense than adult ones, and therefore are so very formative of all later developmental lines. The reason why psychoanalysis is able to be effective is because it is a method which re-enacts deep emotional experiences such that it can match in intensity those of childhood. (In addition it seems extremely likely that in childhood there is not the necessary memory equipment to store the experiences, even those of a less intense nature, but this is not my main theme.)

Piaget considered dreams in the context of the thinking processes of childhood. He believed that children were frequently not aware of certain matters because they quite simply took them for granted; for consciousness of them to be called forth some inner or outer obstacle needed to emerge. As an analyst I feel that this point of Piaget's is confirmed by clinical experience. I would say that a person's deep assumptions, deeply rooted personal philosophies of life, are so much a part of the air he breathes that neither he nor his closest friends notice them consciously; it is one of the analyst's tasks to notice just these, but it may take a very long time. My experience is that the deepest observations are paradoxically the ones that, on reaching awareness, have stared you in the face from the first day of meeting. Piaget's view is that assumptions are unconscious because they are the crystallizations of a particular world that is so familiar that it does not evoke awareness. More important still are Piaget's notions that conscious thinking is antedated by a more primitive form of thinking which occurs through the articulation of imagery, and that this is part of what is occurring in the dreaming process. For Piaget, then, there is an active but primitive process which dreams symbolize.

Certain elements are common to all these thinkers. Firstly, they all rejected Freud's hypothesis that what is being repressed is a hidden wish, and that this repression causes or instigates the dream. Secondly, they all held that a whole mode of mental functioning was being cloaked in the language of the dream. Thirdly, Piaget believed – and this aspect has been taken up by Bion and by Meltzer (1983) – that dreaming is a thinking process. Fourthly, they all held on to the idea that dreaming is a process and not a record of a static fact – a specifiable wish, for instance. Indeed, since it is after all a sequence, a narrative, the manifest content would have us believe this. Lastly, therefore, they all viewed the dream in itself much more positively.

I want now to turn from the psychoanalytic literature to a consideration of the physiology of sleep. In the early 1950s two sleep researchers, Aserinsky and Kleitman (quoted in Richard M. Jones, pp. 24–25), discovered what has become known as the REM state, REM being short for Rapid Eye Movement. They noticed that about every ninety minutes the sleeper went into a physiological state characterized by certain phenomena, one of which was that the pupils of the eyes began to move around rapidly as if scanning the environment, although the eyelids remained closed. Other concomitants of this state, which is triggered by the pontile-limbic system in the brain, were irregular pulse, blood pressure and respiration; penile erection in males; sporadic activity of certain fine muscle groups; near absence of tonic anti-gravity muscle potential; a low voltage desynchronized cortical EEG pattern; high brain temperature and metabolic rate; and a high positive correlation with the ability to report dreams upon being awakened when in this state.

The percentage of REM state is higher in infancy than in adulthood and, as far as can be determined, seems to exist at the foetal stage of development. It is found to exist in all mammals, but there is no trace of it in reptiles or lower forms of life. On close examination this state is found to be as different from NREM (non-REM) sleep as the latter is from waking life, and researchers therefore think it a mistake to call it 'sleep'. They distinguish three physiological states in mammalian life: waking life, the REM state, and sleep. There is a very high correlation between the REM state and the presence of dreams, and very little dreaming occurs in sleep.

This last statement needs a little more clarification. There is complete agreement, in studies of sleepers who have been awakened in NREM and in REM, that reports are quantitatively and qualitatively different. NREM reports tend to be brief, fragmentary descriptions of thoughts that seem close to the thoughts of waking life, whereas reports from REM awakenings describe longer and more hallucinated dramas. In descriptive terms the two types of reports clearly refer to two types of mental processes. We would have no doubt about calling the reports from REM awakenings dreams; but I am doubtful whether the mentation typical of NREM reports can properly be described as 'dreaming' in the psychoanalytic sense of the symbolic narrative that I was discussing earlier.

Freud was not in possession of the knowledge of the REM state that we have. We can now clearly see that dreams are not the guardian of sleep, but the ubiquitous accompaniment of a specific physiological state. The question is: what is the function of the REM state? Several different answers to this question have been suggested. Firstly, that it has a neutralizing function in counteractive relation to some noxious by-product of mammalian metabolism. Richard M. Jones, in *The New Psychology of Dreaming* (pp. 167–189), suggests that there are psychological correlates to all the physiological functions of the REM state, and that the dream, through discharging a noxious wish, becomes the psychological partner to the physiological function. Another view is that the REM state serves a stimulating function to compensate for sensory deprivations during sleep, and that dreaming has a restitutive function in response to recurrent psychological impoverishments imposed by the external and internal conditions that characterize human life. Such a view would be in tune with the finding that subjects deprived of REM become irritable and aggressive, and that in subsequent nights of sleep the amount of REM increases in exact proportion to that lost. A further function may be that of reorganizing the system because of the disorganizing effects of mammalian sleep on the central nervous system. Psychologically a dream increases comprehension and cognitive grasp, and allows new realities to be grasped at a deep emotional level.

A suggested function of particular relevance to psychoanalytic thought is that the REM state alerts the mammal in preparation for flight and fight. (An additional version of this theory rests on the finding that after REM there are a few moments of wakefulness before the animal reverts to sleep.) The idea that the human being is constantly in danger of being overcome by his or her social environment is consistent with Melanie Klein's view that one of the earliest anxieties is that of being overwhelmed by the primary love object. The subject fears psychological annihilation, so the dreaming process serves an inner vigilance by absorbing threatening elements in such a way as to preserve its own subjectivity. The traumatic dreams that led Freud to revise his dream theory would be consistent with this view of the dream's function.

In summary, I suggest that the REM state is the instigator of the dream and that is its purpose: it is a necessary state of affairs for consciousness to exist. If renewal of consciousness comes about through dreaming then I think it possible that REM exists to allow dreaming to take place.

10 THE CLINICAL SIGNIFICANCE OF TRANSFERENCE

As I said in Lecture 5, Freud developed the technique and practice of psychoanalysis between 1892 and 1896. At the earlier date he was still practising hypnotism, but by the latter one he was doing psychoanalysis in a way that was not very different from the methods that psychoanalysts use today. A convergence of different factors led to this transition, but an important moment of crystallization is the one recorded in Freud's *Autobiographical Study* which I quoted at the beginning of the series. Let me quote it again:

> One day I had an experience which showed me in the crudest light what I had long suspected. It related to one of my most acquiescent patients, with whom hypnotism had enabled me to bring about the most marvellous results, and whom I was engaged in relieving of her suffering by tracing back her attacks of pain to their origins. As she woke up on one occasion, she threw her arms around my neck. The unexpected entrance of a servant relieved us from a painful discussion, but from that time onwards there was a tacit understanding between us that the hypnotic treatment should be discontinued. I was modest enough not to attribute the event to my own irresistible personal attraction, and I felt that I had now

grasped the nature of the mysterious element that was at work behind hypnotism. In order to exclude it, or at all events to isolate it, it was necessary to abandon hypnotism. (*SE* 20, p. 27)

Crucial to Freud's discovery of the transference was the fact that he did not attribute the patient's behaviour to his own 'irresistible personal attraction'. The 'modesty' opened a doorway to the thought that he was rather the recipient of affections that belonged to an important figure in the patient's life. At first he considered this to be the first boyfriend or girlfriend of adolescence, then he pushed it back further to the first love objects in the person's childhood; his notion was that it was this love which was transferred to the doctor.

The notion that someone frequently transfers his or her affections to the confidant had been well known for centuries; experienced spiritual directors had written reams about it, emphasizing that confessors needed to be cautious and restrain their own feelings when counselling and advising female penitents. Doctors were also familiar with the phenomenon and, as I mentioned in the lecture on the Mesmer-Hypnotic tradition, the secret report which was submitted to Louis XVI warned of the dangers which could arise as a result of the erotic attraction of the female patient to her male magnetizer.

The dominant note in all the attitudes towards this phenomenon was that it was dangerous, and that if a professional became aware that it was happening then the best course was to flee. It seems that Breuer did just this when the erotic response from Anna O. became too powerful for him to cope with. Freud's attitude was different, however. Firstly, he looked at the matter quite scientifically and asked himself the question: 'What is the explanation for this phenomenon?' Secondly, he did not appear to be emotionally frightened by it, although he was well aware that a powerful transference could be difficult for an analyst. Nevertheless he did not recommend flight as the solution.

The psychoanalyst knows that he is working with highly explosive forces and that he needs to proceed with as much caution and conscientiousness as a chemist. But when have chemists ever been forbidden, because of the danger, from handling explosive substances, which are indispensable, on account of their effects? It is remarkable that psychoanalysis has to win for itself afresh all the liberties which have long since been accorded to other medical activities. (1915a, *SE* 12, p. 171)

Freud came to recognize that the symptoms of the neurosis became converted into a new type of neurosis, which he called 'transference neurosis'. The loving, admiring relation of the patient to the analyst, therefore, he regarded as neurotic. Psychoanalytic treatment sought to work through the phantasies which gave rise to the neurosis. A situation where a patient seemed free of psychosomatic symptoms, but had purely substituted for them a fixated attachment to the analyst, was therefore no real cure; cure was effected only when that particular relation to the analyst had been dissolved. It was the analytic situation itself which caused the patient to fall in love with the analyst.

Freud pointed out that the beginning of analytic treatment consisted largely of allowing a transference to develop. I believe that this is precisely what is most difficult for the analyst, because it means that the analyst must allow the patient to perceive him or her according to some inner repressed configuration. This may sound quite easy, but firstly I know from my own experience that it is not so, and secondly I know from supervising that it is one of the psychical burdens which a therapist or analyst finds most difficult to bear. After all it is not pleasant to be misperceived. Most of us have ideas about ourselves which we cherish. We like to be seen as efficient, or helpful, or easygoing, or sincere, or caring, or humorous, or liberal, or religious, or atheist, or politically committed, or in touch with modern thinking, or educated, or ambitious or unambitious, or well-read, or intellectual, or in touch with our feelings. There is not one of us who does not secretly cherish certain ideas about ourselves.

About two years ago I was supervising someone who was left-wing, anti-authoritarian and favoured an open, flexible approach to patients. I imagine that she prided herself on being non-dogmatic clinically: she made a point of listening to her patients' difficulties, and with one in particular tried not to cram his communications into any particular formula. Now I must tell you that this patient had the audacity one day to say that she was just like Mrs Thatcher. And I must also tell you that the therapist found this quite intolerable. I cannot now remember what the therapist said, but she repudiated the imputation and said that the patient had misperceived the situation, he had not understood the point of her last interpretation. If you are a bright, left-wing, open-minded person it is not agreeable to be called Mrs Thatcher – it might even be the ultimate insult.

This is of course rather a crude example and frequently the situation is much more subtle. For instance, I can remember a time when I used to think that I was rather sensitive and understood my patients' inner difficulties. Then a patient described me as insensitive and slow-witted. I found it difficult to accept but I know that only when I had accepted it did the therapy move on. And when I say that I accepted it I do not mean that I submissively accepted abuse, but actually recognized that an aspect of the patient's perception was true. Only then was it possible to work through a denied part: an insensitive, rather thick aspect of herself.

Now what exactly is it that is transferred or projected on to the analyst? It is a combination of two things: the important figures from the past as they related to the patient, especially in childhood; and the present, repressed, unbearable reality. Now we need to look at this a little more closely. It is the unbearable

psychic quality of both aspects which is projected out, because
it cannot be borne within. It may be easier to grasp this point if
I take a particular case.

A patient described a mother who could never *take* any of his
concerns. He was a man with passionate feelings, but his
mother would always say to him, 'Yes, yes, darling', and
quickly change the subject. This quality of his mother's absolutely exasperated him, for it was a manifestation of her inability
to bear any of her child's anxiety. He described a mother who
seemed unable to cope with any demands from her baby: once
she found herself responsible for *her* baby she just dumped him
on to someone else. This for him was the unbearable response.
Now I think it likely that his mother really *was* like this with
my patient. Accordingly in the transference he perceived me in
the same way. He was sure that I could not bear any demands
from him, and he was certain that I would drop him early on in
treatment. After a time he began to feel that perhaps I would
continue to treat him but only on condition that he was very
compliant.

This was one aspect of the transference, but there was
another. What was much more horrific for him was to discover
that he was also identified with this hated object: to discover
that as soon as I began to put some demands on him he would
reject me. It then became clear that this hated figure or function
was his own way of behaving, but obscured from his awareness. Therefore the question becomes: was this hated way of
behaving a current aspect of himself or was it also the way his
mother had actually behaved towards him? I believe that it is a
combination of both: that there is an object part of the psychic
structure that takes on the form of the external figure, in the
same way that wax will take into itself the impression of a seal.
This object part is then experienced as extraneous to the self,
but at the same time the ego is identified with it; or rather, the
ego becomes lured into the activities of this hated object, which
Fairbairn called a 'bad internal object'. Therefore the analyst is

perceived as the bad object, but he also becomes the recipient of the bad object's activity.

So far I have described only the way in which the analyst has transferred on to him the unbearable things, but the patient also transfers to the analyst the positive yearnings. Freud spoke about transference as a photographic plate projected on to the analyst and therefore stressed the way in which the repressed is put on to the analyst. In a state of regression to an infantile mode of operating the yearnings are also transferred on to the analyst. Every patient approaches an analyst with particular emotional expectations, and with the hope that the analyst will be able to respond to him or her in a way which was more satisfactory than the parents'. I think that in the initial consultation, therefore, every patient gives the analyst some instructions about how he or she wants him to function. In other words, the patient transfers on to the analyst all his or her developmental hopes, an idea which I need to explain further.

One day a patient whom I was seeing for psychoanalysis was disturbed by hearing one of my children crying in another part of the house. She was disturbed in particular by the thought that my attention would be distracted. She was right; it was; and I said to her that it was likely that I would be distracted, and she agreed with this. What was more disturbing to her was the notion that my surface attention was the sum total of all my attention to her: it was just skin deep. From many communications in previous sessions it seemed that her mother's attention to her was of just such a nature: there was no attention in the heart. My patient was concerned to know whether my attention to her was of a deeper nature. Did I really blank her out emotionally as soon as she departed at the end of the session? More especially, when I turned from her to my wife was she blanked out of existence? This was also a question from her about the nature of my emotional intercourse with my wife. Was it of such a sort that it had to blank out others? In other words, was that a surface intercourse as well? It was particularly this that the patient needed to know, because her developmental failure was due to a superficiality of maternal response. She needed to know whether or not I had the emotional capacity to contain her. She knew that if I did not have that capacity, I could not provide what she needed.

I think it will be obvious that such a patient must lead the analyst to a close emotional questioning of himself; for it cannot be that the analyst is sufficiently developed emotionally for the different emotional needs of each patient. Therefore patients who come for analysis put a demand on the analyst that he grow emotionally, and it is for this reason that I doubt whether there is a more emotionally exacting profession. If a particular capacity required by a particular patient is severely lacking in the analyst, then no amount of supervision or technical manoeuvres will be of any avail.

To sum up, therefore: the patient transfers on to the analyst responsibility for emotional development in a failed area. One aspect of this process is that the patient needs to transfer on to the analyst his or her bad inner objects; the other aspect is that the patient requires an emotional capacity in the analyst in the particular area where there has been developmental failure. It is for this reason that the transference is the central locus of cure. It is also the instrument through which the analyst arrives at an understanding of his patient, which is what essentially differentiates psychoanalysis from counselling or other therapies. It is also emotionally what is most difficult, and it is not something that can be *taught* in any training programme.

11 FREUD'S INSTINCT THEORY

In all psychology I doubt whether there is any subject more complex, conditioned by the scientist's view of man, or an ideal target for diverse speculation than that of instinct. There is great variation of view as to the extent to which human beings are dominated by instincts. Some hold that with the development of intelligence, instincts atrophied and now only the most residual traces remain in man. Many late nineteenth and early twentieth century psychologists, however, thought that instincts had a leading place in the determination of human behaviour. William James, William McDougall and Freud, for instance, all thought in this way. Some thinkers, like Herbert Spencer, believed that the instincts were quite blind: forces within the personality that completely bypassed desires or intention. William McDougall, at the other end of this spectrum, thought that instincts were invested with subjective desire, and he argued forcibly against defining instincts as bundles of reflex actions. Freud's solution of this problem is a more complex one and can be properly understood only within his development from the topographical model to the structural one.

A common definition is that instinctive actions emanate from 'inherited knowledge'. Let me take an example. The female mason wasp lays its eggs in a hole, fills it with caterpillars which she then stings in exactly the right place, and seals up the hole. The caterpillars are paralysed so that when the eggs hatch the little grubs have fresh and not rotten flesh to eat. The female mason wasp is not taught to do this; she does it through inherited knowledge or instinct. Because the knowledge is inherited it is not adaptive. In fact as a form of knowledge it is very rigidly circumscribed according to an inner need. The behaviour issuing from it may have been appropriate for a different environment but not so for the present one. Instinct is unable to adapt the environment; it is intelligence in man which has adapted the environment to suit his needs. The adaptation of instincts occurs over many thousands of years along with other evolutionary factors.

Instinctive action is initiated either by a sense impression from without or an internal stimulus, each of which has a meaning for the animal. There is therefore a cognitive aspect to the perceptual apparatus; at least this seems to be so in man and the higher animals. McDougall assumed that instinctive behaviour was attended by some emotional excitement 'peculiar to that kind of behaviour', and considered that the emotional arousal that accompanied instinctive behaviour was part and parcel of the instinct itself. Freud believed that the instinct was not known directly by the subject but only inferred through its representative, which may be a particular arousal state. But before looking at Freud's view I want to look briefly at the current controversy over James Strachey's translation of the German word which Freud used, namely *Trieb*.

Strachey's stated reason for choosing 'instinct' to render *Trieb* – which is normally taken to mean 'drive' – is that it is a vague and indeterminate word, and Freud uses the word *Trieb* in different senses. But this argument could be used of almost any word chosen by him to translate the German original. Bruno Bettelheim, in a recent book, *Freud and Man's Soul* (1983, pp. 103–108), has argued forcefully against translating

Trieb as instinct: he says that Freud uses the German word *Instinkt* on several occasions and that the usage on these occasions corresponds in sense to the English word instinct, but that he deliberately eschews the use of it when talking of human beings. Whenever he uses *Instinkt* he is talking of animals; when talking of human beings as opposed to animals 'drive' or 'impulse' is preferable to translate Freud's *Trieb*.

Bettelheim's central argument against the use of instinct is that an instinct is unalterable, whereas Freud implied a plasticity in the use of *Trieb* which is not accommodated by the word instinct. I am doubtful about this reasoning, as I believe there is both an unalterability and a plasticity inherent in Freud's concepts; I think the most cogent interpretation of the case is simply that Freud used the word *Instinkt* for animals and *Trieb* for human beings and the translation should reflect this usage and therefore the thinking behind it.

Throughout his book Bettelheim's argument is that Freud's translators have done all they can to reduce Freud's humanism to a minimum, where humanism is used to signify the way in which human beings are different from animals. My guess is that they wanted to banish all inconsistencies in Freud and make him 'all of a piece', to quote a phrase from the passage in Somerset Maugham's *The Summing Up* which I quoted in Lecture 3 and would now like to give in full:

> I have been called cynical. I have been accused of making men out worse than they are. I do not think I have done this. All I have done is to bring into prominence certain traits that many writers shut their eyes to. I think what has chiefly struck me in human beings is their lack of consistency. I have never seen people all of a piece. It has amazed me that the most incongruous traits should exist in the same person and for all that yield a plausible harmony. I have often been asked how characteristics, seemingly irreconcilable, can exist in the same person. I have known crooks who were capable of self-sacrifice, sneak-thieves who were sweet-

natured, and harlots for whom it was a point of honour to give good value for money. (1938, p. 40)

I have no doubt that Maugham is right about this, and that there is a strong desire (shall we call it an instinct or a drive?) to make men conform to a particular image, a stereotype, and to make them more uniform than they are. This goes also for great thinkers: there is a drive in their followers to make them conform to some presupposed uniformity. There is a resistance to accepting that the great thinker is a mixture, and Freud is no exception. There was a humanist aspect to his thinking which is quite different from that of Freud the Darwinian scientist. I do think the translators wanted to iron out the humanism, but it would not surprise me if some new translator arises who will want to erase the Darwinian scientist. To avoid perpetuating Strachey's error, I am going to use the word 'drive' for the rest of this lecture.

Early on in his thinking Freud did not draw a distinction between a drive and its psychical representative. Later he drew a sharp distinction, saying that the drive itself cannot ever be known, only its psychical representative or idea (*Vorstellung*) can be. I think it is worth reflecting upon the psychological nature of this 'idea' or 'psychical representative', for I doubt whether Freud meant a purely intellectual idea. I think that 'representative' refers to the reality that is apprehended by the subject. It might be an idea, but it might also be an emotional state or a phantasy: it is that which is subjectively known but the status of the known thing may vary within the personality. I imagine that Freud was influenced by Kant's distinction between 'noumenon' and 'phenomenon'. The latter is known directly by the subject; the former is inferred, but ultimately unknowable.

Freud said that a drive was a concept on the frontier between the mental and the somatic. It is therefore something that binds both these aspects of man together; Marie Jahoda suggests that

Freud's thinking is focused on precisely those concepts which make a bridge between these two aspects of man. (Pleasure has a central role in Freud's thinking for the same reason.) As a concept, however, the drive is still very difficult to grasp. Let us start with Freud's formulation: a drive finds its source in a somatic process occurring in an organ or part of the body and is the representation of that in mental (*seelisch*) life. At this point it is worth reverting to another of Bettelheim's criticisms of Strachey.

Strachey's word 'mental' is his rendering of Freud's *seelisch*, which means 'of the soul', and I think Bettelheim is right (pp. 74–78) to decry this translation of Strachey's. 'Mental' suggests something devoid of emotionality, something quite untrue of the word 'soul'; I think Freud's usage gives strength to my contention that the representative of the drive may be a phantasy or an emotional state. Somehow there is a translation of a somatic stimulus in an organ of the body into an emotional state, a phantasy or an idea.

We are here of course into the conceptually very difficult area of the mind–body problem, which philosophers have grappled with for centuries. The theory which Freud follows has been called psycho-physical parallelism, the view that a physical happening in the body is always paralleled by a psychical one in the mind. These two constituents are separate but lie parallel to each other and activity in one is always paralleled in the other. For Freud, however, somatic activity has priority; that is where things begin.

When he later developed the theory of the ego I do not think he ever definitely formulated where this agency was located, but he seems to have placed it on the surface of the body – on the interface between the organism as a whole, and the external and internal worlds. It was the receptor of stimuli from both and became the organizer of them into some coherent whole. Naturally every mind–body theory has its own problems; I will consider the ones that I think are generated by Freud's position in a critique at the end.

Freud, as I said, has the *source* of the drive in a somatic process. Then the *aim* of the drive is satisfaction: for Freud the achievement of happiness is the aim of human striving. A drive achieves its aim through an *object*; the aim cannot be satisfied without an object. The organism is in a state of tension which is associated with the emotional state of unpleasure. When the object comes in contact with the organism and satisfies the drive, there is a reduction of tension which is associated with pleasure. Hunger is such a state, and the satisfying of it through eating is pleasurable.

Early on Freud was fairly dogmatic about this but he later says that this homeostatic theory, or theory of constancy (the term was Fechner's) or nirvana principle (the term was Barbara Low's) does not explain those occasions when pleasure is associated with an *increase* of tension, such as sexual activity prior to orgasm. Thrill is associated with increase of tension, and this clearly has a pleasure component in it.

To recap. In every drive there is the source, in some somatic stimulation; the aim, which is the satisfaction of the drive associated with reduction of tension, subjectively experienced as pleasure; and the object, that through which the aim is achieved.

After these general remarks about Freud's definition of drives I want to look first at his early theory and then at his later one. In his early writings (1905, *SE* 7, p. 168) Freud differentiates between a stimulus or impulse and a drive. A stimulus in this context is a single impact that operates a single action, whereas a drive is a constant source of patterned activity. (This distinction seems to be a good reason for *not* translating *Trieb* as 'impulse', as Bettelheim would have us do.) Freud believes that in the course of phylogenesis external stimuli have demanded of the organism that it develop drives, or rather that those with drives were better fitted for survival. Through the drives organisms are endowed with a half-born intentionality which remains constant; given a certain inner and outer ecology, the drives come into operation with a certain predictability.

I recently had a patient who wanted to get in touch with an underlying drive which was constant through his life. He functioned extremely well in his professional life, but his private life had suffered a severe crisis. When I started seeing him the immediate crisis was over but he still wanted to come for analysis. Yet for a period after each session he felt depressed and found that analysis interfered with his wish to concentrate well at work. So then there was a period when he could not see any reason for coming to analysis: it interfered with his professional functioning, made him depressed and he could see no benefit from it. Yet he still came. Over time it became clear that his capacity to love was severely interfered with. That drive which enables the couple to function and be fruitfully together was forbidden by a tyrannical inner object. It was nevertheless the erotic drive which kept him coming to an analyst. This point may become clearer when we get to Freud's later theory.

In his early theory Freud is vague about any difference in quality between drives. He believed that all drives were qualitatively alike and that they owed their differences to differing amounts of excitation. Apparent qualitative differences were therefore attributable to differences in quantities of excitation at the somatic source. There does seem to be some sort of contradiction, however, because he then makes a division according to sources of drives, and claims that here there *is* a qualitative division (1915c, p. 123). In his later theory, of the death instinct and eros, which I come to in the next lecture, he says that there must be some other differentiating factor than the quantitative one but is content to say that what it is remains mysterious.

So Freud makes a division at source into two main drives: the ego or self-preservative drives, and the sexual drives. Between the claims of these two drives is a conflict of interests, a constant state of war, which is particularly manifest in obsessional neurosis and hysteria. The conflict he sees as being played out between the claims of these two statements: 1. The individual is the principal thing and sexuality is one of its needs; 2. The process of generation is primary, and the individual is its temporary appendage.

Are there no other drives in Freud's schema? There are but they are always subservient to these two, and he calls them component drives. He therefore sees the drive situation within the personality as one of conflict between two main sets of drives. A warring for dominance goes on between them and all other drives are subsidiary. Now in thinking of these two sets of drives it is helpful if we consider them within the context of the life cycle, something which Freud does not seem to do in his early theory.

In the early years of struggle and establishment it is likely that the individual is the principal thing and that sexuality is one of its needs: sex is often regarded in this way by adolescents and young adults. It is subservient to the individual's own needs, his or her ambition. Somewhere in the midlife crisis there seems ideally to be a change-over, so that the process of generation becomes primary and the individual its temporary appendage, as Freud puts it. The individual gears him- or herself to the next generation. It may be that in the female this occurs sooner, at the time of giving birth to her children; if so this might account for the frequently repeated notion in our society that men are all out to get it (i.e. sex) whereas the women are more concerned with the emotional bonding and the babies.

The main component drives are: sadism/masochism, scopophilia/exhibitionism, love/hate, and relation of hate to ego drives. Sadism consists in the exercise of violence or power upon another person, and includes within itself pleasure in inflicting pain. Freud gives no account of its purpose or evolutionary meaning; he just dogmatically states his case. In his early theory sadism is primary and masochism occurs through a reversal of the drive. (Indeed all drives are capable of reversal.) In masochism the object has been reversed, the subject himself has become the object, and the external person has taken on the role of torturer. The person concerned still derives sadistic pleasure through identifying with the external person who tortures. Masochism, therefore, according to the early theory, is sadism directed towards a particular object.

At this stage, then, Freud is fairly certain that masochism is not primary. (As we shall see in the next lecture he changed his view about this.) Pity for an object is a reaction formation against sadism, where reaction formation is the reversal into an opposite so that the subject does not consciously experience the primary drive. In other words, pity is a cover for sadism; and my own experience tells me that anyone who shows pity towards someone is in fact acting sadistically, though this is not consciously known. Pity confirms a state of affairs: says it is unalterable, nothing can be done about it, and therefore contains a final judgement. There can be no hope of development for the person who is pitied; for pity contains within it the cruel desire to block the person's possibilities of growth. Graham Greene, in his novel *The Ministry of Fear*, makes his protagonist say this:

> . . . he looked everywhere and saw reflected in the crowded court the awful expression of pity: the judge's face was bent, but he could read pity in the old fingers which fidgeted with an Eversharp. He wanted to warn them – don't pity me. Pity is cruel. Pity destroys. Love isn't safe when pity's prowling around. (1943, p. 233)

I have no doubt that pity is a death judgement upon its victim.

Yet, despite the fact that Freud says that sadism is primary he involves himself in a contradiction. He says that there is a primary stage of auto-erotic satisfaction which he calls narcissism, which is linked to a passive state of affairs. Sadism occurs when the state of narcissism is left behind, and an external object is found and adhered to; masochism occurs when the state of narcissism still reigns supreme. This is in clear contradiction to his earlier statements (1905, 1915c) that masochism is secondary. Freud applies the same developmental schema to his other pair of component drives: scopophilia and exhibitionism. At first, he argues that scopophilia is the pleasure in looking, which starts with pleasure in looking at a sexual organ, and that this develops into a whole object being viewed with pleasure. Then the reversal of this is to oneself or part of oneself being looked at. Later, he says that this pair of drives starts with oneself at the narcissistic stage, and progresses to active scopophilia; exhibitionism then occurs when the person remains fixated at the narcissistic stage. Freud makes the point that both pairs of drives, the sadistic/masochistic and the scopophilic/exhibitionistic, do usually exist in concert with one another. (In later theory it became clear that both of these were coincident with the stage of infantile dependence.)

When Freud turns to love he candidly admits that he is unwilling to consider this as a component drive of libido. Instead he wants to see it as an expression of the *whole* sexual current, and it seems to me to be one of the cases where what one might call a basic belief does not fit his model, which still has a physiological basis. For Freud clearly believed that love was the supreme guarantor of mental health and stated this in his paper on narcissism (1914, *SE* 14, p. 85). It was a goal of human striving and had enormous importance, but it did not fit his rather restricted model. It is clearly linked, though, to the sexual drive and Freud's belief that the term love could only be applied to a phenomenon if it was bound closely to the sexual drive and a particular object.

The opposites of loving are hating, being loved and being indifferent; the latter two states are based in the narcissistic stage of development. Hate occurs when the loved object becomes the source of unpleasure – for instance, if the subject is rejected or abandoned by the loved object. But hate is also linked closely to the self-preservative drive (whereas love is not) and is closely linked to the narcissistic stage of development. In love the ego makes a leap whereby it places its survival largely in the custody of another; in the narcissistic stage the ego repudiates any such notion. We can see therefore that in the narcissistic state the sexual drive is subservient to the self-preservative, and is dominated by it. In the state of love, by contrast, the ego drive becomes subservient to the sexual drive.

This then is Freud's early theory. You will note that there is no mention of aggression, or a destructive drive in itself. After the First World War, however, Freud recast his whole theory and aggression was given a much bigger place. We have to leave this topic to the next lecture.

12 FREUD'S INSTINCT THEORY
Part 2

In 1920 Freud wrote *Beyond the Pleasure Principle*, in which he radically reformulated his drive theory. I want first to consider what it was that made him change over from his previous theory to this final one. As I said at the end of the last lecture, Freud had greatly underestimated the place of aggression and destructiveness in human beings. By the time he came to write *Civilization and Its Discontents* in 1930, however, he had devoted much anxious attention to the problem, and had also looked at how religion had tried to deal with destructiveness within the human species. His particular concern was how the individual organism dealt with an excess of destructiveness; he now came to see it as being used against external threats.

But how did this change come about in Freud? Truly we cannot answer such a question, although I suspect that it was due to the progress of his self-analysis. One can speculate that certain external events were challenging his self-analysis to take account of aspects of human reality which had hitherto been ignored. The fact of the First World War has often been mentioned; but I think that there is little doubt that Freud also believed that accompanying the enormous scientific progress of this century and the last there had developed a capacity for managing crude, brutal impulses. I will quote some passages from his paper 'The Disillusionment of War', written about six months after the outbreak of the war:

> We were prepared to find that wars between the primitive and the civilized peoples, between the races who are divided by the colour of their skin – wars, even, against and among the nationalities of Europe whose civilization is little developed or has been lost – would occupy mankind for some time to come. But we permitted ourselves to have other hopes. We had expected the great world-dominating nations of white race upon whom the leadership of the human species has fallen, who were known to have worldwide interests as their concern, to whose creative powers were due not only our technical advances towards the control of nature but the artistic and scientific standards of civilization – we had expected these peoples to succeed in discovering another way of settling misunderstandings and conflicts of interest . . . The enjoyment of this common civilization was disturbed from time to time by warning voices, which declared that old traditional differences made wars inevitable, even among the members of a community such as this. We refused to believe it; but if such a war were to happen, how did we picture it? We saw it as an opportunity for demonstrating the progress of comity among men since the era when the Greek Amphictyonic Council proclaimed that no city of the league might be destroyed, nor its olive-groves cut down, nor its water supply stopped; we pictured it as a chivalrous passage of arms, which would limit itself to establishing the superiority of one side in the struggle, while as far as possible avoiding acute suffering that could contribute nothing to the decision, and granting complete immunity for the wounded who had to withdraw from the contest, as well as for the doctors and nurses who devoted themselves to their recovery. There would, of course, be the utmost consideration for the non-combatant classes of the population – for women who take no part in

war-work, and for the children who, when they are grown up, should become on both sides one another's friends and helpers. And again, all the international undertakings and institutions in which the common civilization of peacetime had been embodied would be maintained. (1915d, *SE* 14, pp. 276, 278)

And in his paper 'On Transience' he said:

A year later the war broke out and robbed the world of its beauties. It destroyed not only the beauty of the countrysides through which it passed and works of art which it met with on its path but it also shattered our pride in the achievements of our civilization, our admiration for many philosophers and artists and our hopes of a final triumph over the differences between nations and races. It tarnished the lofty impartiality of our science, it revealed our instincts in all their nakedness and let loose the evil spirits within us which we thought had been tamed for ever by centuries of continuous education by the noblest minds. (1916a, *SE* 14, p. 307)

I think it is clear from these quotes that Freud had been under an illusion until this time. But if one asks what the illusion was, then the answer is not as straightforward as it may first seem. It is not that he thinks that human beings have no aggression or destructive potential; it is clear that he knew of the brutality that had existed through history. It is also clear that he thought it still existed in more primitive races, yet not among the cultured races of Europe. In 'The Disillusionment of War' his expectation that there would never again be a barbaric war was based not only upon the technical advances, but the artistic and scientific standards of civilization. It is strange to realize that it was Freud who believed that a high state of civilization had rescued man from the baser and more brutal drives still manifest in less advanced cultures. So where does the illusion lie? To answer this it is necessary to go off on a little journey which is speculative but also, I think, enormously important in our attitude to social matters and to revolutionary hopes in particular.

The Christian and Jewish religions, Islam and Buddhism all share one idea in common: that man exists in a state from which he needs to be rescued; he needs to be saved. The inference is clear that he needs to be saved from his present situation. I think a further inference is that man dimly perceives that it is intolerable to think about his present social and individual reality. Now it is difficult to find the right language to express this, but one could say that man feels that something is gravely wrong, his situation has some intolerable quality at its very centre, it cannot be that man is to remain as he is, things must improve, somehow the situation in which he finds himself just cannot be accepted as such. Surely some god will come from Mount Olympus, or Mount Sinai, or from the lotus plant, and save man from his plight. Now I am not sure how all of you regard these myths; whether, for instance, you believe that there must be some rescuer. I cannot proceed here without sharing with you my belief that these are illusions.

Now I should like to make it clear that I do not think man can live without illusions, and that they do serve a helpful purpose; but nevertheless that the 'rescue' desire, if really believed, is an illusion. I think Freud had this illusion; he believed that twentieth century European man had been saved from the state of brutality through the 'scientific and artistic standards of civilization'. I do not think it is profitable to go into what lies behind Freud's thinking here, but it is clear that this something enjoyed by European civilization had 'saved' a portion of mankind from . . . I will say 'brutality'. (Let us not get into casuistry over what I mean by 'brutality'. I think we all know the appalling brutalities of war.) It was the events of the First World War which shattered this illusion.

This point leads me on to the second reason why Freud abandoned his original drive theory. In order to concentrate, even over the most mundane matters, the person normally screens out a vast mass of stimuli from the outside world, the internal world, and the memory. This screen Freud called the 'stimulus barrier', and it is very closely allied to illusion. If the stimulus barrier is suddenly shattered – the personality is flooded by an enormous shock – or an illusion is suddenly smashed, then the personality resorts to 'returning to the scene of the crime' in order to try to master what has happened. The emphasis here is on the adverb 'suddenly': when there is a shock to the system through some untoward event the person goes back and back over it, trying to make what occurred different.

Until recently I lived next door to a lady whose fourteen-year-old granddaughter was killed by a car on her way back from school. I would meet the grandmother, a woman whom I liked, on the street or in her flat from time to time, and I noticed that in every conversation of any length there was some mention of this granddaughter, and always a remark of this sort: 'As soon as I saw this flat of ours I knew it was for us, but then since Janie died I have often wondered if we had bought another house whether it would have happened.' 'Yet perhaps if Mary had sent Janie to a boarding-school the accident would never have happened.'

Freud noticed that people who had been at the front during the war dreamed again and again of any horrific event which they had undergone. Prince Myshkin, in Dostoevsky's *The Idiot*, relates how he saw a man guillotined while on a visit to France and adds: 'It is a month since I saw it, and I can still see it as though it were happening before my eyes. I've dreamed of it half a dozen times.' I think one can speculate that the First World War was just such a shock to Freud and that the reformulation of his drive theory was his attempt to master a terrible event. It is the only way in which I can really understand the significance of the concept of a repetition compulsion.

I call this the second reason for Freud's revision of the theory, but I think it is understandable only if one sees it as

Freud's own realization of what he was doing in trying to master a shocking event among the nations of Europe. The difficulty for him was probably heightened when Karl Abraham and Sandor Ferenczi were acting as physicians to the men in the trenches on the German side, while Ernest Jones was now one of the 'enemy'. Indeed in one of his letters Freud conveys to Abraham his sense of shock at this truth.

The third reason for the reform of the theory was Freud's clinical experience of the 'negative therapeutic reaction'. When analyst and patient come together and real, joint understanding seems to occur, and something is cemented between the two partners in the analytic endeavour, it frequently happens that in the following session the patient will react violently against both the analyst and the analysis. I can think of many examples. The most violent and most tragic was in a session when hopeful understanding occurred and for the first time for some years a glimmering of hope dawned. The next session I could tell that something had gone wrong, and then the patient, a woman, committed suicide.

In another case, a man had a good session, I grasped a difficult nettle in it and he went out much relieved. The next session I might have expected pleasure or relief, but no; the patient was absolutely furious and said that I was quite useless and had done nothing useful, and so on. Now the interesting point is that until the previous session he would have been right, but he was not right on that Thursday because I had definitely been useful and competent on the Wednesday. Another patient would have a very profitable session in which there was clearly helpful mutual understanding; then she begins the next session saying, 'Last session you *said* I seemed to have overcome my sexual rage with my boyfriend, and then at the weekend I threw a picture at him.' As she said 'you said' I felt myself fill with rage, saying to myself, '*I* didn't say any such thing.' The design was to get a bloody good argument going and mess up the previous session.

The most exaggerated example of the same type was a patient who, after a session where a new realization and consolidation had occurred, came in and said, 'In a session at the end of the summer term last year you did not take my demand for more sessions seriously.' She went on to tell me a regular catalogue of my serious failures. I do not think she was wrong in content; it was the timing.

Of course it is often the case that when an analysis makes a stride for the better then the wasted time and the failures are felt more acutely, but there is an added dimension in the cases which I have mentioned: there is an attempt to disrupt the analysis. Sometimes it succeeds, as in the first case which I mentioned. Freud was shocked by these cases and came to the conclusion that there must be some very powerful anti-life force in the personality, something whose aim was to destroy the fertile coming-together of analyst and patient – of eros, in other words.

Now, to proceed to a description of Freud's reformulation. The new pair of drives became the death drive and eros. I want to explain what Freud understood by the death drive: it is that all organisms tend towards the inanimate state. This notion is also consonant with Freud's view that the goal of drives is to conserve an earlier state of affairs. All life on this planet emanated from inanimate nature, and the goal of the death drive is to re-establish this earlier state of affairs. The paradox, however, is that the self-preservative drive is a component of the death drive. The death drive wishes to bring about the termination of the organism according to its own internal processes of dissolution. Listen now to the way Freud describes it; I shall quote from the Strachey translation and therefore use the word 'instinct':

> In the last resort, what has left its mark on the development of organisms must be the history of the earth we live in and of its relation to the sun. Every modification which is thus

imposed upon the course of the organism's life is accepted by the conservative organic instincts and stored up for further repetition. Those instincts are therefore bound to give a deceptive appearance of being forces tending towards change and progress, whilst in fact they are merely seeking to reach an ancient goal by paths alike old and new. Moreover it is possible to specify this final goal of all organic striving. It would be in contradiction to the conservative nature of the instincts if the goal of life were a state of things which had never yet been attained. On the contrary, it must be an *old* state of things, an initial state from which the living entity has at one time or other departed and to which it is striving to return by the circuitous paths along which its development leads. If we are to take it as truth that knows no exception that everything living dies for *internal* reasons – becomes inorganic once again – then we shall be compelled to say that '*the aim of all life is death*' and, looking backwards, that '*inanimate things existed before living ones*'. (1920, *SE* 18, p. 38)

What then becomes of the self-preservative drives? Freud sums the matter up in the following passage:

The hypothesis of self-preservative instincts, such as we attribute to all living beings, stands in marked opposition to the idea that instinctual life as a whole serves to bring about death. Seen in this light, the theoretical importance of the instincts of self-preservation, or self-assertion and of mastery greatly diminishes. They are component instincts whose function it is to assure that the organism shall follow its own path to death, and to ward off any possible ways of returning to inorganic existence other than those which are immanent in the organism itself. We have no longer to reckon with the organism's puzzling determination (so hard to fit into any context) to maintain its own existence in the face of every obstacle. What we are left with is the fact that the organism wishes to die only in its own fashion. Thus these guardians of life, too, were originally the myrmidons of death. Hence arises the paradoxical situation that the living organism struggles most energetically against events (dangers, in fact) which might help it to attain its life's aim rapidly – by a kind of short-circuit. Such behaviour is, however, precisely what characterizes purely instinctual as contrasted with intelligent efforts. (*SE* 18, p. 39)

I have quoted these passages at some length as Freud's formulation of the death drive is quite different from Melanie Klein's. Klein did not recast the drive theory as Freud did in *Beyond the Pleasure Principle*; she accepted his earlier drive theory but added to it a destructive drive which she and her followers named the death drive. Thus it is not the same as Freud's death drive which, paradoxically, preserves the organism against assaults upon its existence from outside. For Freud, as we saw, the aim is to preserve the organism so that it will return to inanimate existence according to its own internal processes of dissolution. Although there is an aggressive component in Freud's death drive that wards off external dangers, its aim is to bring the organism back to the inorganic state: 'Thou art dust and to dust thou shalt return'. The death drive is thus in opposition to any drive to maintain life beyond the individual's own existence, and so comes into conflict with the other great drive: eros.

Eros seeks to maintain life indefinitely through male and female coming together, in coitus, so that a fertilization takes place and new life continues. Freud believed that through eros a binding occurred, a certain union leading to a new entity, and Talcott Parsons has pointed out (1964, pp. 18–19) that this binding substance – eros – in Freud's thought is similar to Durkheim's conception of society as an organic unit with individuals integrated into an organic whole through value systems which have a cementing effect. I would suggest that it is through eros that people who work in a firm or an institution – like the Tavistock, for instance – have some form of group identity; and that this identity lives on beyond the lives of the individual members.

The death drive – often called thanatos, by followers of Freud – and eros war within themselves. How, though, does it come about that the death drive gets turned inwards so that the individual becomes the object of attack? That in the extreme case of suicide the aim of the death drive is not achieved? Freud's explanation of this goes as follows. The erotic drive is aimed towards another, but it can happen that this drive takes the individual's own subject as its libidinal object. We call this situation narcissism. This, says Freud, has the effect of lassoing that component aspect of the death drive whose purpose it is to attack external marauders, and draws it on to the subject's own ego. The sequence is not quite convincing to me, but more of it shortly.

I want now briefly to pass to a personal critique of Freud's theory under three main headings. In the first place I think there is evidence for a moral sense in man; Freud gives no place for such a notion. However, a number of psychoanalysts since Freud have believed that man has a moral sense which is primary and not just derived: Bion and Winnicott explicitly make this point, and I think it is implicit in Melanie Klein, Fairbairn, Balint and others. Winnicott's delightful paper 'The Observation of Infants in a Set Situation' (1941), for instance, gives convincing evidence for an innate moral sense. The paper seems to demonstrate its existence in numerous cases at the age of seven to thirteen months, and nor does it appear to be due to the internalization of parental injunctions. Freud's view that the achievement of happiness is the goal of man's life does not, I think, give sufficient place to those people who are motivated by corporate values and ethical ideals.

My explanation for the conjunction of narcissism and an attacking superego, for instance, is that there is a moral sense which demands concern for others; and that when others are obliterated through narcissism then the superego attacks the individual violently. If it is the death drive turned inwards then why should narcissism effect it? I can see no alternative except to suggest that there is a moral sense which dictates concern for others, and that if this is disregarded at a deep level then the death drive is directed towards the subject. Freud leaves this out, and I think it leaves an unwelcome gap in his theoretical work and also in his clinical understanding; I know that in treating a patient with a severe superego it is safe to assume that he or she is damaging the feelings of others.

Secondly, psycho-physical parallelism does not seem to me to be a satisfactory philosophical account of the human entity. I think that man is a single entity, not composed of body and soul in parallel with each other. Freud's view is that the drives have a somatic source – a source in the body which is then paralleled in the psyche. The drives are known in the psyche through the idea or representative – *Vorstellung*. I on the other hand follow the theoretical framework of the Aristotle-Aquinas-Husserl-Heidegger tradition, in which it would not be possible to make the sort of division which Freud makes here, and which is especially striking in the area of the drive theory.

Thirdly and lastly, I do not think that the death drive and eros are similar phenomenal entities; they cannot, therefore, both be categorized as drives (or instincts, or whatever). It seems to me that the death drive is genuinely instinctual according to Freud's definition – to return to an old state of affairs – but I cannot see that eros fits this definition. Eros is surely linked to something more primary than instinct; it is surely life itself. Life in its innermost nature goes we know not where. What Freud is talking about in the death drive is a restriction or limiting factor; eros is in another category altogether. I believe that placing them both under the same logical heading leads only to confusion.

13 THE TOPOGRAPHICAL MODEL

The most distinctive feature of Freudian theory is the radical distinction it makes between consciousness and the unconscious. I said in Lecture 6 that Leibnitz was the first scientific thinker to posit the existence of an unconscious. Between Leibnitz and Freud, a period of over 150 years, there were many thinkers who assumed the existence of an unconscious, one of the most influential being J.F. Herbart, who taught that ideas which were not congenial to a person's conscious self-image were forced to remain unconscious. Freud therefore did not discover the unconscious, but he was the first to chart its territory and investigate it scientifically.

Freud infers its existence, in his paper 'The Unconscious' (1915b), on a logical basis. Activity that we do not consciously initiate flows out of us: this activity comes from 'another', just like the actions of another person. We infer, says Freud, that there must be a source of such actions; it is therefore an area of which we have no self-awareness. I should emphasize that it is not really true to say that we are not conscious of this area: we are conscious of it but do not have self-consciousness of it.

I can remember a patient telling me in the initial interview that when she got into a love relation she soon started to attack and be cruel to her boyfriend; consequently all her relationships broke up. Now when she told me this she was quite *conscious* of this activity, but the *inferred* statement was that it proceeded from some part of her which was outside her management, and she had no self-consciousness of it. There is also a hint here that the *capacity* for management is closely linked to self-consciousness, a point which is related to something I said in the third lecture, 'Psychoanalysis: The Science of Meaning'. That one of the analyst's tasks is to *bear* the patient's projections so that the patient's inner management of self can be increased, and, therefore, his consciousness as well. Capacity for consciousness becomes coextensive with the emotional strength of the self.

At any single moment of time my awareness is confined to a very small area: a particular focus like the beam of a searchlight on a small spot in the midst of the night. At that moment all the rest of the mind's contents are unconscious. There is a large area that is capable of recall, however – the searchlight can beam in on it when it wants. Freud named this part of the mind the preconscious and it shares the qualities that we attribute to consciousness. It is unconscious only because attention absorbs all our energies on to one spot and the rest of the mental territory is then not in sight. Freud next wanted to differentiate between this area and one which is kept unconscious by the force of repression. It is this latter area which clinically we refer to as the unconscious, and in order to get some understanding of it we need to have a look at repression.

In his early work Freud spoke about a 'censor' (1900, *SE* 5, p. 505), imagined almost as a personality, standing at the gateway between the two territories of the unconscious and consciousness. I say a 'personality' yet it was a mechanistic notion in that it was not rooted in the ego, which Freud did not formulate until 1923. But by 1915 he had begun to work out a more elaborated idea of repression and the process by which it happened. We tend, because of the imagery of the word, to see a force pushing something down into the unconscious like a hand thrusting a sponge under water, but Freud did not see repression in this way.

For something to be invested with consciousness it has to be possessed of a certain quantum of energy. Repression occurs through a withdrawal of this necessary parcel of energy. This is then taken over and used against the idea or its representative to keep it in the unconscious, and in fact in Freud's earlier formulation (e.g. 1915b, pp. 180–185) it is activity on the part of the agency of repression which creates the unconscious. In other words the entire contents of the unconscious are those elements which have been withdrawn from consciousness.

Later Freud acknowledged that the unconscious was also the repository of elements which had never been past personal happenings and thus were not repressed in the way I have been describing. Here he was acknowledging, somewhat grudgingly, his debt to Jung who believed that apart from the personal unconscious there was also a collective unconscious which is inherited. We shall look further into this issue when we come to consider Jung, but for the moment let us just remember that the topographical model is constituted by the three terms I have been defining: conscious, preconscious and unconscious.

When Freud came to formulate the structural model – I come to this in my next lecture – he attached the activity of repression to the ego. One of the difficulties with his repression theory, however, lies in the difference between the nature of an idea in the unconscious and the form of its existence in consciousness; so we now need to consider something more about the nature of the unconscious as Freud described it. Perhaps its most important characteristic is that unconscious ideas have no 'word presentations' attached to them: in the unconscious there is no language, as we normally understand the word. This is one of the reasons why dreams do not communicate their message in a straightforward grammatical sentence.

You need to think of the unconscious as a deaf and dumb per-

son whose only method of communicating is by drawing pictures. The unconscious, like the deaf and dumb person, is very
skilful in the employment of its pictures and their chosen symbolism. All the features of this interesting world remain unconscious until meaning is attached to them through words; at that
moment, they become conscious. I had a patient once who
painted, and she conceptualized to herself, at the unconscious
level, her sense of abandonment and loneliness; the sense of this
was clear from her paintings, but in her conscious life she was a
bustle of social activity and was liked by many people.
Nevertheless she was unable to get this affectivity into words.
Her words remained quite unconnected to her affective life,
which remained disconnected from her social presentation of
herself. (It seems that happiness is partly a product of the world
of the unconscious permeating through into conscious life and
across the boundaries of personal space to reach the other.)

The reason words had been kept out of contact with my
patient's affective life was that she had not been spoken *to* as a
child but always spoken *about*: 'Geraldine wants to study
French; Geraldine does not like milk for breakfast; Geraldine
wants to be a hairdresser when she grows up.' The girl came
from an extended family, and people somehow assumed she
was this and was that. She became anxious that her own personal affective life would be taken over by the group, and that
she as a person would sink without a trace. At the same time she
became bitterly hostile towards these dangerous words, hence
they were kept at a great distance from her affective life; she
consequently became incapable of using words as vehicles for
carrying her feelings and emotions.

There is no doubt that a person feels deeply unhappy if there
is a severe disjunction between the aspirations of his or her
unconscious life and the conscious. The conscious presentation
of the self is then formed almost totally by the identification of
the surface or object part of the personality with the hated
figures of the immediate environment. If an analyst then makes

contact with the hidden unexpressed part of the self, the figures of identification which form consciousness rage against the birth of the hidden self. It seems therefore that identifications which form consciousness take place around the sound images of spoken language; and that patients in whom the disjunction I have spoken about is most obvious are consequently extremely sensitive to the analyst's tone and manner of communication. If he or she should happen to speak in the same way as the hated figure of the past there is either an angry outburst, a silent withdrawal or, worst of all, a submission entered into out of despair.

The unconscious is also not place-related, a concept which is rather difficult to grasp. The unconscious is an emotional source. For instance, one of the ways we have of thinking about the transference is to describe it as a situation where expression of the unconscious is far more encouraged than in normal daily undertakings; as a result the person acts according to the emotional inner world. The fact that the analyst is Dr Smith living at 100 Finchley Road is ignored, and the analyst is felt as the mother who is living in Timbuktu. Certain communications by Dr Smith will 'tune in' to the emotional world within that is in a state of receptivity to the mother. The unconscious is not receptive to the message that says, 'No, this cannot be my mother because she lives in Timbuktu, but I am at the moment at 100 Finchley Road', because it is not able to make a deduction of this sort. It is peopled by static visual images.

I used to visit an old man who was senile and lived in a private nursing home. We met in a sitting-room that had round coffee tables with easy chairs around each table. After we had been sitting for a little while a male nurse wearing a white coat came in and asked us if we wanted a coffee or a drink. When he left the senile man said, 'I think I'll go up to my cabin and get a cigar'. Now I knew that this man had often been on passenger liners; I looked around and realized that our surroundings were just like the lounge of a steamer – and who has ever heard of a nurse coming and saying, 'Would you like a coffee or a drink?'! How did I know that we were not on a steamer on the high seas? Well, in reality I had driven up in my car some minutes before, parked, and walked into the building and along the corridor into the sitting-room. So my consciousness had to do some work and suppress the rather pleasing phantasy of me and this old man having a drink in a lounge on the old *Queen Mary*. For the unconscious is tuned to the images and the emotional world that they represent, and these are not located in a geographical place. I know it is difficult to grasp this idea; but the more we can the better are we able to 'feel' the meaning of the patient's communications.

The unconscious is also not located in time: it exists just in the present or, more accurately, out of time. To return to the Dr Smith example: it may be that the patient's mother died some years ago, but the unconscious tunes into Dr Smith as mother. The senile old man was on a steamer many years ago. These memory-images are stored and conceptualize our experience in the here and now. When you suddenly 'remember' something it is because a constellation of events is now represented by the memory of it.

In the last session before a Christmas break, a patient of mine spoke about her sexual difficulties. She had a strong puritanical conscience, she explained, so that the only way she could get into bed with a man was to get drunk first. It was significant that she had always felt too inhibited with me to speak about anything sexual, and this area was always awkwardly avoided. I pointed this out and she agreed that she felt differently about it today. Then I said that, strange though it might seem, I thought she felt that we were lovers and so she had not mentioned any sexual relations with other men because these incidents were felt as infidelities to me.

The patient agreed that something of this sort seemed to be the case; but went on to say that she felt freed from her father for the first time. She was therefore correcting or amplifying

my statement: it now said that we had been lovers, but incestuous ones. I was her father and she my daughter, and we were in
an incestuous bondage. My experience of that session was that
the patient became much more free; I felt her to be more
friendly and spontaneous, and to be with her was a pleasure
rather than something of a burden.

She returned from the break withdrawn, and eyed me with
distrust. I had the feeling that she felt betrayed by me. I said to
her that she was feeling and behaving quite differently towards
me; we had had a good session before the break, and I thought
she felt that I had then just turned my back on her and dumped
her. Then she said that as soon as I said that, she suddenly
remembered that before Christmas some years before, when
she had been abroad, she had gone to a party and then slept with
her boyfriend. The next day he had gone off back to England
for three weeks, and then when he returned to her she would
not speak to him.

In this incident you can see how she is experiencing me as
people from past times – first her father, then her boyfriend. A
constellation of past memories is evoked by a series of cues in
the present, whose emotional tone is similar enough for the past
to be experienced as the present. The past has coalesced in the
present. The emotions in the unconscious that are evoked are
not in time, as I said before. A debate is often heard in clinical
discussions as to whether the analyst should interpret the present reality of the transference or the patient's past. I think that
this debate occurs in the first place only because of a failure to
grasp sufficiently the way in which the emotions in the uncon-
sious are out of time; and I think the clinical example that I have
given illustrates this point.

Freud says that our perception of the external world is
embodied in consciousness and that the unconscious is
removed from this external world. He makes two statements,
however, which contradict this idea:

I have good reason for asserting that everyone possesses in his own unconscious an instrument with which he can interpret the utterances of the unconscious in other people. (1913b, p. 320)

It is a very remarkable thing that the *Ucs.* of one human being can react upon that of another, without passing through the *Cs.* This deserves closer investigation, especially with a view to finding out whether preconscious activity can be excluded as playing a part in it; but, descriptively speaking, the fact is incontestable. (1915b, p. 194)

In some ways these two statements upset the apple-cart altogether, since the rest of Freud's topographical model seems to deny the point that they make. Yet Freud asserts the phenomenon with conviction in the two passages, especially the second. According to his view, then, a communication between human beings can take place which is unconscious to both. In fact this is clearly the case in an analysis, where an unconscious communication may be made at the initial interview, continued in the first session, the second session and continuously for the first five weeks, and then the first five months. But only in the fifth year does it become conscious to the analyst – nevertheless it was there from the beginning.

I have tried, in a rather idiosyncratic way, to describe the topographical model, but you will notice that one area of the mind has been mentioned only by inference: consciousness. We should note that this is also the way Freud attends to the matter: he hardly says a word about consciousness directly. I will just make some personal comments about this complex matter, but they will have to remain as suggestions to you. Firstly, I want to take an example from experimental psychology. Gordon G. Gallup (1970) anaesthetized four wild chimpanzees and some monkeys, and while they were asleep he painted bright red spots on their faces with an alcohol-soluble dye. He then exposed the two groups to mirrors: the apes touched their own faces, and the red spots in particular. The monkeys poked at the mirrors, but no amount of exposure to the mirror aided them in realizing that they were seeing their own faces in it. Gallup's conclusion was that the apes had a degree of self-consciousness whereas the monkeys did not, and I quote this to suggest that the roots of consciousness lie in some preverbal capacity.

Secondly, there would seem to be degrees of consciousness. A child's awareness of place and time grows, as does its acquisition of language. There can therefore be different areas of consciousness, and different levels of achievement of consciousness. Thirdly, self-consciousness emerges through contact with another, and intimacy is a challenge to greater self-consciousness. In analysis the growth of the two factors goes hand-in-hand, while connected to this idea is the observation that narcissism is correlated with a low degree of consciousness. I would like to leave you with the suggestion that the presence of the other in the subject's unconscious is the guarantor of a developing consciousness.

14 THE STRUCTURAL MODEL

When I start to speak about ego, superego and id, I am greeted immediately with expressions betokening familiarity. Everyone knows that model of the mind and yet, of all the constructs within psychoanalysis, it is the most complicated. Widely differing opinions about it are held, and in this lecture I shall only be skimming the surface of a complex issue. For although *The Ego and the Id* (1923) formally defined what we call the structural model of the mind, Freud introduced a concept of the ego very early in his psychoanalytic thinking, even before he had conceptualized his notion of psychosexual drives.

Freud's first formulation concerned the ego as discharge-regulating, and appeared in the 'Project' of 1895. Here behaviour is ultimately the expression of discharge of the accumulated pressures of internally and externally generated tensions. Discharge is the primary function of the psychical structures within the organism, and we have seen how this notion is also central both to Freud's conceptualization of pleasure as the reduction of tension and of his drive (or instinct) theory. Various permanent structural arrangements or agencies develop in the organism in the service of finding the most effective means of this discharge, with the ego as one of these secon-

dary functions. In the discharge through the neuronal pathways the ego is defined as the totality of the cathexes (stored-up
emotional energy) coming from the impermeable neurones in
which a permanent component can be distinguished from a
changing one. The ego has evolved as a permanent agency regulating the discharge.

All functions of thought are ultimately instruments of this
secondary function. The ego was conceived as an

> . . . essential structural means of accomplishing the secon-
> dary function of effective discharge, one that could respond
> simultaneously to the demands of energic tension and to
> environmental conditions suited to tension reduction, one
> that could monitor motoric instrumentalities of discharge
> (because effective discharge is achievable only through
> action), and that could be implemented by perceptual-cog-
> nitive operations which guarantee the proving of reality, or
> 'reality testing'. (George S. Klein, 1976, p. 124)

The ego therefore had the role of perceiving the environment,
regulating the discharge of energic tension, and matching the
inner to the outer. I suggested in the lecture on Freud and the
physicalist tradition, however, that we might do well to dis-
pense with the homeostatic model implied by the reality testing
function of the ego such as Freud conceived of it at this stage. If
we exchange the homeostatic model for a motivational one, we
can see the ego as having a role in testing the objects of the environment to determine whether they will prove satisfying and
will promote a person's development.

Next we need to consider two intermediate papers, both of
which extended Freud's thinking about the ego, namely
'Mourning and Melancholia' and *Group Psychology and the
Analysis of the Ego*. 'Mourning and Melancholia' was written in
1915, though only published two years later. Freud begins by
comparing the emotional state which we find in mourning with
that encountered in melancholia. In a state of mourning a per-

son loses interest in the outside world, has no interest in forming a new love relationship, and turns away from activities that
are concerned with the lost object of love. Similarly in melancholia there is painful dejection, loss of interest in the outside
world, loss of the capacity to love and an inhibition of all activity. To this extent the two emotional states are similar, but
there is an important difference: in the state of melancholia a
lowering of self-regard is found which is not present in normal
mourning (though it usually is in pathological mourning).
Freud states it pithily thus: 'In mourning it is the world which
has become poor and empty; in melancholia it is the ego itself'
(1917, *SE* 14, p. 246).

Freud goes on to say that the self-denigrating, self-accusing
statements of the melancholic patient are a correct description
of his psychological situation. They begin to make sense only if
you consider that they are intended for someone else. They are
the typical accusations of a person who has been jilted by his or
her lover, the plaintive cries of one abandoned by his love
object. The love object is then accused and vilified. Now in
Freud's paper there is an inference, though not explicit, that
something of this nature has happened before and that the person is fixated around some event, or series of events, where the
infant had been abandoned by its primary love object (I should
mention that the conceptualizations that make my statement
about a primary love object possible came after Freud – with
people like Melanie Klein, Donald Winnicott and Michael Balint). What Freud says is that the shadow of the lost object falls
upon one part of the ego. The ego splits into two: one part
becomes identified with the lost object, and the other becomes
the accuser.

Freud gives a description which tallies with the clinical
phenomenology, but without saying why it occurs quite like
this. However, he makes a further point which is crucial, and
has become a focus of attention in recent psychoanalytic
research: it is that the original love for the love object could not

have been very robust and was not able to sustain much of a blow. In other words the attachment to the love object was narcissistic – and narcissistic object choice is not a secure foundation for mental health (Freud, 1914). Why the attachment was narcissistic, however, remains the $64,000 question.

Freud brings up a further point: that the ego's earliest attachment to the love object is by identification. He develops this idea in *Group Psychology and the Analysis of the Ego* (1921), and I want next to draw your attention to one thing he says about the ego there. It is that in identification the ego becomes the object, and that this frequently has a hostile colouring. The shape of the ego, as it were, is moulded by the child's early models, something which a psychoanalyst can experience in his relations with his patients.

I will try to give an example of what I mean. A patient frequently complained that she was bullied by her husband. When this patient first came to see me she had told me that a previous therapist kept on interpreting her erotic feelings towards her father, and how unhelpful these interpretations had been. She made it quite clear that I was not to make such interpretations. For quite some time I went along with this until some things she was saying made it clear that an interpretation about her erotic feelings towards her father was called for. I made the interpretation; she was furious, and told me that I was a typical psychoanalyst dishing out something from the textbook. I stuck to my guns, however, by saying that the textbooks were sometimes right. She tried in every way to make me retract what I had said, but I remained obdurate.

There was now no doubt that she was trying to bully me. Whatever else it may have been, her ego was a bullying ego. After a few sessions some psychological realization that I was not going to shift in my opinion dawned, and so she gave up. In the very next session she told me that the previous evening her husband had tried to persuade her to write a letter to the headmaster of their son's school demanding that he be allowed to start French classes before the normal age, and my patient said: 'And it was strange because for the first time I stood up to him and said I wouldn't, and I stood my ground, despite all his persuading.' It was quite clear to me that there had been a change in her ego and that she recognized that this was new behaviour for her. Now we shall try to understand in psychoanalytic terms exactly what had happened.

The change came about through a conjunction of two factors: the transference, and the nature of the object which she found in the analyst. Through the transference the analyst became an inner object which the patient tried desperately to alter according to an emotional preconception. After some attempts at this her ego gave up and accepted the object as it was: that is, as one which would not submit to bullying (was not masochistic, in the jargon). In some way the object part of the personality identifies internally with this object, and the object 'feeds' the ego with a new vitality. Let us say that a new identification has taken place, and there has been a transformation of an area of ego functioning. However, it usually takes a long time in psychoanalysis before such a moment of crystallization can be reached.

It is clear then that the quality of the ego arises out of a process of identification, and this in turn depends on the nature of the object to which the subject is libidinally attached. In other words, a healthy ego results from identification with mature and responsive objects; a crippled ego results from identification with an object which has failed the infant in some crucial way. Although these observations give some information about the emotional health or illness of the object, they do not tell us about the function of the ego as Freud came to conceive of it in *The Ego and the Id*, and we must now pass on to that.

If it were possible to imagine a human being suspended in outer space, totally removed from reality, then (according to Freud's conceptualizations) there would be no ego. The ego is, as it were, moulded by surrounding reality. That part of the organism on the boundary between the organism and reality is the ego. It is like the skin of the organism, receiving the sensations from the outer world. It is also the projected surface of the organism, a psychic skin. The ego processes the stimuli of the outer world but also those of the inner world. It is like a radar screen that registers and patterns the stimuli from within and from without, and it is psychic reality.

The ego has no energy of its own, however; the repository of energy is the id. Id is the Latinized jargon translation of *Das Es* (a term borrowed from Georg Groddeck), which properly translates as 'The It'. To get some flavour of what Groddeck meant by the It it is necessary to read some of his imaginative books, but I will quote one passage which gives some idea of what he meant by the It:

> The It of a particular man starts, since we must start somewhere, with fertilization. It embraces all the powers which govern the formation and further development of the individual man. The outstanding fact of this being is that without a brain it fulfils the most difficult functions of life, and indeed, that the brain, and with it the power of thought and later of consciousness, and the Ego itself are created by it. The It is the deepest nature and force of the man. It accomplishes everything that happens with and through and in the man; it is responsible for his existence, gives him all his organs and functions, helps him out of the mother's body into the light of day, does everything which the man appears to do. In accordance always with its own infallible purpose it creates speech, breathing, sleeping, work and joy and rest and love and grief, always with correct judgement, always purposefully, and always with full success, and finally, when he has lived long enough, it kills him.' (1951, p. 40)

I think you can probably see why this idea attracted Freud: it grounded the activity of the human entity in the non-personal drives by which we are lived. Man is rooted, for Freud, in the biological organism governed by drives. This is the basic datum that we are all born with. Differentiation gradually occurs and the ego becomes separated out from the id. The id is ruled by the pleasure principle; the ego by the reality principle – its function is to bring the organism into harmony with reality.

I want now to pass on to Freud's explanation of the superego. 'Mourning and Melancholia' describes the way in which the ego splits, and one side is set off against the other. Then in his paper 'On Narcissism' Freud describes an ego ideal which is the object of the ego's narcissistic love. In *The Ego and the Id* he first refers to that split-off part of the ego as the superego. It is the moral agency in the mind, and is closely related to the ego ideal but is not the same. The ego ideal holds an ideal in front of the ego for the ego to strive after, but the superego reproves the ego when it does not behave as it should. In this sense the superego is like the conscience.

How does the superego come about? Freud describes the process in the young boy, seeing it as the outcome of the Oedipus complex. Initially the young boy is libidinally attached to his mother and positively identified with the father. As he begins to see his father as his rival, however, the identification takes on a hostile colouring. The superego is therefore a precipitate of the identification, but also of the prohibition against the incestuous desires. It is established in the personality after the upheaval of the Oedipal crisis, which Freud placed in about the third or fourth year of life.

In *Civilization and Its Discontents* Freud developed further a notion that he had adumbrated in *The Ego and the Id* – the idea that the superego, or a part of it, can be unconscious. A person may not feel consciously guilty, but be terribly sensitive to criticism. The criticism cannot be borne because it strikes at an already persecuting inner figure. So also the person who is always blaming others is projecting his inner, persecuting feelings outwards. Similarly with the person who is always bringing disasters on his head. In the analytic situation the phenomenon is manifested in what is called the negative therapeutic reaction. In all these cases the person is not conscious of feeling guilty; in fact he or she feels quite innocent; but in the unconscious there is a persecuting superego.

Now the question I want to ask is: for what reason is the superego so mercilessly attacking the ego? Is the ego quite innocent? I believe that this is an important question, because we do not modify a superego by reassuring a patient that he is good and need not feel the way he does. Quite often a therapist says to a patient, 'Perhaps you feel you have hurt your mother/husband/me', but the statement contains the implication that the therapist believes that the patient has *not* hurt mother, husband or analyst.

My experience is that a severe superego is closely associated with an inner narcissism; that inwardly other people do *not* exist for the patient. The patients I can think of who had the severest superego were externally full of care and concern for those around them, but as the analysis progressed it became clear that inwardly people did not exist for them emotionally as *persons*; people as persons were completely blotted out. It is for this that the superego is accusing the individual so severely.

I believe that this understanding has important clinical implications. With the patient who has a severe superego the analyst can feel a very strong temptation to react in a similar way, i.e., to the patient not as a person. Then you have a situation, not where two people are interacting with one another, but one of two cardboard people, as a friend of mine used to express it. What I am saying is that the clinician has to be very wary of enacting the fierce superego with such patients.

By the time Freud came to write *Civilization and Its Discontents* he had come to realize the destructive virulence of the superego, and saw it as the seat of the death instinct in the personality. We will see later that Melanie Klein and Winnicott both thought that the superego formed a long time before the third or fourth year; Winnicott had controlled experimental evidence for it from the age of seven months, and Melanie Klein saw it developing in the very earliest months. Klein also believed that the Oedipus complex made its appearance much earlier than Freud had conjectured; and that the superego's harshness was partly attributable to hostile projections originating in what she called the paranoid-schizoid phase of development. I will define these terms later, but for the moment will simply note that this is in line with what I suggested earlier about the obliteration of the object.

Freud sketched out the structural model as a rough guide to the inner processes. He was well aware that it did not fit all the facts with exactness, so I want to end this lecture with the following passage from the *New Introductory Lectures*:

> I am imagining a country with a landscape of varying config-uration – hill-country, plains, and chains of lakes – and with a mixed population: it is inhabited by Germans, Magyars and Slovaks, who carry on different activities. Now things might be partitioned in such a way that the Germans, who breed cattle, live in the hill-country, the Magyars, who grow cereals and wine, live in the plains, and the Slovaks, who catch fish and plait reeds, live by the lakes. If the partitioning could be neat and clear-cut like this, a Woodrow Wilson would be delighted by it; it would also be convenient for a lecture in a geography lesson. The probability is, however, that you will find less orderliness and more mixing, if you travel through the region. Germans, Magyars and Slovaks live interspersed all over it; in the hill-country there is agricultural land as well, cattle are bred in the plains too. A few things are naturally as you expected, for fish cannot be caught in the mountains and wine does not grow in the water. Indeed, the picture of the region that you brought with you may on the whole fit the facts; but you will have to put up with deviations in the details. (1933, *SE* 22, pp. 72– 73)

Here we take leave of Freud himself and turn to some of his early followers.

FREUD'S
CONTEMPORARIES

15 KARL ABRAHAM AND CHARACTER FORMATION

Karl Abraham was one of Freud's most loyal disciples, yet strangely Freud was rather critical of him. He praised Abraham for his 'clarity, solidity and power of carrying conviction' but regretted that he lacked the spark of Ferenczi and complained that he had no 'dash'. Freud did not like those who went to the extreme of rebelling against any of the central tenets of psychoanalysis, but equally he did not like passive submission. Abraham built on Freud's theories and modified them in places, but remained faithful to his master.

He was born in Bremen, Germany in 1877 and was therefore two years younger than Jung and twenty-one years younger than Freud. He came from a well-established Jewish family and studied medicine in Berlin. He was a man of wide education and, apart from his mother tongue, he spoke English, Spanish and Italian fluently and had a good command of French, Dutch and Danish. At the Psycho-Analytical Congress in The Hague in 1920, before the days of instantaneous translations, he surprised his colleagues by addressing them in perfect Latin. He also knew Greek well and in his last illness entertained himself by reading Greek drama in the original.

After qualifying as a doctor in 1901 Abraham worked for four years as a physician in the state hospital at Dalldorf near

Berlin. He then spent three years at the Burghölzli psychiatric asylum at Zurich and was there at the same time as Jung, with whom he came into conflict and seemingly always distrusted. Although the conflict apparently centred around the aetiology of schizophrenia, I cannot help but wonder if it was a clash of personalities. In modern parlance Abraham was a 'straight' guy, whereas Jung was emotionally more effervescent. There has been a recent book, for instance, about Jung's supposed sexual affair with Sabina Spielrein, one of his patients, and this would have occurred during the time that Abraham was at the Burghölzli. It is difficult to think that their professional outlook and characterological attitudes were not very different. We do know, from the correspondence between Freud and Abraham, that Abraham warned Freud against Jung and, at that stage, it was Freud who tried to assure Abraham that Jung was all right.

From Zurich Abraham returned to Berlin and set up in psychoanalytic practice there. Hanns Sachs and Franz Alexander joined him, as did Sandor Rado, whom he started by analysing. Others came for analysis with him, the most famous being Alix Strachey, Edward and James Glover, Helene Deutsch, Theodor Reik, Karen Horney, Ernst Simmel and Melanie Klein. Reik and Sachs both objected to his excessive rigidity and complained about his 'orderly, methodical and surgical approach to the unconscious'. He died after a short illness on Christmas Day 1925 when he was only forty-eight. He was deeply mourned by his colleagues and Freud said that the psychoanalytic movement had lost a great light.

Karl Abraham wrote on a wide variety of topics, but he is best known for his papers on character formation. The most famous and comprehensive of these is 'A Short Study of the Development of the Libido, Viewed in the Light of Mental Disorders', which he wrote in 1924, and in which he traces the individual's libidinal development from the first oral stage, in earliest infancy, to final maturity with the establishment of genital sexuality. Abraham was in fact the first psychoanalyst to shift his attention from symptoms to character, although the definitive work on this topic was to be Wilhelm Reich's *Character Analysis*, written in 1933.

In the early days of psychoanalysis the analyst focused on the symptom and instructed the patient to free associate; when the patient had difficulty in doing this he was merely encouraged to persevere. It was Reich who recognized that the patient's resistance to associating needed to be analysed itself, for it meant that the analyst was up against some obstacle in the structure of the personality. What the analyst was asking of the patient went against a deep-seated mode of communication. But it was Abraham who recognized that these immature modes of communication derived their colouring from the individual's bodily relation to his or her earliest objects. A fixation at one of these bodily stages structured future emotional responses to the social environment.

Maturity, for Abraham, is an emotional relationship with a stable love object together with a capacity for genital-sexual relationship. When this state has been achieved the person lives in a friendly harmony with his social environment, a different view of the relationship between society and the individual from Freud's. Freud thought that there was an ineradicable opposition between the individual and society. He held a Hobbesian view of man 'in the state of nature': that if the pressure of civilization is removed then all man's lusts and savagery are released. Abraham's view is different: it is that this is the case with immature man, but not with individuals who have reached psychological maturity. With mature man the requirements of civilization and man's individual needs dovetail into each other and together form a consistent pattern.

The aim of the analytic endeavour is therefore to help the individual to full maturity; those who present themselves for analysis have done so because, in some important area of their lives, they are not living properly as adults. They have remained stuck at one of the six developmental stages identified in Abraham's 'Development of the Libido', which are as follows:

1. Earlier oral stage – Auto-erotism, pre-ambivalent
2. Later oral stage – Narcissism, oral-sadistic
3. Earlier anal-sadistic stage – Partial love with incorporation
4. Later anal-sadistic stage – Partial love
5. Earlier genital stage – Object love with exclusion of genitals
6. Later genital stage – Object love

Freud had noted and named a stage of development which he called the 'anal', but Abraham thought that this was too general a term and that the aetiology of melancholia and obsessional neurosis required a division of the anal stage into two: an earlier and a later. He then bisected both the genital and the oral stages in a similar way. He divided the oral into the times prior to and after the eruption of teeth, here following Van Ophuijsen (1920), who believed that certain neurotic phenomena were due to a regression to this point, and further that the appearance of sadism coincided with it. But whereas Abraham's division of the anal stage was made in order to explain a particular clinical situation, it is more difficult to see the value of the division in the oral stage of development. What is certain, however, is that he makes many observations which pertain to the oral stage as a whole, and I will treat of these first.

In melancholia, he said, there was a regression to a state of longing for the mother's breast, although the relationship to the breast was always an ambivalent one. On the surface the breast was usually idealized but underneath it was denigrated. Abraham gives the example of a patient who was continually looking for mother-of-pearl buttons in the street, and whose associations took him to a mother-of-pearl shell which was all shiny on one side but dirty on the other. The object which is both repudiated yet desired is symbolized in coprophagia: the desire to eat shit. Shit is the repudiated object which stands both for the child's repudiation of the mother, and the mother's rejection of the child.

Abraham was the first analyst really to signal the importance of this early relationship of the child to its mother and in particular the mother's breast – Freud had been much more concerned with the father – and he stresses two things which need to be brought together. The first is that melancholia stems from some great disappointment that the child has suffered, particularly in the case of a first child who felt himself to be his mother's favourite, and then when another sibling has come along, has felt shattered. The loss is irreparable, and efforts to direct love to the father have somehow failed. The second is Abraham's view that a regression to the oral stage takes place when the child has been either overindulged in its pleasure in sucking, or deprived. The child then remains stuck at that stage.

Yet Abraham does not make a further point which would link the two. That the mother either deprives or overindulges her child when she herself feels unable to *give* herself in love to her infant. I say that he does not make this link, but the object-related nature of his understanding still seems clear. With the melancholic patient, full of self-reproaches, Abraham followed Freud in thinking that the reproachful voices were directed against the lost object which is identified with the ego. It is the child part that is identified with the lost object, but Abraham brings the process to a more archaic level than Freud did, for he sees the withdrawal of the mother's breast as the primal castration. Here there is a sense that what is being talked about in castration is most fundamentally a looting of the ego.

In all this it is not difficult to see how much Abraham influenced Melanie Klein. He does not quite come to a formulation of part-objects in so many words, but he reaches the content of what Melanie Klein later elaborated. For in this primal castration state the child, he says, is not focused on the mother as a whole but on a part. The infant has partial love, which he describes as a fetish: a part of the mother assumes total importance psychically and the rest of the person is thereby obliterated. Klein, who was analysed by Abraham, followed in greater detail this fetishistic relation to the mother's breast, particularly by giving more attention to the aggression which is projected into the breast.

I want to move on now to the specific features of the earlier oral stage, and the most important point that Abraham makes about it is that the child cannot distinguish between its own self and the external object:

> 'Ego' and 'object' are concepts which are incompatible with that level of development. There is as yet no differentiation made between the sucking child and the suckling breast. Moreover the child has as yet neither feelings of hatred nor love. (1924, p. 450)

Frustratingly, however, he does not follow his thinking about this any further. Winnicott also believed that at this early stage the child cannot differentiate between itself and its mother: the two together form an agglomerate. Melanie Klein, on the other hand, differed on this point. She held that there was an ego from the beginning and that it was object-related from the start. She also differed from Abraham in saying that there was hostility from the start; for Abraham the sucking stage, prior to the eruption of teeth, is pre-ambivalent. In fact I would have expected Abraham to connect confusional states to a regression to this stage of development, but he does not do so. I also think the position taken on this matter is clinically important: Melanie Klein's and Winnicott's views lead to important differences in technique. (The notion of an undifferentiated state at the beginning of life was also the view of Heinz Hartmann and those who followed him, the 'ego psychologists'.)

Abraham went on to say that pleasure in sucking gets transferred to the anal and urethral sphincters, the action of which is modelled on the lips. If pleasure has been either too indulged or too deprived at this stage it fastens with particular intensity on to the possibilities of pleasure from the next stage. Pleasure in soiling or retention of faeces, therefore, can be the response to overindulgence or deprivation at the oral stage. That is, anal traits develop from the ruins of an oral erotism whose development has miscarried.

One could look at the anal stage as a screen that cloaks the more intense feelings of the earlier stage when the infant was at the breast. When we come to Fairbairn, for instance, we find that he knocks the anal stages out altogether because they are not object related. However, it might be more accurate to say that object-relatedness comes from the oral stage but receives a particular colouring from the anal stages.

Neurotic parsimony, for Abraham, comes from an inhibition of the craving for objects: pleasure in acquiring has been repressed in favour of holding fast on to possessions. The parsimony is therefore a turning away from objects, but the anal stage does not sufficiently explain it and it is therefore necessary to look for its origin in the first oral stage. A person who has had too much pleasure in sucking, he says, becomes sunk into a form of passivity connected to a belief that all will be well.

Optimism and confidence in the face of life are qualities deriving from this stage, but they become pathological when they are mustered in the service of an inner passivity. I once had a patient who believed that all would be well, but there was no hint of determined activity that might help towards the hoped-for goal. He was completely passive and expected from the bottom of his soul that a saviour would stoop from the skies and rescue him from his nightmare world where his private and public life were steadily crumbling. Abraham says of such people that 'they expect the mother's breast to flow for them eternally'.

He also instances people who renounce all ideals in favour of receiving an assured and regular income, so that the sole aim in life consists in having means of sustenance. People who are always asking for something also have a fixation at the sucking stage. They plead and insist and will not be put off by hard facts or reasonable argument: they cling like leeches to others. Then there are people who have a need to communicate orally on and on, demanding the other's attention. Somerset Maugham describes such a person in one of his short stories: 'Mr Harrington was a talker. He talked as though it were a natural function of the human being, automatically, as men breathe or digest their food; he talked not because he had something to say but because he could not help himself, in a high-pitched, nasal voice, without inflexion, at one dead level of tone' (1951, p. 182). Note that Maugham has picked up the oral significance of such dependent talking. You will notice that one of the things with such people is that it is often difficult to get away, and I have met patients who start just such a flow a few minutes before the end of a session. I had a patient once who talked incessantly, never stopping, going from one topic to another. You certainly could not have accused him of failing to free associate.

I want now to move on to the later oral stage. Covetous impulses derive from this stage because their source is in the desire to rip the good breast from a rival sibling. Covetousness is therefore object-related (whereas acquisitiveness finds its source in an obliteration of the object and so belongs to the earlier anal stage). In particular, envy is aroused when a baby sees its sibling suckling at the breast. I cannot resist quoting to you a passage from St Augustine's *Confessions*:

> I have myself seen jealousy in a baby and know what it means. He was not old enough to talk, but whenever he saw his foster-brother at the breast, he would grow pale with envy. This much is common knowledge. Mothers and nurses say they can work such things out of the system by

one means or another, but surely it cannot be called innocence, when the milk flows in such abundance from its
source, to object to a rival desperately in need and depending
for his life on this one form of nourishment? Such faults are
not small or unimportant, but we are tender-hearted and
bear with them because we know that the child will grow out
of them. It is clear that they are not mere peccadilloes,
because the same faults are intolerable in older persons.
(p. 280)

St Augustine wrote this in the year AD 397, so envy of the breast
has been known for a long time. Abraham held that the sight of
the rival at the breast reinforced the envy; here is the notion of
a very primary force at work. As we shall see when we come to
her, Melanie Klein considered this envy to be destructive,
destroying the good breast as source of creativity and good,
from a very early stage.

Abraham further said that those who were fixated at the oral-
sadistic stage were hostile and malicious, and also tended to
have a morbidly intense appetite for food and oral perversions.
Oral-sadistic tendencies were the source of the mental suffering
found in depressed patients. It is the oral-sadist who attacks
with hurtful and cruel language. At this stage of development
there is incorporation of the object but at the same time
destruction of it, and the destruction comes out in the form of
hatred, resentment or bitterness.

I had a patient who hated his mother, in particular the way in
which she turned her back on his own interests due to her self-
preoccupation. In fact he had incorporated her, because he was
self-preoccupied himself. This patient did not become depressed when he became conscious of it, because by that time he
was much less self-preoccupied; but I can think of another
patient who got a flash of insight into her own cruel suppression of others, and she became depressed for some weeks. For
Abraham also says that in the later oral stage is to be found the

beginning of ambivalence: if, during this period, there is a crashing disappointment, the hostility towards the mother is greatly intensified, leading ultimately to melancholia.

I shall now move on to anal erotism. Abraham reminds us that there is pleasure in the release and in the retention of faeces. When the faeces first come out and rest upon the baby's buttocks in his nappy they are warm and pleasurable. The retention of faeces also provides an erotic pleasure. (In adults the pleasure is repressed and only comes to light in psychoanalytic investigation.) There is also considerable pleasure in messing with faeces; this is usually met with severe reproach from the mother and a reaction formation sets in, whereby it is replaced with a love of cleanliness.

When this is the case there is an external conformity, but analysis always reveals that underneath there is bitter resentment; you can be certain that a severe obsessional neurosis only gives way after a long and determined analysis. I say determined, because I have so often encountered clinicians who feel so helpless in the face of these patients that they give up.

Together with the love of cleanliness go tidiness, orderliness, parsimony and miserliness over money. (It is always a much more difficult business to put up the fees of an obsessional patient than of any other.) In the case of the child who smears faeces for his mother to clear up, it is fairly clear that the smearing is a hostile attack on the mother whom he feels to be controlling him. In particular, however, it is a reaction to an obsessional mother, and Abraham gives the instance of a mother of this obsessional kind:

A mother drew up a written programme in which she arranged her daughter's day in the most minute manner. The orders for the early morning were set out as follows: 1. Get up. 2. Use the chamber. 3. Wash, etc. In the morning she would knock from time to time at her daughter's door, and ask, 'How far have you got now?' The girl would then have to reply, '9' or '15', as the case might be. In this way the mother kept watch over the execution of her plan. (1924, pp. 376–377)

Of course the emotional attitude of such a mother is sensed by the baby from birth onwards, and my experience has been that a child's obsessional neurotic attack is an attack on tyrannical control of this nature. I also think we all know how cleanliness, orderliness and miserliness can be and usually are an unconscious attack on those around. You may have had the experience of going to someone's house and after you have sat down your hostess immediately straightens and pats the cushions. You are encouraged to feel that you are a dirty smelly creature. The attack is powerful though it is subtle, and again the best description of it that I know comes from that same short story of Somerset Maugham's, 'Mr Harrington's Washing':

Mr Harrington was a bore. He exasperated Ashenden, and enraged him; he got on his nerves, and drove him to frenzy. But Ashenden did not dislike him. His self-satisfaction was enormous but so ingenuous that you could not resent it; his conceit was so childlike that you could only smile at it. He was so well-meaning, so thoughtful, so deferential, so polite that though Ashenden would willingly have killed him he could not but own that in that short while he had conceived for Mr Harrington something very like affection. His manners were perfect, formal, a trifle elaborate perhaps . . . but though natural to his good breeding they gained a pleasant significance from his good heart. He was ready to do anyone a kindness and seemed to find nothing too much trouble if he could thereby oblige his fellow-man . . .

It was only when he was dressing that Mr Harrington was silent, for then his maidenly mind was singly occupied with the problem of changing his clothes before Ashenden without indelicacy. He was extremely modest. He changed his linen every day, neatly taking it out of his suitcase and neatly putting back what was soiled; but he performed miracles of dexterity in order during the process not to show an inch of bare skin. After a day or two Ashenden gave up the struggle to keep neat and clean in that dirty train, with one lavatory for the whole carriage, and soon was as grubby as the rest of the passengers; but Mr Harrington refused to yield to the difficulties. He performed his toilet with deliberation notwithstanding the impatient persons who rattled the doorhandle, and returned from the lavatory every morning washed, shining, and smelling of soap. Once dressed, in his black coat, striped trousers, and well-polished shoes, he looked as spruce as though he had just stepped out of his tidy little red-brick house in Philadelphia and was about to board the streetcar that would take him downtown to his office . . .

Mr Harrington was absurd, but lovable. It was inconceivable that anyone should be rude to him, it would have seemed as dreadful as hitting a child; and Ashenden, chafing inwardly but with a pretence of amiability, suffered meekly and with a truly Christian spirit the affliction of the gentle, ruthless creature's society. It took eleven days at that time to get from Vladivostok to Petrograd, and Ashenden felt that he could not have borne another day. If it had been twelve he would have killed Mr Harrington. (1951, pp. 187–189)

You catch a flavour here of the nature of the attack that Mr Harrington inflicted on Ashenden. Ashenden was amiable outwardly but chafing inwardly, and this is a mirror of Mr Harrington's unconscious psychological state. One could say that Ashenden feels it through projective identification, which will become clearer when we consider Melanie Klein's work. One might imagine that as a baby Mr Harrington was forced to be toilet-trained and that he conformed outwardly but was bitterly resentful inwardly.

When someone reaches mature genital love he or she accommodates to the other person. In the obsessional there is no accommodation, but rather a powerful desire to control the other and make him or her conform to his own mode of behaving. The obsessional unfailingly has a most severe superego, and in the transference, when you get behind the polite exterior, the analyst will be experienced as a tyrannical figure whom the patient feels ruled by and whom he hates.

Another quality of this kind of patient is that changeable man-made rules are always experienced as acts of parliament. This is because the violent feelings within are projected on to the authority figures of the surrounding environment. The bank manager, the policeman, the headmaster or the MP are figures whose words are carved in stone; there is no possibility in his mind that he could talk with any one of these figures so that agreement could be reached. Indeed in a long analysis it is very tiresome to be relentlessly treated as an unapproachable figure. I always get the sense, with these patients, that there is no spontaneous source of life at the centre.

Let me make one last observation about this kind of patient. An obsessional longs to get some sense of what the analyst feels himself. What he wants to know is 'Does the analyst really want to be with me? Does he have any natural feelings of affection for me?' I think that the yearning for this knowledge hails from a longing to know what the mother, behind all her rituals, felt for the baby. It is only when the patient knows what the analyst feels that he is freed of his chains. If you agree with this then I think you will see that it must lead the analyst to search creatively into his revered technique – that is, it may at times be appropriate for an analyst to convey what he feels for such patients.

Abraham believed that there was an important divide between the earlier anal and the later anal stages. The pleasure of the earlier anal stage lies in the expulsion of faeces which, in particular cases, is the infant's reaction to loss of the object. The loss is reacted to directly in a somatic way, rather than experienced emotionally; the faeces become a symbolic object which the infant actively expels as a way of mastering the trauma of the loss. In the later anal stage the person retains his object though with an ambivalent attitude. He is now object-related. If a patient is regressed to the later anal stage he is on the side of neurosis, but a regression back to the earlier anal stage denotes a psychotic state, and if someone has regressed across that important divide he will certainly cascade back to the oral stages. Melancholia has its origins in a regression back across the psychotic divide whereas obsessional neurosis remains on the neurotic side of it. However, Abraham noted that someone is not necessarily fixed on one side or the other but will frequently oscillate across the divide. This is the reason why in depression there is always a component of obsessional neurosis and vice versa.

The goal of the preceding stages is object love combined with the capacity for genital sex. This is the final stage: the later genital stage. However, Abraham does interpose between the anal stages and the later genital stage the phallic or earlier genital stage, in which object love towards the other does not include the genitals. In other words the genitals are cathected with narcissistic love; that is, there is a desire for sex, but the meeting of the sexual organs of the pair is in the service of narcissistic pleasure. Narcissism is finally given up only in the last libidinal stage. So a developmental move has been going on throughout: from narcissistic love which starts in the later oral stage, to true or genuine love that is only finally consolidated in the later genital stage. It is in the final stage, when the ego feels robust, that it can love. This view is consistent with my experience that narcissism always blankets a person's own personal creative capacity.

I think it is probably necessary to say that even in the most mature person there remain vestiges of the preceding stages and hence of narcissism; in crises we all regress to more primitive modes of functioning. It is also important to note that object love exists in the earlier stages. We must avoid the obsessional's love of carving things up too neatly.

16 ERNEST JONES' THEORY OF SYMBOLISM

The psychoanalytic theory of symbolism is traditionally associated with the name of Ernest Jones. In this lecture I will concentrate on Jones' work in this area, and in the next I will move on to examples of symbolism from my clinical experience. In his classic paper of 1916 on the subject Jones says that interpretation of symbols calls forth the greatest resistance of all in psychoanalytic work, and I do not think there can be any doubt about the factual reality of this statement. I do not know the reason for it, but I can make some suggestions. It is very devastating if the object of love is shown to be a sign pointing to a part of the person's own self, and so patients often hate transference interpretations of this nature; they realize that they point to a self-centred narcissism. Related to this is the fact that self-esteem is directly correlated with a capacity to love; if the latter is shown up to be illusory it is a shattering blow. In a similar way if the object someone hates is shown to be a sign pointing to a part of the self, or the self's immediate environment, it robs the manifestation of its altruistic pretension. However, the symbolic is not entirely illusory: when interpretations imply that it is, the patient repudiates them with justification.

The word 'symbolism' is used in connection with a wide variety of phenomena such as emblems, amulets, tokens, badges, flags and trophies. The word is also used to indicate figures of speech and modes of thought such as the simile, metaphor or allegory, apologue (allegorical story), metonymy (attribute or part substituted for the thing meant – crown for king), synechdoche (whole equalling the part – little man equals penis). In a general sense 'symbol' is often used synonymously with 'sign'. It is also used in ritual and liturgy: in the Venetian ceremony, the Doge wedded the Adriatic with a ring which symbolized the naval power of Venice. In Frankish law the seller of a plot of land handed the buyer a single stone from the property as a symbol of the transaction. In ancient Bavarian law a twig was used to symbolize the sale of a forest. In the ceremony of Ash Wednesday in the Catholic Church the priest anoints each member of the congregation with ash, to remind them that they came from dust and that they will return to it after death. (No doubt Freud would have been pleased with this particular bit of symbolism!) I remember on an occasion when I gave up smoking that I took a cigar and broke it and threw it into a wastepaper basket: it symbolized the actuality of the decision.

These are the generalized senses in which the word symbolism is used. Ernest Jones, however, gives the word a more specialized meaning and he notes six differentiating factors:

1. A phenomenon of primary significance is represented by a lesser essential idea.
2. The symbol represents the primary element through having some perceptual element in common with it. This perceptual element has gone underground and is not consciously understood, though it is often [always?] recognized unconsciously.
3. A symbol is sensorial and concrete but may represent a relatively abstract idea. It has its roots in childhood when matters are concretely represented.
4. Symbols are primitive modes of thought and represent a reversion to an earlier stage of mental development.

5. Usually the symbol is a manifest expression of a hidden idea.

6. Symbols are produced spontaneously and are productions of the unconscious.

Ernest Jones does not enlarge on all these but I would like to go over them in some detail.

A phenomenon of primary significance is represented by a less essential idea. The symbol may in fact be quite a paltry thing. A flag, for instance, is just a piece of material printed with certain colours. However, Independence Day in Tanzania, when the Union Jack was lowered outside Government House and the Tanzanian flag raised in its place, was a moment of emotional significance both for the British and the people of Tanzania. The symbol is always a receptacle of considerable affect, positive or negative, and I think it would be more correct to say that a phenomenon of primary emotional significance is represented by a phenomenon of lesser emotional import. A symbol (a true symbol rather than a sign or emblem) is always a receiver of affect.

The symbol represents the primary element through having some perceptual element in common with it. This perceptual element has gone underground and is not consciously understood, though it is often recognized unconsciously. The perceptual link is through some portion of the symbol being identical, or nearly so, with some portion of the matter symbolized. Children see the perceptual link between things where adults do not, and this is because adults have qualified their primitive vision with cognitive structures.

I will give you two examples of this, both of which come from a holiday spent in Portugal when our elder son was three years old. Close to where we were staying a farmer had caught a wild boar and penned it up. On hearing this we went with our young son to see it. Naturally after that first visit we had to visit it every day. On one occasion, after visiting it, we continued on for a walk alongside the edge of a wood. Our son suddenly pointed out some dried-up ferns and said, 'Look, that looks like the wild boar'.

At first I thought he was quite crazy, but then I realized that the ferns were exactly the colour of the hairs on the wild boar's back and had the same straggly formation. I was quite blind to this perceptual link because with my intellectual (and I would almost say Linnaean) education I had the idea that it would be hard to find two things more dissimilar than a wild boar and a dried-up fern. I had to strip my mental apparatus of all this cognitive rubbish before I could see what a child (or a painter) can see with unlearned immediacy.

I don't know if a fern has ever symbolized a wild boar, but if it ever has then you will understand the reason why. There is always a perceptual link between the symbol and the thing symbolized. The other example is that one day we were on the beach and our son picked up the shell of a mussel that was greyish in colour with black edging and said, 'Look, it's like a gramophone record'. I am happy to tell you that this was subsequent to the wild boar incident, so I did not think my son was mad, and I 'saw' the similarity as soon as he had pointed it out. It was in both the black colour and the small grooves.

A symbol is sensorial and concrete but may represent a relatively abstract idea. It has its roots in childhood when matters are concretely represented. This notion is closely related to the above quality of symbols. As a bearer of emotion the symbol needs to be concrete and individual. The crucifix is single and individual, but it represents human suffering, God's love for man, goodness in man clashing with evil, the culmination of man's history on earth, the diversity of Christian traditions through the last two thousand years, and so on. Emotion can only ever be felt fully towards the concrete and individual. A symbol has as part of its purpose, therefore, to take the individual from the narrower concerns to the wider values of the group, the nation and even perhaps the human race.

Symbols are primitive modes of thought and represent a

reversion to an earlier stage of mental development. Again the reversion is to a child stage of mental life, before conceptualization has emerged. Thinking is embedded in the perceptual. Vision, for instance, is an activity as well as a passivity, and thinking is contained in it. An enormous amount of intelligent activity enters into our comprehension of the visual field: the constancies in it – of size, shape, and colour – are the product of this intelligent activity. The brightness or darkness of objects arises out of relational comparisons – they are not absolutes. Symbols arise out of this stage of thinking; this stage, tied as it is to the perceptual, is the bearer of emotion. Hence the perceptual link is suffused with thinking. Symbol formation is thus the emergence of thinking in its earliest form.

Usually the symbol is a manifest expression of a hidden idea. Here Ernest Jones is talking in particular of the sorts of ideas that are encountered clinically in the practice of psychoanalysis, often in a dream. I once had a woman patient with a violent hatred of the penis. On one occasion, she told me, she had gone to Mont-Saint-Michel and while there had begun to be overcome by a dark and tyrannical mood. It was clear that Mont-Saint-Michel was a symbol of the penis which she hated so much.

Symbols are produced spontaneously and are productions of the unconscious. An emblem which is consciously elaborated is not a symbol. Symbolization takes place spontaneously and unconsciously. This process can be disturbed, however, and we shall give some attention to it in the next lecture.

Ernest Jones says that a characteristic of the 'true symbol' is that when it is interpreted it evokes surprise and repugnance. He gives the example of Punchinello (Punch of Punch and Judy) being interpreted as a phallic symbol. Yet, he goes on to say, the conception of the penis as the 'little man' is extremely widespread. It becomes personified through a process known to mythologists as 'decomposition': it becomes separated and given an independent existence, as in the penis becoming the 'little man'. The decomposition of the penis leads to the dwarfs, gnomes and goblins of folklore. These little men tend to be deformed, ugly caricatures of men, wicked and even malign, yet sometimes willing to be friendly and yield services on certain conditions. Jones quotes Maurice Sand as follows:

> 'His heart is as dry as his cane, he is an egoist in every sense of the word. Under an appearance of good humour, he is a ferocious being; he perpetrates evil for the sheer pleasure of it. He cares as much for human beings as we would for a louse . . . he fears neither God nor the devil, he who has seen so many societies and religions pass beneath his crooked and scabby nose . . . yet despite his blemishes and small size hardly made for seducing, though he is caustic, persuasive, enterprising and insolent, he has great success.' (Jones, 1916, pp. 93–94)

Jones goes on to show that Punchinello is a piece of matriarchal symbolism: there is a tie to the mother in this revolutionary son, the upstart, the court jester and critic of the patriarch. The patriarch is symbolised by the eagle and the bull.

Jones then specifies the six attributes of true symbolism as put forward by Rank and Sachs in a paper entitled 'Die Bedeutung der Psychoanalyse für die Geisteswissenschaften' (1913, 'The Significance of Psychoanalysis for the Humanities').

1. *Representation of unconscious material.* It is not so much that the concepts symbolized are not known to the individual, as that the affect attached to them is repressed. The process of symbolization is carried on unconsciously. What does this mean? That the representative link is not apprehended, and I would like to take an example from *Crime and Punishment*. Raskolnikov violently kills an old money-lender woman, and

this may stand for Dostoevsky's murderous attack on his mother. At the end of the book, through Sonia's love and devotion, Raskolnikov begins to repent of his bitterness towards women and start a life of emotional love. Lovingness replaces bitterness, and I think this symbolized a change in Dostoevsky himself. Now presumably he was aware of the intensity of passion and could also see himself in Raskolnikov, but did he *consciously* recognize his hatred for his mother and choose this incident to represent it? I would hardly think so. When a story is used to convey a conscious intent the result is poor literature. Ergo . . .

2. *Constant meaning*. A given symbol will have a restricted meaning and this holds across cultures. So a room will symbolize a woman, or a womb, or a part of the body. A house will symbolize the body, and so on. Variation in meaning is restricted, which seems to be consistent with what I said earlier about the way in which constancies are formed through cognitive-perceptual processes. This tendency – to the restriction of meaning – will be built into man's cognitive-perceptual manner of constructing the world around him. This was really Ernest Jones' argument against Jung's belief that archetypal symbols were inherited; I agree with Jones' basic position, though he lacked psychological understanding of these very early mental and perceptual processes.

3. *Independence of individual conditioning factors*. The individual cannot give a regular symbol a different meaning from that given it by everyone else. Jones says that the universality of symbols is due to the uniformity of the fundamental and perennial interests of mankind, which furnish the source of symbolism. As I have said above, the universality of symbols is due to the psychological processes involved in the cognitive-perceptual construction of the world which is basic to symbolism, combined with the fact that symbolizing takes place unconsciously, at an early stage of development, and therefore uninfluenced by any individuating factors.

4. *Evolutionary basis*. Jones says he intends to discuss this later in the paper, but then does not do so. We know that animals are able to apprehend symbols: Pavlov's dogs are proof of this. In stimulus-response theory the symbol is referred to as the conditioned as oppposed to the unconditioned stimulus. The sight of the meat is the unconditioned stimulus, the bell announcing the appearance of the meat is the conditioned stimulus or the symbol. Whether there is a perceptual link or not would take us too far from our subject; I also regret that I am not sufficiently *au fait* with animal studies in this area to be able to say anything helpful about the evolutionary factors governing the genesis and operation of symbols.

5. *Linguistic connections*. In a symbol there is always a connection between the symbol and the signified, and this connection is a perceptual one which may not be immediately conscious to our sophisticated minds. The perceptual cue of similarity may just be related to a part of the object, as I have already mentioned. The two examples I gave earlier related to visual cues, but they can also be auditory. I remember that on that same holiday in Portugal our son said to me while walking up a path one day, 'What's that?' and I said, 'It's a stone', and he replied, 'That's like a phone, isn't it, Dadda?' Here the similarity was in the auditory sphere and again he was right.

A patient who was due to see me for a further two years told me of a dream in which there were two bears. When I asked her what she thought they meant, she said, 'Well, bears sounds like years, doesn't it?' Linguistic connection capitalizes on both onomatopoeia and visual connections, and the study of etymology shows that although the word denoting the symbol may have no connotation of the idea symbolized, its history always shows there is a connection. The best I can do here is quote an example from Ernest Jones:

The name Punchinello is an English contamination (see below) derived from the Neapolitan *pol(l)ecenella* (modern

Italian *pulcinella*), which is the diminutive of *pollecena*, the young of the turkey-cock (the modern Italian *pulcino* means pullet, *pulcinello* being its diminutive): the turkey-cock itself is a recognized phallic symbol, as, indeed, is the domestic cock, both ideationally and linguistically. The Latin root is *pullus*, which means the young of any animal; the phallus is often, for obvious reasons, identified with the idea of a male child, a little boy or little man. The reason why the name came to be used in this connection is thought to be the resemblance between the nose of the actor and the hooked bill of the bird, and again it may be pointed out that both nose and beak are common phallic symbols.

The name *polecenella*, or its English variant 'polichinello' (derived via the French *polichinelle*), was contaminated with the English word 'punch', the main meaning of which is a tool for perforating material, with or without the impressing of a design – e.g., to pierce metal or stamp a die; it is used to mean a dagger (another common symbol). The word is short for 'puncheon', which used to mean a bodkin or dagger, and is now used in carpentry to denote 'a short upright piece of timber which serves to stiffen one or more long timbers or to support a load'; it comes from the Latin *punctiare*, to prick or punch. Pepys, in his *Diary*, 30 April 1669, calls punch 'a word of common use for all that is thick and short', and refers to a gun (by the way, yet another phallic symbol), 'which, from its shortness and bigness, they do call Punchinello'. Suffolk punches are thickset draught horses with short legs.

To sum up, the four ideas that keep recurring in connection with the name 'punchinello' are *one*, a caressing name for male offspring, equivalent to 'little man', *two*, a projecting part of the body, *three*, the motion of piercing or penetrating, and *four*, that of shortness and stoutness – four ideas that admirably serve to describe the male organ and nothing else; indeed, there is no other object to which the curious combination applies of stoutness and pricking. Finally, I may add that two common expressions become more intelligible in the light of the interpretation just given. 'To be as proud (or pleased) as Punch': overweening pride is intimately associated in the unconscious with exhibitionistic self-adoration. 'He has plenty of punch in him': in this modern Americanism the word 'punch' is used as a synonym for the colloquial 'backbone', 'spunk', 'sand', etc. – i.e., symbols of the male organ and its product. (1916, pp. 99–100)

6. *Phylogenetic parallels.* Jones mentions the remarkable ubiquity of the same symbols both across cultures, and also across centuries and millennia. For instance, teeth represent childbirth both in dreams in the present and also in ancient literature and mythology. In the 'Song of Songs' of the *Old Testament* we read: 'Thy teeth are as a flock of sheep, which go up from the washing, whereof everyone beareth twins, and there is not one barren among them.' The idea of the snake symbolizing the phallus is well known. That king and queen symbolize father and mother is also well known; I have had many patients who have had dreams of the Queen (even the most anti-monarchist patients, much to their shame!). Jones goes on to note that there are thousands of symbols, but the number of ideas symbolized are few. Ultimately he says that:

> All symbols represent ideas of the self and immediate blood relatives, or the phenomena of birth, love and death.

self = the whole body or any separate part of it, not the mind.

relatives = father, mother, brothers and sisters and children and various parts of their bodies can be symbolized.

birth = ideas of giving birth, of begetting or of being born oneself.

death = lasting absence. Always refers to others. One's own death is inconceivable.

love = sex, excretory acts and all the concepts associated with Freud's theory of sexuality. (1916, pp. 102–103)

Jones then goes on to discuss the genesis of symbols. He gives passing mention to the view held by Pelletier, Jung and Silberer, that there is cognitive immaturity in the infantile or primitive mind. Jones does not dismiss this as a reason for the genesis of symbols, but thinks it an unimportant factor. A second reason, he says, is that when a new experience presents itself, the mind seizes on the resemblances; and this seems to be patently true. The mind cannot move to something new except by the bridge of the known and familiar. When we try to grasp something new we try first to do so through the experience of something we already know.

Quite how we then move to the new is mysterious. Ernest Jones links this phenomenon to the pleasure principle, or a subordinate aspect of it, known as 'the law of mental inertia' or 'the law of the least effort'. The inference is that this process is more active in the infantile mind. (Is this true?)

His third reason, a development of the above idea, is that man's primitive interest is in matters sexual and only under duress is man dragged away from them to work. Hence work is endowed with sexual symbolism – ploughing the earth, tools, fields, and so on; unconsciously man is still intent on the sexual activity underlying the symbolic acts. In other words, the sexual activity becomes sublimated. In this context Jones quotes Sperber, a Swedish philologist, who apparently argued with some force that all language originated in speech sounds for calling a mate.

In seeming contradiction, however, Jones notes that it would be incorrect to think that the infantile or primitive mind does not differentiate. It does, but its categories are different from adult ones. The primitive mind, he says, differentiates according to interest. Arabs are supposed to have five hundred words to designate lions in various aspects, but no word for lion itself. They are also supposed to have 5,744 words for camels, but none for camel. Most of us call 'horse' any of those familiar four-legged animals that bear men on their backs; but for a horse dealer the word 'horse' is just one variety of many – mare, stallion, jennet, mule, gelding, donkey, pony, filly, and so on.

I know that when my younger son says he wants his white police car to play with; when it can't be found, and I say why not play with the white Citroën, he takes a dim view of my unconcern over the difference between the two cars in question. Connected with this is the fact that what a child names may not be the identifiable form of the adult category. A young child sees a duck landing on the Serpentine and calls out 'quack', but it denotes for him the shape of the wing and the spray of water, so that the next time he sees some frothy water he calls out 'quack'. Again the conclusion seems to be that the primitive categories are different – they are much more closely tied to the perceptual sphere.

Adult categorization of forms, on the other hand, is more removed from perceptual cues. It is also interesting that the adult definition of categories always includes the concept of an exception. So, for instance, the difference between butterflies and moths is said to lie in the fact that the antennae of the butterfly have a blob on the end, whereas those of the moth do not; but the moth known as the burnet is an exception to this. Also moths generally fly by night and butterflies by day; but there are several moths that fly by day, and so on. Scientists evidently find value in this more abstract categorization. This adult categorization is written deep into the mind; it is one of the tasks of the painter to banish these categories and see the colours and forms in front of him – to recapture the vision of the child. (I believe this is also the psychoanalyst's task.)

Therefore symbol formation is an activity in which identification and differentiation do go in concert. If either process is defective then there is a breakdown in the process as a whole. We shall come in the next lecture to consider the effects of a breakdown in the process through lack of identification. Does the opposite occur? Yes, in relation to the self where it cannot be categorized – i.e., when the self is merged and cannot be differentiated (the notion of the omnipotent self that cannot accept a role).

Why is it that, of two ideas unconsciously associated, one symbolizes the other and never vice versa? So a church spire may symbolize the phallus and never vice versa, and the eye symbolize the penis but never vice versa? Ernest Jones says that in the repressed part of the mind the psychic interest remains in the bodily self, relations of family, birth, love and death, and that energy is centrifugal and never centripetal. It is from the centre that the whole pool of psychic energy originates.

I want to end with just two main criticisms of Ernest Jones' theory. One is that I think it is too 'mentalistic' or cognitive: Jones does not give sufficient weight to the emotion-bearing quality of symbols; an indicator of this cognitive bias lies in his frequent use of the word 'ideas' for what is symbolized. My second criticism is a related one, and is that the matter symbolized is not the concrete entity – the penis, say – but the emotional *significance* of the penis and the self's relation to it. In the next lecture I hope to show you what my criticisms are based on from clinical work.

17 FURTHER THOUGHTS ON SYMBOLISM

Some years ago I was engaged in treating a man who was mentally handicapped. Like many mentally handicapped people he could not understand a joke, and what was said would be taken literally. If he was standing with some mates when a police car came by and one of them said to him, 'Harry, they're coming to pick you up', he would break out into a hot sweat. He did not realize that they were just pulling his leg. Of course in most jokes of this kind there is often an element, even if not very great, of aggression or sadism, and I think we all know the phenomenon where someone says something jokingly, but it is just a bit too loaded, and it is not experienced as funny.

Harry's trouble was that he was intensely sensitive to any hint of aggression or sadism, however small. It was selected out from the surrounding context and experienced as extremely persecuting. Harry and I had managed to understand this quite well: he was being punished for his intense fury towards his father but, ultimately, his even greater unconscious rage towards his mother. Somewhere a vengeful figure was out to destroy and obliterate him, so the slightest hint of his independent activity could not be borne.

I had understood this much but I realized in some inchoate way that I was missing some other element. Harry also realized this, so one day he came into the session and asked if I had any paper. There was a stack of rough paper on my desk so I pointed to it. He picked up a sheaf of these papers and put one down on a little coffee table saying 'That's Charlotte'; he placed another over a book on my desk and said 'That's George'; another on a chair saying 'That's Mary'; another over an ashtray saying 'That's Peter'; and staked out about a further five papers, each time naming someone by his or her Christian name. As he was doing this I was not exactly sure what was going on, but I knew the names were those of members of staff at the day centre he attended. When he had finished he said:

Well, that's all of them with their white coats on.

He went on to say:

When they have got their white coats on I do not know whether I am at the centre or in Friern Barnet.

(He had had a breakdown ten years previously and had been treated as an in-patient at Friern Barnet mental hospital in North London.) Amazed, I whistled a gasp of comprehension and he put his face right up against mine and said:

So now do you understand?

The implication that I was dim, in fact mentally handicapped, so obtuse as not to understand so obvious a fact, was the unavoidable conclusion. So, just to get it quite clear I asked him:

So, if you came in here one day and I had a white coat on you would think you were in Friern Barnet?

Well, I'd be very worried.

Then he went on to say that on a previous occasion when I had mimed being dead, he had truly thought for a few moments that I was.

How are we to understand Harry's delusion that he was in

Friern Barnet once a member of staff at the centre had a white coat on? The first important psychological fact was that his time at Friern Barnet had been a living nightmare for him. The next was that his mother was there as an in-patient at the same time. We all know that if we have had a very bad experience, we begin to shake when we find ourselves surrounded by signs reminiscent of it. For instance, I know a man who had been a prisoner of war during the Second World War. The corridors in his prisoner-of-war camp were long, painted brown from about the waist downwards and painted cream from there to the ceiling. Whenever, in later years, he came across corridors in an institution with similar decor he found that a shudder went through him.

We can well understand Harry shuddering at the staff member with the white coat on. It is almost certainly true too that there was an identity of meaning behind the white coats of the staff at Friern and at the centre. I do not know the history of doctors wearing white coats, but for Harry the white coat signified: someone in a white coat had the power to imprison him; a white coat was authority; a white coat was intelligent; a white coat was pure; a white coat was far superior to him. Probably the essential combining element here is the power that the white coat symbolizes. (I think that white coats are mostly worn to distinguish staff from patients. Therefore there is some message that says, 'I am different from you', but I cannot resist mentioning that the previous chairman of the Tavistock Clinic, Dr Robert Gosling, was once asked by a visitor how you could tell the difference between a patient and a member of staff. He answered as quick as lightning: 'The patients get better'.)

The white coat in the two places contained an identical emotional communication. Harry, like a child, was sensitized to the emotional communication of the white coat that takes us sophisticates some time to reach. Georg Groddeck, in *The Meaning of Illness*, says: 'The adult does not understand symbolism easily, and only occasionally does he succeed in grasp-

ing the symbolic connections that some piece of human under-
taking has with the unconscious. The child possesses this
understanding intuitively, a fact which should be borne in mind
in theoretical or practical studies of children' (1922, p. 163).
There is a greater quantum of emotionality in a visual symbol
than in the spoken word. The white coat for Harry was an emotional scream.

We may say that this is rather absurd, because a white coat is
only an article of clothing worn by a member of staff. It is not
the person him-or-herself, only a piece of clothing, and therefore quite external to the person. However, I think we need to
pause before we accept such a statement with too much non-
chalance. After all, we do express ourselves through clothing,
and I will tell you about something that occurred to me when I
was treating a psychotic patient.

In some sessions she would be warm and co-operative, and in
others full of rage. For a long time I could not detect what
triggered these alternations until I discovered that when I was
wearing a brown suit with a brown tie she was positive, but
when I was in a grey suit with a blue striped shirt and a blue tie
she fell into a fury. You may say that it was absurd of her to
behave in this way; I do not think it was, because the clothes I
wear express me and also stimulate a certain aspect of me. Different clothes express differing identifications, and these are
real. The patient was unable to hold on to the me that wore the
brown suit on Monday and the grey one on Tuesday. She was
overwhelmed by a part of her which was aroused by a part
of me.

In the case of Harry it is also significant that all the members
of staff wore white coats. The centre and the hospital are therefore clubs with a uniform: the individual is merged into the collective. It is this merging which is a source of such terror,
because Harry's own individuality is itself merged with his
primary love object or, put more simply, with his mother. At
the beginning of therapy, for instance, he used to be brought by

his social worker and then by his mother. Only later did he feel able to come on his own. One day I asked him why he had felt the need to come accompanied, and he said he was afraid of being mugged. I acknowledged that this was a danger but noted that he seemed more afraid of it than normal. He replied by saying that if he were killed it would kill his mother, and the way in which he said this made it clear that he was not speaking figuratively. The object of his love is so deeply located in him that killing him actually kills her. He is overwhelmed by the stage of the emotional before the individual has emerged.

This stage of the emotional is shared by both mother and child. Normally there is a development in which an individual begins to grow on the surface of each through a process of weaning-mourning. The emotional is the soil out of which the plant which is the individual grows. The emotional is essentially a group-embodied phenomenon. The emotional is inflamed by the partial personality. It is a world of part-object encounters. The symbol occurs only as an ego begins to be differentiated out from the emotional morass. It straddles two systems: the individual-thinking and the emotional-corporative. It is a link between these two systems; in the link meaning emerges. I will try to look at this a little more closely.

Meaning is essentially individual *and* emotional. A cry of 'Oh, I *see* what you mean' is not just an act of intellectual understanding. It is definitely a phenomenon in which my 'I' is engaged. But it is also emotional, and in fact I can feel the excitement which signals the presence of emotion. (You may remember that when Archimedes realized how he could discover whether King Hieron's crown was made of pure gold or an alloy he jumped out of his bath and ran through the streets of Syracuse shouting 'Eureka, eureka'.) The link between the emotional and the personal is via a symbol; if someone is still submerged in the amorphous morass of emotion then what is seen is not a symbol. If I am merged with my primary love object then I cannot distinguish between symbol and the object symbolized. Hanna Segal says: 'Disturbances in differentiation between ego and object lead to disturbances in differentiation between the symbol and the object symbolized' (1957, p. 52). I think it was significant that when Harry was in Friern so was his mother.

When a woman is carrying the foetus inside her womb, it is part of her: it feeds, drinks and breathes through her. At birth the infant is still herself psychically; there is a symbiotic reciprocity in the two parts of the unity. Thus a postpartum depression is frequently a despairing grief over the loss of the primary love object which had been invested in the foetus. In this state of affairs there is emotion, but no subject or object; and in Harry some part of this state still obtained. He was not differentiated from his mother, nor was the object in the perceptual field. Hence the two white coats spoke the same emotional field. Now when I asked him if he would have thought he was in Friern Barnet if I had been wearing a white coat, and he answered that he would have been very worried, I think this denoted a slight shift: some personal object was dimly showing in the mist. It is when this merged state of affairs is not negotiated that symbols are not formed. Symbols form as soon as an 'I' begins to separate out from the morass. The symbol remains as a link containing both emotion and the personal.

I said in the last lecture that a consciously elaborated emblem, such as a heraldic shield, was not a symbol. This is because it does not draw directly on the emotional. However, I used 'directly' because below the surface there is usually the presence of the symbolic. If you ask why the Union Jack flag is as it is, we are still in the realm of the emblematic if we offer the explanation that it is a conjunction of the flags of Scotland and England dating from the time at the beginning of the seventeenth century when James VI of Scotland became James I of England. If an enquiring child begins to ask why the flag of St George is a red cross on a white background, and we come to blood and the dragon, we verge on the land of symbolism. The symbol draws our affect, although it is not without cognitive content. It structures the unconscious emotional currents within; but it is at the moment that I understand consciously that a symbol yields meaning. A symbol therefore combines intellectual and emotional understanding.

Can man live without symbols? Let me go back to Harry. Could he live without being looked after? I think not; anyway not as I encountered him. To be able to live an autonomous life man needs symbols, for the symbol takes the individual beyond his or her immediate relations and primary objects, enabling him to make contact with the wider world. Without this capacity, or at least some measure of it, life in the maelstrom of the adult world is not possible. People need to draw constantly from the reservoir of emotional life to make contact with a constantly changing world; this contact is made by the formation of symbols. Through symbols humanity imaginatively forges towards a beyond. Without this capacity we stay stuck, clinging to the immediate, like survivors to a raft. Those early months when the bedrock is being formed, and in which symbols grow, are therefore crucial to a person's development over the rest of his or her life. A personal life of meaning depends on them.

18 FERENCZI – A FORGOTTEN INNOVATOR

Sandor Ferenczi is almost forgotten today but he is probably one of the greatest of Freud's followers, if not *the* greatest. He is almost forgotten, because he did not found a school. I think this was because he believed profoundly in the freedom of the individual and in his personal life seemed to be remarkably free of narcissism. Another reason for the neglect of Ferenczi could be that Ernest Jones blackened him in his biography of Freud, but the evidence suggests that this was unjustified calumny. Ferenczi has also been branded as the one who was seduced into a dilution of psychoanalysis.

However, Ferenczi did have his followers; the most famous of these was his analysand Michael Balint, to whom we shall devote Lecture 28. Balint particularly followed through Ferenczi's thinking on and practice of the therapeutic value of regression in psychoanalysis. During this lecture I shall quote from time to time from a book called *Difficulties in the Analytic Encounter*, whose author, John Klauber, also followed some of Ferenczi's techniques and ways of thinking about patients.

Sandor Ferenczi was born in Miskole, a city not far from Budapest, in 1873. His father had migrated as a young man to Hungary from Cracow in Poland; his mother was also of Polish origin. His father ran a bookstore and a lending library and had also established an artists' bureau. It was a large Jewish family, of twelve children: seven boys and five girls, Sandor being the fifth son. All the children grew up in close association with the bookstore, and throughout his life Ferenczi's greatest pleasure was reading, both prose and poetry, the latter of which he particularly loved.

After finishing his schooling he went to Vienna to study medicine; he qualified as a doctor in 1894 and then served as a military physician before turning to neurology and psychiatry, which he practised in Budapest. By 1907, when he came to take an interest in psychoanalysis, he had already published about thirty papers in Hungarian and German medical journals. Indeed he was always a prolific writer. Freud, whom he first met in 1908, loved Ferenczi and thought he was the most imaginative of all his followers. Once, when speaking about Abraham to a friend, Freud sighed and said: 'Oh, if only he had Ferenczi's flair'. As I said in the lecture on Abraham, Freud did not like those of his followers who were too dependent upon him; he preferred them to have independent minds and judgements of their own.

In 1923, for instance, Ferenczi published *The Development of Psycho-Analysis* in collaboration with Otto Rank. In it they stressed the communication that went on *between* patient and analyst, and the need for an analysis not to be just an intellectual reconstruction, but an emotional reliving. Freud did not find the book entirely congenial to his way of thinking, but he wrote to Ferenczi in the following way:

As for your endeavour to remain completely in agreement with me, I treasure it as an expression of your friendship but find this aim neither necessary nor easily attainable. I know that I am not very accessible and find it hard to assimilate alien thoughts that do not quite lie in my path. It takes quite a time before I can form a judgement about them, so that in the interval I have to suspend judgement. If you were to wait

so long each time there would be an end of your productiv-
ity. So that won't do at all. That you or Rank should in your
independent flights ever leave the ground of psychoanalysis
seems to me out of the question. Why shouldn't you therefore have the right to try if things won't work in another way
from that I had thought? If you go astray in so doing you will
find that out yourself some time or other, or I will take the
liberty of pointing it out to you as soon as I am myself sure
about it. (quoted in Roazen, p. 365)

It is worth mentioning that Freud wrote 2,500 letters to
Ferenczi in the course of his lifetime, more than to any other
person. Ferenczi had a great generosity of mind and heart and,
even though relations between the two men became severely
strained when Ferenczi began to develop his 'relaxation'
technique, Ferenczi never broke with Freud. When Ferenczi
died in 1933 at the age of sixty-two Freud said of him in his
obituary that he was the greatest of his followers, and that
Ferenczi's written works had made all analysts his pupils.

With such a creative and prolific writer it is impossible to give
even an idea of the many subjects that he treated in considerable
depth. I have chosen therefore to talk about the technique
which he developed in the last ten years of his life, and to refer
particularly to the following papers: 'The Problem of the Termination of the Analysis' (1927), 'The Elasticity of the Psycho-
Analytic Technique' (1928), 'The Principles of Relaxation and
Neocatharsis' (1930), 'Child Analysis in the Analysis of
Adults' (1931), and 'Confusion of Tongues between Adults
and the Child' (1933).

I have selected this focus for two reasons: firstly, because
both Freud and Michael Balint said that healing of the sick was
Ferenczi's vocation: it was the passion of his life and gave a pattern and meaning to everything else he did; secondly, the matters of technique which captured his interest in the last decade
of his life deserve, I believe, our special attention, and I shall try

to explain why. Ferenczi thought that aspects of our somewhat distant and sometimes severe technique re-enact, for the patient, his or her original trauma and therefore do not bring healing. I hope that as the lecture develops the meaning of this brief statement may become clear.

Ferenczi took on the most difficult patients: when other analysts despaired of a patient they referred the patient to Ferenczi as a last resort. He refused to give up and would not accept verdicts such as 'the patient's resistance was unconquerable' or 'the patient's narcissism prevented him penetrating any further'. In 'Child Analysis in the Analysis of Adults', he says he had told himself that 'as long as a patient continues to come at all, the last thread of hope has not snapped' (1931, p. 128). And in the same paper he asks: 'Is it always the patient's resistance that is the cause of failure? Is it not rather our own convenience, which disdains to adapt itself, even in technique, to the idiosyncracies of the individual?' (p. 128).

His belief, therefore, was that it was necessary, with certain patients whom today we would diagnose as either psychotic or borderline, to adapt some element of the classical technique in order to get the analysis unstuck. This point is made by John Klauber in *Difficulties in the Analytic Encounter*, and I want to quote from it at some length:

> With patients in whom a serious depression dominates the clinical picture from the start the regression is likely to go further, and demands may become too primitive for the ego to mediate. Miss L. was a senior business executive who was failing in her work following a period of intense grieving for a lover who had died. She developed early the symptom of being unable to leave my consulting-room, and, some time later, would instead pour abuse on me for my inability to say anything conceivably designed to help her, though she only wanted a little sympathy. Such a denial of the analyst's situation in reality was already highly suggestive of psychosis. A

considerable period followed in which she voiced typical
paranoid delusions in a tentative form. One of the few signs
that some perception of the reality of the analyst's character
remained was demonstrated by the fact that she would
periodically insist on giving me a cheque with which she paid
in part for the extra time she had exacted from me. In this
phase analytic work proved impossible. Her behaviour was
to some extent a reaction to a realistic anxiety. The lunch-
time analytic hour we had agreed upon reduced the much-
needed time available for her work. It was necessary eventually to recognize the impossibility of her ego's mediating her
demands – and that the analyst could be capable of making
an unsuitable arrangement – and I gave her a time which
would both enable her to come late (as she always did) and to
have extra time at the end. Miss L.'s attitude then began to
change. She brought her sympathy for the birds she watched
in her garden, and, through this medium, for her outcast father, who had attempted suicide and died in a mental hospital, despised by herself and the rest of the family. It was not
too long before she was able to cry for him in sympathy . . .

It may seem contradictory that a modification of standard
technique should be advocated after previously emphasizing
the danger of being seduced by the depressive patient's
dependency. But such an acceptance of her need at this phase
of the analysis enabled guilt and aggression which had been
mobilized to be recognized instead of projected: first, it
reduced the disruption due to the burden of her realistic anxiety; second, it showed that I did not consider myself infalli-
ble, but was prepared to listen to her in spite of her abuse. All
this paved the way for the interpretation of her fantasy that
she had killed her father by her unawareness of his need.
(1966, pp. 104–105)

I will tell you of two small instances some years ago where I
adapted the classical technique with a psychotic patient. At the

end of one session the patient refused to leave; I got hot under the collar about it to start with, but then agreed to leave the room. From then on I allowed her to stay in my room after the session ended. When I examined myself I realized that on the four times that I saw her each week I did not need my room immediately after seeing her, so I let the arrangement stand. About six months later, as it happened, it became inconvenient to have her in my room on a Tuesday after her session: I had a seminar straight after. I then asked her if she would leave on Tuesdays, and this she agreed to do without a murmur. What she had been clamouring against was being fitted into a stereotyped routine for no reason other than my obsessional narcissism.

At another stage in her treatment she flatly refused to start off the speaking in the session. Similarly, after some thought, I recognized that there was no sacred reason why the patient needs to start the talking, so quite frequently I would start. In this latter respect the patient freed me from an unnecessary rigidity, for which I have always been grateful to her. When I let up on the rigidity it became possible to analyse her own powerful stereotypes, which emerged quite clearly in the sessions. Previously she had been able to project them into me entirely, in the manner that Klauber talks about.

Ferenczi stresses again and again the need for the analyst to divest himself of his narcissism, but particularly as it adheres to his role and the rules and procedures that are attached to it. Object-relatedness demands adaptation. We all know that in a love relationship there has to be a continual process of adaptation, because without it there can only be self-love or narcissism. Where narcissism is dominant the tendency is to control the object to make him or her conform, whereas in object love there is adaptation. Ferenczi subjects classical technique to the same object-related demand. In cases of the kind I have mentioned, like Klauber's and my own, the analyst has felt that interpretations alone would not suffice.

When Freud gave up his theory that neuroses were triggered by the seduction of a patient by her father or another close male relative, he came to the truth that phantasied wishes were the source of the mental disturbance. For a time the idea that there had been a seduction of the child in reality was given up, but Ferenczi resurrected the notion. He said that although the precautions of the hysteric and the avoidances of the obsessional neurotic have their explanation in their phantasy life, the first impetus towards abnormal lines of development has always originated from real psychic traumas, and conflicts with the environment. I have myself frequently come across cases where a patient feels, with good reason, that he or she has to carry the mother or father, particularly the mother.

Ferenczi does not spell this idea out clearly, but we do meet many patients who have suffered real trauma at the pregenital stage. Ferenczi stresses the trauma unconsciously inflicted by a remote and distant parent; I have often found that when one goes into this a little more deeply, the patient has the feeling that the parent cannot control his or her incestuous impulses towards the child, so the only way that they can be managed is to withdraw emotionally.

One meets this in particular when a parent – usually but not always of the opposite sex – becomes anxious because his or her child has reached puberty. I had a patient who complained bitterly about the way her father was so withdrawn from her. At first it looked just as if he didn't care, but I had noticed from the early days with this patient that she did not feel safe with me, from which I inferred that she was apprehensive at a genital level that I would attempt to rape her. Below that I sensed there was a horrific anxiety that I would emotionally assault her, and that she would then disintegrate. The problem is that the analytic situation is one of extreme intimacy, yet at the same time the sexual expression of feelings is not permitted; in this way it exactly repeats the situation of child and parent. If there has indeed been some sexual advance from the parent towards the

patient as a child, then the patient will be enormously apprehensive that the analyst will abuse his professional role.

I had a patient who panicked if she heard me move during a
session; the patient whose father had withdrawn from her also
felt that I as her analyst was very withdrawn – and for the same
reason that she attributed to her father's withdrawal. So
Ferenczi stressed that the distant attitude in sessions was not
helpful to the patient because it so often re-enacted a past
trauma. In 'The Principles of Relaxation and Neocatharsis' he
says: 'We found that the rigid and cool aloofness on the
analyst's part was experienced by the patient as a continuation
of his infantile struggle with the grown-ups' authority, and
made him repeat the same reactions in character and symptoms
as formed the basis of the real neurosis' (1930, pp. 117–118).

I think it is particularly the case with the obsessional neurotic, who, in his or her illness, largely mirrors the attitudes of the
deliberately distant analyst. I once observed to such a patient
that, although she knew I was married, she excluded from her
communications any mention of or allusion to my wife. She
replied by saying that from my attitude and demeanour she
thought she was not supposed to know of my wife's existence,
let alone mention her. This seemed to me to be a fair point. Let
me repeat a point of Klauber's which I quoted in my second lecture:

> Psychoanalysis has both traumatic and therapeutic ele-
> ments. The clearest indication of its traumatic quality lies in
> the fact that it regularly induces a flight from reality. This is
> the most dramatic feature of analysis, and we describe it as
> the development of transference . . . A not infrequent exam-
> ple is by starting a sexual relationship at the beginning of
> analysis which may end as marriage as a defence against end-
> ing the analysis – that is, against the full power of the trans-
> ference at all stages. (1979, p. 112)

To counteract this 'traumatic quality' Ferenczi recommended

warmth and friendliness, even embracing the patient or kissing him or her. This last activity worried Freud, because he thought it was a short step from kissing to sexual intercourse and also that there was a danger of psychoanalysis getting a bad reputation.

Klauber further believed that the analyst should address himself to detraumatizing the patient:

> The sudden, traumatic development of transference creates a distance between the patient and the analyst. The patient feels that he is not his own master, while the analyst is elevated to a magical superiority. The essential craft of the psychoanalyst consists in undoing this distance by identifying the unconscious impulses that spill over to form the patient's image of him . . . Spontaneous exchanges humanize the analytical relationship by the continual interchange of partial identifications. It is this human quality of the relationship which is the antidote to the traumatic quality of the transference as much as or more than the acceptance of impulses by an analyst who reinforces the benign qualities of the superego. (1979, pp. 114, 116)

Two particular forms of trauma were of special concern to Ferenczi. He identifies a stage of tenderness in the young child, during which too much love can cause a trauma, i.e., a flooding that the ego cannot deal with. Trauma could also be caused by what he called the 'terrorism of suffering'. Here a mother binds her child to her by complaining of all her miseries, and so turns her child into a mother substitute. As adults such patients are very concerned in the transference to protect and look after the analyst.

Closely related to this is Ferenczi's idea that children have a compulsion to put right all disorder in the family. Harold Searles, in his paper 'The Patient as Therapist to his Analyst' (1975), put forward the hypothesis that innate among man's most powerful strivings towards his fellow men, beginning in the earliest years and even earliest months of life, is an essentially psychotherapeutic striving. It can be so intense in a patient who has experienced the 'terrorism of suffering' that his or her own development has been crushed. (But when someone comes out of a trauma in analysis it can be very sudden, and the effect can appear to be like a miracle.) Searles also makes the interesting point that a trauma can bring about a precocious maturity. I have come across patients, and other people for that matter, who give the appearance of maturity, but this has come about through identification and not through personal experience. There is a world of difference between a maturity that comes about through living through life's experiences, and precocious identification with a figure or group of figures in childhood. In individuals where this kind of identification is dominant, it is usually the case that the ego is very immature.

In a trauma, Ferenczi goes on to say, there is always a split whereby a part of the personality regresses to the pre-traumatic state; it does seem to me that it is necessary with such a patient to reach the good which has been so overladen with reverberations from the original trauma. Finally, he states that no analysis is complete if it has not penetrated to the traumatic level; the inference here is that an analysis that never does reach this level can be conducted. It is a point which Betty Joseph has made: 'correct' interpretations can be made and the analysis goes on, but the deepest level is not reached (Personal communication).

There needed to be a contrast, Ferenczi held, between the analytic situation and the original one in infancy. Only if there is this contrast between the two can the patient be helped towards recollecting instead of repeating the trauma. The patient needs to have an experience which is different from the original. He therefore recommended that the analyst be more involved than has generally been thought advisable in classical psychoanalysis, and his reasoning is like this. The first reaction to a shock is at least a transitory psychosis in which there is a turning away from reality. (Indeed when we discover this we can suspect that there has been a trauma.) The turning away from reality is very provocative and tempts the analyst too to turn his back on the patient. The trouble is, however, that it may not even be conscious in the analyst. For instance, the analyst does not feel warm and friendly towards patient A. and he does to patient B., or he nurses some prejudice against patient C. The analyst in these cases is under the sway of the patient's trauma. Something needs to be done, said Ferenczi, to relax the patient so that the pre-traumatic state can be reached. He counselled a form of general relaxation that encouraged the patient to sink down into his or her primitive emotions and feelings, a more elemental state than one which allowed free association. I will say more about this process towards the end of the lecture.

Ferenczi believed that one of the most necessary qualities of an analyst was tact, which he thought was a blood relative of empathy. His paper 'The Elasticity of Psycho-Analytic Technique' states that it is a question of psychological tact as to whether one should tell a patient some particular thing and if so in what form; whether one should wait for further associations; when to be silent and when silence would cause the patient useless suffering. In this regard he says:

> Nothing is more harmful to the analysis than a schoolmasterish, or even authoritative, attitude on the physician's part. Anything we say to the patient should be put to him in the form of a tentative suggestion and not of a confidently held opinion, not only to avoid irritating him, but because there is always the possibility that we may be mistaken. (1928, p. 94)

He recommended a spontaneous natural attitude towards patients. It has struck me quite often, when walking down a corridor of consulting-rooms at the Tavistock Clinic, that it is usually possible to see immediately if a clinician is waiting for a

patient rather than a visit from a colleague: there is a certain
stiffness of poise when the therapist is waiting for a patient. In a
similar way Ferenczi said: 'One must never be ashamed unre-
servedly to confess one's own mistakes' (1928, p. 95). And in
the same way he warned against professional hypocrisy.

Here he was speaking in particular about a situation where an
analyst disliked a patient, even found he could not bear him. He
thought it was hypocritical to pretend that he liked and was
sympathetic to the patient; in these cases he believed it was the
truthful path which had to be followed. He would tell the
patient how he felt; he found not only that it did not hurt the
patient but, contrary to what he might have thought, the
patient was immensely relieved. Having said this he then told
the patient that the situation had a meaning which it was their
task to investigate. The result of such an intervention was to
free the patient: 'Something had been left unsaid in the relation
between physician and patient, something insincere, and its
frank discussion freed, so to speak, the tongue-tied patient'
(1933, p. 159). Similarly, if a patient's behaviour was unpleas-
ant and provocative it was better to point it out, and then search
for the meaning.

By the time Ferenczi was writing these papers it had become
the practice for analysts first to undergo a training analysis, but
he stressed again and again the need for the analyst to go deeper
and deeper into himself: 'When we have gradually learned to
take into account the weak points in our personality, the
number of fully analysed cases will increase.' In this connection
he also recognized that certain patients have a very refined sen-
sitivity to the wishes, tendencies, whims, sympathies and
antipathies of their analyst, although the analyst may be completely unaware of this. Such patients 'show a remarkable,
almost clairvoyant knowledge about the thoughts and emotions that go on in their analyst's mind' (1933, p. 161).

This point is rather close to my heart and I wrote a paper on
the subject (Symington, 1983). In it I claim that an emotional

shift in the analyst is unconsciously perceived by the patient; and that, when it is one enabling the analyst to be inwardly freed of a previously held conception, then the patient too makes a developmental shift. Ferenczi notes that there is frequently resistance not only in the patient, but in the analyst also; and that it can be an extreme source of frustration to a patient – sometimes leading to depression and submissiveness – when he realizes that his own analysis is more far-reaching than the analyst's own.

As I said earlier, Ferenczi recognized that some patients, in order to find healing, needed to regress and to go into a state beyond communication by free association. The technique of free association, he found, was too much a conscious selection of thoughts, so he recommended a deeper relaxation and a more complete surrender to the impressions, tendencies and emotions which spontaneously arose in the patient. The patient needed to fall into a more trance-like state. I will not dwell further here on the very important topic of regression in analysis, since we come to this again with Michael Balint. I will just mention that when spontaneous rapport developed between analyst and patient Ferenczi found that he 'played' with his patient, and I can remember an occasion in my own analysis when my analyst sang me a song.

Ferenczi had enormous respect for the individual's free choice. He said that if a patient was doubtful about psycho-analysis, and wondered about other methods of treatment, then let him try out the other methods first:

> In other cases we may suggest that they try one of these much-promising methods before coming to us. But we cannot allow to pass the objection usually made by patients that they do not believe in our methods or theories. It must be explained to them at the outset that our technique makes no claims to be entitled to such unmerited confidence in advance, and that they need only believe in us if or when

their experience of our methods gives them reason to do so. (1928, p. 91)

My own opinion is that it is always a mistake to tell a patient that he or she needs psychoanalysis. It is a very godlike judgement to make. How can I know that someone needs psychoanalysis? How do I know how his or her life will be without psychoanalysis? How can I know that psychoanalysis is going to benefit this person? You can be sure of this: that if you tell a patient that he needs analysis, nine times out of ten he will inwardly, if not outwardly, resent it. For instance, a patient was referred to me once who had been told that unless she came for psychoanalysis she would have an impoverished middle age and a sad or tragic old age. I started seeing her regularly, but she so resented my possessiveness (although it was not I who had made this *ex cathedra* statement) and my demand that she have psychoanalysis that she told me she wanted to leave treatment, and then asked if she could come once a month, to which I agreed. After a time she asked if she could come once a week, and finally she came more frequently.

On another occasion a patient was sent to me with a similar harangue and after a while she stopped altogether, but then came back two years later – this time of her own accord. In both these cases the treatment went ahead by leaps and bounds once the women were coming out of subjectively felt need. Moreover I have quite often found it valuable with certain patients to sum up what has been achieved so far and then let the patients decide whether they want to go on further, and what other aims they have set themselves.

Let me return to Ferenczi. By the time he came to write the papers I have drawn on, Ferenczi did not idealize psychoanalysis. He recognized the need to interpret the patient's negative feelings towards both the analyst and also towards psychoanalysis. He thought, for instance, that free association was an ideal that could not be fulfilled until an analysis had ended:

The patient's pride, his fear of losing the analyst's friendship
by disclosing certain facts or feelings, invariably and without
exception whatever betray him into occasional suppression
or distortion of facts. Observations of this nature have convinced me that calling on all our patients for full and complete free association from the outset represents an ideal
which, so to speak, can be fulfilled only after the analysis has
ended. (1927, p. 79)

To convey the idea that you expect the patient to be able to do
so gives him or her the feeling that he or she is useless. Again
Klauber echoes Ferenczi:

One thing is certain; no patient tells or can tell his analyst
everything, even of what consciously occurs to him. Every
patient keeps his secrets, whether from a desire to keep an
area of his life unanalysed, to convince himself of his own
power to contain his deepest fears, or because he fears to
hurt the analyst excessively. But whatever his motive, it
implies a considerable area of reserve. (1971, p. 33)

If we recognize what we are ourselves capable of, and are truthful to ourselves, we will not impose the sort of burdens on our
patients which will make them feel hopeless. Ferenczi tried to
encourage patients to free themselves from the words and
attitudes of the analyst; of analysts in general he said this: 'We,
[Freud's] disciples . . . are inclined to cling too literally to
Freud's latest pronouncements, to proclaim the most recently
discovered to be the sole truth and thus at times to fall into
error' (1930, p. 108). He also wondered how advantageous it
was, for the analyst, to have knowledge passed on instead of
gained through personal struggle: 'I really do not know
whether I envy our younger colleagues the ease with which
they enter into possession of that which earlier generations won
by bitter struggles. Sometimes I feel that to receive a tradition,
however valuable, ready-made, is not so good as achieving

something for onself' (1930, p. 111). He was followed in this by Bion, who stressed the same point again and again.

In brief, then, Ferenczi recommended for analysts that they strive after patience, humility and self-knowledge. All these qualities are beyond technique and cannot be taught. I don't know how they are acquired. Do you?

19 THE BREAK IN THE FRIENDSHIP BETWEEN FREUD AND JUNG

I have chosen in this lecture to talk about the personal break between Freud and Jung in order to provide a context for the next, where we shall look briefly at some aspects of Jung's theories and general approach. I think the most unfortunate effects of these schisms, which have belaboured psychoanalysis since its beginnings, are that good and rich insights are lost along with the founder of them. Each time another great figure is banished from the centre of orthodoxy, what I would call our capital resources become diminished and our understanding impoverished.

It would be quite false to think that Jung broke with Freud after having been his devoted friend and admirer for many years. Jung first met Freud when he was thirty-two, and finally broke with him six years later. His professional and academic orientation were already well formed by the time that he met Freud. Although Freud's revolutionary insights came as an illumination to him, from the first time they met Jung had an area of reserve which lasted throughout the period of their close association.

The association was a passionate affair that ended as suddenly and as violently as it began. At their first meeting, in March 1907 in Vienna at Freud's house, they spoke almost nonstop for thirteen hours, having started at ten in the morning, and finished only an hour before midnight. From this moment Freud saw Jung as his successor, as a St Paul who would bring his teachings to the Gentile world. It was important to him that Jung was not Jewish; Freud's own inferiority feelings were entangled with his Jewishness and he saw Jung as a figure who would compensate for his own sense of alienation and thereby rescue psychoanalysis from the ghetto.

Carl Gustav Jung was born in the little village of Thurgovia in Switzerland, and at the age of four moved to Klein-Hüningen, a small peasant village. At that time this was near the shores of the Rhine in the country, but today it is an industrialized suburb of Basle. His father was a Protestant pastor and, like many of our own Anglican clergymen, was very poor yet lived in a large old house with a garden and stables which had originally belonged to an aristocratic family. His father taught him at home as a young child; at the age of eleven he started at the Gymnasium in Basle, doing well in all subjects with the exception of mathematics. In his autobiography, *Memories, Dreams, Reflections*, Jung says that mathematics was totally incomprehensible to him, and that he got through it only by visually memorizing the various algebraic formulae that the teacher wrote up on the blackboard.

There are two childhood experiences of Jung's which are significant. When he was twelve he started to have fainting fits and moped around in a state of lassitude. His parents had him seen by various doctors. One of these thought he might have epilepsy, the others scratched their heads but did not know what to make of it. Nothing that anyone did could move him to apply himself, and then one day a friend came to visit his father. The two men sat talking out in the garden and little Carl hid behind a bush to listen in to their conversation. The visitor asked after Pastor Jung's son and he said in reply that he did not know what to do; he himself had no money and if Carl could not apply himself and work he did not know what would become of the little boy.

The young eavesdropper was stunned and then shocked into action. He rushed up to his study and started working on his Latin. After about a quarter of an hour a fainting fit came over him. He told himself he was not going to give in. Another fainting fit began to take hold an hour later and again he refused to give in to it, and similarly a third time an hour later. From then on he never had any further fainting fits; he was well and a good student from then on. He says in his autobiography that he knew then what neurosis was; and further that all his life he was influenced by the individual's need to face up to the demands of pragmatic reality. He took this attitude to himself during his 'creative illness' and later he adopted this attitude towards his patients.

The other experience was a more internal one. He came to experience himself as divided into two people: the person who went to school and did his lessons, and another, very superior person who had great knowledge and lived in the eighteenth century. This was the 'Other' person who seemed to have experiences independently of the pragmatic schoolboy. His eighteenth century self was his first psychological tasting of the surface of those deep waters which stretched away down the centuries into the prehistory of primitive man and beyond: those deep forces whose patterned images govern the great ideological and religious movements of mankind. The later Jung came to call these the archetypes.

Jung was genuinely religious from these earliest days, and this religion of his sprang from a personal experience. In fact, he found himself at odds with his father who, he thought, just relayed official Christian doctrine, and I think it is worth describing his experience. He had the feeling that a thought was pushing its way towards consciousness, and he tried desperately to push it away, but eventually he took courage and let it through. He saw God sitting on his golden throne, high above the world – and from under the throne an enormous turd fell upon the sparkling new roof of the cathedral, shattered it and also broke its walls asunder.

He then felt enormous relief, and had the experience of participating in God's freedom. He felt himself to be in a responsive dialogue with a personal God. The shattering of the cathedral was a shattering of all the ritual and dogma of the Church with its condemnatory attitudes. From now on all the ritual and dogma seemed nonsense to him – like abstract analytic theory quite unrelated to a real encounter with a patient. He felt a living personal encounter with a real God. In this sense Jung remained religious all his life, and it was a source of deep conflict in his relations with Freud.

There is another point worth noting in his description of this incident. He speaks of a thought trying to push its way through to his conscious self; the thought is looking for a self in which it can find a welcome habitation. He spoke later on of thoughts having their own life:

> He (a personalized inner figure) said I treated thoughts as if I generated them myself, but in his view thoughts were like animals in the forest, or people in a room, or birds in the air, and added, 'If you should see people in a room, you would not think that you had made those people, or that you were responsible for them.'

This rather strange theory is one that was shared by Bion and we shall come to it again at the end of the series. At the moment I only want to draw your attention to it and leave it for you to think about. Thoughts are not self-created but find a home in a personality that can bear to think them.

During his time at the Gymnasium at Basle Jung immersed himself in the philosophers of the nineteenth century, especially Schopenhauer and Nietzsche. It is noticeable with Jung that he immersed himself in a subject when it echoed his emotional mood; later in life he immersed himself in mythological writings and also alchemy. This philosophical orientation was quite contrary to Freud, who eschewed philosophy and was always suspicious of it.

After finishing school he decided to study medicine, and his father secured a free place for him at the University of Basle. He completed his medical studies in five years, and during that time immersed himself still further in philosophical and psychological writings. He was very interested in Mesmer and (as with Freud) Goethe was one of his heroes, and Nietzsche's *Thus Spake Zarathustra* made a deep impression upon him. He also read as much as he could on spiritualism and parapsychology.

When he had finished his medical studies he decided to specialize in psychiatry, a decision influenced partly by reading Krafft-Ebing's textbook on the subject. Jung said that psychiatry was a new inspiration to him, but in fact his grandfather had been deeply interested in retarded children, and his own father had been chaplain to a mental hospital, so it is probable that these had their influence too.

Having made this decision he applied for a post at the well-known Burghölzli psychiatric hospital in Zurich. The director of this hospital was the famous Eugen Bleuler, who gave the name 'schizophrenia' to that familiar disease entity and wrote several valuable papers on the subject. He also wrote a very good introduction to psychiatry. Bleuler was a hard-working and humane man who effected remarkable cures with his schizophrenic patients. He worked from eight in the morning until ten at night and was in constant contact with his patients; when the doctors met with him at eight in the morning he expected them already to have made a ward round and to be able to report to him. So it is strange that in his autobiography Jung makes no mention of Bleuler, but actually states that 'the psychology of the mental patient played no role whatsoever'. As Ellenberger says, this assertion is contradicted by every other person who came into contact with Bleuler. It is difficult not to come to the conclusion that Jung found it difficult to acknowledge people who had a formative influence upon him, perhaps starting with his own father.

Jung worked at the Burghölzli for nine years, from 1900 to

1909, and during that time gained enormous experience of psychotic patients. His experience of severely ill patients was in fact much greater than Freud's. He studied them very carefully and, at the same time, read extensively on psychiatry, being particularly concerned with the inner mental world of the patients. There can be no doubt that during this time he wrestled to understand the meaning of the hallucinations and delusions of psychotics and noted the frequent incidence of religious imagery in their utterances. He came to realize that much of this imagery symbolized inner states and had a meaning.

It was during this time that he started to experiment with Word Association tests. He presented the patient with a hundred stimulus words to which an immediate association was requested. The reaction time was measured, as were also the recorded and the enunciated word. With repetition he built up a pattern of normal responses, and when there was a deviation he knew that an unconscious factor was intervening.

It was also during this time that he first read Freud's *Interpretation of Dreams*. The first time he read it he was not able to take it in properly, but on a second reading some time later he was bowled over by it. Finally, after an exchange of letters, a first meeting took place, and a firm friendship was instantly forged. As I said at the beginning of the lecture, Freud decided that Jung would become his successor, and Jung was soon president of the young International Psycho-Analytical Association.

We know more about the break between Freud and Jung from Jung's angle as Freud did not leave any written record of it other than what is in the published correspondence between the two men. In a chapter entitled 'Sigmund Freud' in his autobiography, Jung says that Freud had made a dogma of sexuality. He writes of an occasion when Freud begged Jung never to have any doubts about his theory of sexuality, saying that sexuality was a 'bulwark against a tide of black mud and occultism'. Jung felt that Freud was like a pastor saying to his son, '"Promise

me, my lad, that you will never abandon your faith and that
you will always go to church every Sunday.'" Freud was
antipathetic to anything spiritual, Jung comments, yet he had
himself created a new dogma just as rigid as the religious one
which he had rejected.

It is certainly true that the person who violently rejects a particular value or ideal always espouses it secretly, though under
a disguised covering. The American psychologist J.B. Watson,
for instance, violently repudiated his Baptist upbringing but
replaced it in his adult life with a new creed which he named
behaviourism. Jung always held that if we are to be whole and
healthy people we have to acknowledge our background with
its values and attitudes, and come to terms with it and be, as it
were, on friendly terms with it.

For instance, I have come across patients from working class
backgrounds, from middle class backgrounds and the aristoc-
racy, all of whom in their different ways have repudiated their
roots with hatred. In truth it has only been when they have
entered into friendly relations with their origins that they really
become sympathetic to the new grouping which they espouse.
In fact I would always suspect the person who has repudiated
his or her background, whether it be in terms of class, national-
ity or religious value system. Someone can truly move on with
an inner freedom only when he or she has first had a friendly
dialogue with the inner and outer figures of his or her
background. Jung emphasized this again and again.

Jung felt that Freud had failed in this regard and he also
thought that his dogmatizing of sexuality was in the service of a
power drive; that Freud saw himself as the patriarch of a new
ideology whose disciples he could control as long as they all
subscribed to the ideology and it was not questioned. Jung said
that inwardly the break came when he was helping Freud to
analyse one of his dreams in the boat on their way to America in
1909. Jung had gone some way into analysing the dream, and he
then asked Freud for some further associations. Freud replied

that if he were to reveal any more it would risk his authority. Jung was horrified and knew that he could not remain a follower of Freud because 'Freud was placing personal authority above truth' (Jung, 1963, p. 154).

Jung was also frequently preoccupied with Freud's bitterness, which he attributed to Freud's having been thrown off balance by a numinous experience. I will try to explain what Jung means by this. He takes the term 'numinous' from Rudolph Otto's *The Idea of the Holy*: the numinous is an internal and external experience in relation to which the whole of man's psyche stands in awe. Jung says:

> Whenever the psyche is set violently oscillating by a numinous experience, there is a danger that the thread by which one hangs may be torn. Should that happen, one man tumbles into absolute affirmation, another into an equally absolute negation . . .

> The *numinosum* is dangerous because it lures men to extremes, so that a modest truth is regarded as *the* truth and a minor mistake is equated with fatal error. (1963, p. 151)

Jung thought that man is thrown off balance by powerful emotional forces issuing from one of the archetypes, and that this had happened to Nietzsche and, in a lesser way, to Freud. Freud had been thrown off balance by eros and power. Jung thought that ultimately these were not entities in themselves but sons of a single father or products of a single motivating force, and that Freud's interest in sex and in incest was too concrete. Jung believed that incest had a religious aspect and that with sex it was necessary 'to investigate, over and above its personal significance and biological function, its spiritual aspect and its numinous meaning'. Sexuality, said Jung, is the expression of the chthonic spirit – the dark side of the god-image.

Jung says that Freud was persecuted by the idea that Jung had death wishes against him, and in this connection there were two occasions when Freud had a fainting fit. One was in 1909 in Bremen, just before Freud, Ferenczi and Jung left by boat for America; the second was in 1912 at the Psycho-Analytical Congress in Munich. On both occasions Jung was there, and both times there were references to corpses, death and the obliteration of the names of fathers.

Bettelheim gives another interpretation of these fits which I think needs to be given some consideration. To explain this I need now to speak briefly about Sabina Spielrein, about whom a book came out in 1984 (Carotenuto, 1984). Sabina Spielrein, who was Russian, was a patient in the Burghölzli whom Jung encountered in a psychotic state. He treated her and managed to bring her to health but, at the same time, became sexually involved with her. We must take into account the positive things which Jung did for Sabina Spielrein: it seems he did cure her of her severe illness and did also encourage her to study medicine, which she did. She subsequently became an analyst and practised in Geneva (Piaget was analysed by her). But it seems certain that when Sabina fell desperately in love with Jung and wanted to have a child by him, Jung became frightened and withdrew.

In his introduction to the book about her Bettelheim has some harsh words to say about Jung. Jung's wife, it seems, wrote to Sabina Spielrein's mother, who in turn wrote to Jung asking him to stop seducing her daughter and not to undo the good work that he had done. In response Jung wrote that as he was not being paid, he could not have been expected to treat Sabina in a professional manner. This extraordinary statement probably came out of panic and certainly Jung dropped Sabina like a hot potato. Sabina's mother was threatening to take the matter to Eugen Bleuler, and Bettelheim suggests that Jung resigned from the Burghölzli at this time in order to pre-empt a dismissal. It would have been a professional disgrace to be sacked from the Burghölzli.

It was at this same time that Sabina wrote to Freud, who at

first would not see her. Jung admits to Freud in a letter that he had acted like a knave. He admits to having written to Sabina's mother saying that he was not the seducer of her daughter. Bettelheim puts it that Jung was intent on saving his own skin rather than considering the feelings of Sabina. In the end Freud did see Spielrein, and so by the time of the first fainting fit would have known how shockingly Jung had treated a woman who had put her trust in him. Bettelheim suggests that this is the reason for Freud's fainting fit – it resulted from his effort to prevent himself from being abusive to Jung when he wanted Jung to be leader of the international movement. In the second fainting fit in Munich, Freud admitted that repressed feelings directed against Jung played the main part. It seems fair to assume that they may have played quite a large part in the first fainting fit also.

Jung married Emma Rauschenberg in 1903 and had five children over the next few years. She was a wealthy woman, so from the time of marrying her, he had no further financial worries. It seems that he also had several affairs and he said in one of his letters to Freud: 'The prerequisite for a good marriage it seems to me is the licence to be unfaithful' (quoted in Brome, 1980, p. 130). One of his most long-lasting affairs was with Antonia Wolff. She became a psychoanalyst and was an extremely intelligent woman who was Jung's intellectual equal, which Emma was not. When Emma was very distressed about this relationship she spoke to Freud, and they corresponded about her difficulties. Jung came to know of this correspondence because one day he saw an envelope addressed to his wife in Freud's hand.

There seem to have been two movements going on between the two men. In Freud a growing distrust towards Jung: both over his personal way of behaving towards his patients and his wife, and also over his theories. And in Jung a growing resentment towards Freud, whom he experienced as powerful and interfering. Emma Jung could see the break coming and tried to warn Freud. The personal break came first and, for a while, the two men tried to maintain professional relations, but finally in 1914 Jung resigned as president of the International Psycho-Analytical Association and Abraham was appointed in his stead.

As I said at the beginning Jung was a very different person from Freud. His background was different, his intellectual formation was different, and his personal values were quite different. Theoretically Jung rejected Freud's libido theory. Whereas Freud thought that there was a *re*-eruption of sexuality in adolescence, Jung thought that it emerged then for the first time; and he also thought that libido was a generalized energy which received a sexual colouring in some of its currents at the time of adolescence. Jung also considered that the religious dimension, along with mythologies, archetypes and symbols, had been unjustifiably cut out of Freud's system. I think, however, it should be clear that between the two men there were massive unresolved transferences and, as I implied at the start of the lecture, these were set in motion right at the beginning of their relationship. When the break came it was with bitterness on both sides. It was also clear on both sides that the two men tried to deny the differences between them. Both tried to hold back and deny a deeply felt antipathy, but finally it broke through.

Jung's concept of the unconscious is far richer than Freud's, because it embraces those deep desires and aspirations which have underpinned human motivation down the centuries. He referred to this as the 'collective unconscious' and distinguished it from the 'personal unconscious', and his view is that the thoughts and feelings of the personal unconscious stretch down into the collective unconscious. Today we are very used to talking about parts of the self as if they existed as separate personalities – or in object relations language we talk of split-off parts of the object together with split-off parts of the ego – but Jung was one of the first analysts to characterize this phenomenon clearly. He spoke about these parts as 'complexes', and I will quote at some length what he says about them:

> A complex is an agglomeration of associations – a sort of picture of more or less complicated psychological nature – sometimes of traumatic character, sometimes simply of a painful and highly toned character. Everything that is highly toned is rather difficult to handle. If, for instance, something is very important to me, I begin to hesitate when I attempt to do it, and you have probably observed that when you ask me difficult questions I cannot answer them immediately

because the subject is important and I have a long reaction time. I begin to stammer, and my memory does not supply the necessary material. Such disturbances are complex disturbances – even if what I say does not come from a personal complex of mine. It is simply an important affair, and whatever has an intense feeling-tone is difficult to handle because such contents are somehow associated with physiological reactions, with the processes of the heart, the tonus of the blood vessels, the condition of the intestines, the breathing, and the innervation of the skin. Whenever there is a high tonus it is just as if that particular complex had a body of its own, as if it were localized in my body to a certain extent, and that makes it unwieldy, because something that irritates my body cannot be easily pushed away because it has its roots in my body and begins to pull at my nerves. Something that has little tonus and little emotional value can be easily brushed aside because it has no roots. It is not adherent or adhesive.

Ladies and Gentlemen, that leads me to something very important – the fact that a complex with its given tension or energy has the tendency to form a little personality of itself. It has a sort of body, a certain amount of its own physiology. It can upset the stomach. It upsets the breathing, it disturbs the heart – in short, it behaves like a partial personality. For instance, when you want to say or do something and unfortunately a complex interferes with this intention, then you say or do something different from what you intended. You are simply interrupted, and your best intention gets upset by the complex, exactly as if you had been interfered with by a human being or by circumstances from outside. Under those conditions we are really forced to speak of the tendencies of complexes to act as if they were characterized by a certain amount of will-power. When you speak of will-power you naturally ask about the ego. Where then is the ego that belongs to the will-power of the complexes? We know from our own ego-complex, which is supposed to be in full possession of the body. It is not, but let us assume that it is a centre in full possession of the body, that there is a focus which we call the ego, and that the ego has a will and can do something with its components. The ego also is an agglomeration of highly toned contents, so that in principle there is no difference between the ego-complex and any other complex.

Because complexes have a certain will-power, a sort of ego, we find that in a schizophrenic condition they emancipate themselves from conscious control to such an extent that they become visible and audible. They appear as visions, they speak in voices which are like the voices of definite people. This personification of complexes is not in itself necessarily a pathological condition . . .

All this is explained by the fact that the so-called unity of consciousness is an illusion. It is really a wish-dream. We like to think we are one; but we are not, most decidedly not. We like to believe in our will-power and in our energy and in what we can do; but when it comes to a real show-down we find that we can do it only to a certain extent, because we are hampered by those little devils the complexes. Complexes are autonomous groups of associations that have a tendency to move by themselves, to live their own life apart from our intentions. (1935, pp. 71–73)

Although the complexes derive primarily from the personal unconscious, they stretch down into the collective unconscious wherefrom they draw their power. So we must now turn to the collective unconscious.

All men have a common psychic substrate, and this is inherited. Jung pointed out that this theory of his was not different in principle from Freud's, since Freud believed that we inherit an instinctive deposit that is shared by all men. Where there is a difference is that Jung held that the instinctive deposit is shaped into a variety of symbolic images. Even here, though, the difference from Freud is not so great since Freud said that we know the drives through their representatives. In other words, there is some image through which the instinct or drive becomes known to us. Jung suggested that if Freud thought through his instinct theory he would find himself in agreement with him.

Within the collective unconscious are the unconscious images of the instincts, and Jung named these the 'archetypes'. Whereas Freud stressed the repression of the personal wishes and desires, Jung stressed that our imagination, perception and thinking are influenced by inborn, universally present formal elements, or archetypes. How far back does this line of inheritance go? I think there is no doubt that Jung thought it went back through all the known stages of civilization and to stone-age man and earlier, and probably back to our prehuman ancestors.

There are as many archetypes as there are typical situations in life. Endless repetition has engraved these experiences into our psychic constitution. These experiences are not inherited as images, however, but as *forms without content*, representing the possibility of a certain type of perception and action. The archetype therefore exists as a potentiality for actualization. When an external situation corresponding to a given archetype arises, that archetype becomes activated, gains the quality of a compulsion and gains its way against all reason.

An inner drama exists, which man discovers by means of an analogy with the processes of nature: myths are man's subjective 'mad' experience grasped through a complementarity with nature. Water, for instance, always represents the unconscious. I once had a patient who was terrified of the water and had never learned how to swim, but she had many dreams in which water played a prominent part. In one dream water was flooding into her bedroom and she and the bed were raised from the floor and began to float on the water; then more and more water flowed into the bedroom. In another dream she was in the water, and a man was attacking her from under it. She was terrified of his vicious attacks and the revenges that were wrought on her; water represented the unconscious, and therefore she was terrified of it. It was deeply invested with the frightening contents of her unconscious.

As the analysis proceeded and she was able to look at the shadow side of her (the denied 'bad' part of the self), as Jung would call it, she became less afraid of the water. So it was significant, when she came to a session after the summer break, that she had been paddling in the sea. Now you might say that this was something quite personal, yet water always has this significance for us. This particular patient felt that she had no firm ground beneath her feet, she did not feel that I was behind her and wanted her welfare. I would say then that the archetypes were flying around everywhere within her stricken self.

I will tell you another of her dreams. The patient woke one morning to find an envelope and in it some little eggs. Out of one of the eggs came a little moth which started to fly around the room, growing to an immense size. She woke up as it was about to devour her with its huge beak. The moth represented her greed for money, which had been fanned by something I had said in the previous session, but this monster (and others) were in her unconscious to start off with. She hated avarice in others, but worked in the City among money-grasping people to whom she was polite on the surface but of course loathed inside. Yet greed, symbolized by the moth which eats away good clothes, was powerfully active in her.

In this analysis there emerged more than once the very danger of which Jung warns – that of the archetype being inflamed into action and overwhelming the patient. Now greed is a universal human plight, and we all know that whole cultures or social groups are under the sway of it. The archetype symbolizing this drive can stir a whole society and overwhelm it, particularly through the intuitions of a leader who is in tune with the deep currents of his people. But I continued to analyse my patient as an individual and to discover the individual roots of her greed, and in this I was being Freud's loyal disciple.

Jung would take exception to this procedure. He believed that it was wrong to convey to the patient that she was in some way peculiar to be afflicted with greed when it is such a widespread, even universal phenomenon. Confronted with such blatant archetypal imagery Jung would explain the nature of the archetype that was afflicting her, and guide her towards one of the world's great psychotherapeutic systems, namely the great religions. In other words, he tried to incorporate the person into a community whose symbols and affective life were geared towards combating that archetype. The idea that the individual alone cannot combat the full force of a powerful archetype is central to Jung's thought: the individual needs to understand that he is suffering from a condition with which many others are afflicted. To feel himself part of a community with a shared archetype in itself militates against omnipotence and despair. To feel that one is part of the human condition is healing, and particularly in relation to the shadow side of man. When Jung came across an archetype of this kind he would explain to the patient what it symbolized, and then try to incorporate the person into a grouping cognate with the person's inner resonance. He specifically mentions that he usually recommended that his Catholic patients return to the confessional and the other sacraments of their Church.

Let me make some personal comments on this. I do not agree with Jung's 'advice' to the patient to associate him- or herself with a particular religious organization; I would favour an approach that enables the patient to find his or her own way. It is a fact that inner change alters someone's relation with the outer world, and in particular with the grouping that has some echo for the person's inner world. The patient will find this naturally, therefore, as an outcome of good analysis. However, I think Jung's wish to convey to the patient that he or she is not alone in the world but very much part of the human community is a healing one.

I know that I am greedy, envious, jealous, spiteful, vain, vengeful and proud, and particularly so under certain conditions. I know that I do not help a patient if I convey, however subtly, that he or she is greedy, envious, jealous, spiteful, vain, vengeful and proud but that I am not. I do not mean that I have to make a great confession à la Rousseau, but to speak in such a way that the patient feels that I know from personal experience what he or she is talking about. I think therefore that this aspect of Jung's approach is salutary (and not unlike Ferenczi's), but that he lacked faith in the individual's capacity to find his own way.

Jung stressed that in each of us there is a collective element and an individual element, and that if either overwhelmed the other there would be a deterioration in our mental condition. Individuation, for Jung, is the process by which the two elements are integrated into one hegemony of management. The neurotic condition is one where the collective is denied and pushed under, and the psychotic is one where it is the archetypes which have erupted and destroyed consciousness. As life proceeds different archetypes are roused to life by biological and environmental changes, and it is the ego's task to integrate them – neither to push them away nor to be overwhelmed by them. Individuation is a lifelong developmental process, and it includes the transformation from a state where the person is controlled by the collective unconscious, to one where that attachment is loosened. In other words the person is *in relation to* the archetypes rather than being merged with them.

I will give an example of such a transforming moment as it was conveyed to me by a patient some while ago. The man had been brought up in Scotland in an extremely puritanical house-hold, and he felt God to be a powerful tyrant under whose control he lived. He did not feel that he had any free, individual selfhood. As quite often happens under such a superego he went to the extreme of fasting for a whole week 'because he had to'. During the subsequent exhaustion he suddenly felt one day that God was not a mechanical figure whose puppet he was, but a person; and that he himself was a freely responding individual who could choose, or not choose, to respond to God. Here was a transformation typical of the individuation process. Whenever a person 'has to', he or she is under the power of the collective unconscious.

I had another patient who was *told* to invest a recently earned windfall of £2,000 in a profit-bearing life assurance. Because he had been told to do this he 'had' to do what he was told, but he resented it bitterly inside. Happily, as the analysis proceeded the patient was able to repudiate the insurance man, who a year later suggested that he invest a further £1,000 in another bond of some kind. There is therefore a connection between the external figure, whether God or the insurance agent, and the relation of the ego to a godly archetype. That is, when the merged relation is loosened so that the ego has a relation *to* the archetype, the external figure assumes ordinary proportions. When the individual is invested with these powerful imagos he or she becomes an embodiment of the collective. For it is the collective which is so powerful and overwhelms the ego, just as the ecstatic excitement of the crowd contaminates and over-whelms the individual. So the transformation is the essential developmental ingredient in the individuation process.

Jung says that the archetypes stretch down to the sympathetic nervous system, and that this gives the individual a knowledge of the innermost life of other living beings. He stressed that when this faculty was highly developed it gave the person a link with the inner life of other living beings, principally humans but also animals; a successful stockbroker, as well as a successful hunter of big game, needed this quality.

I don't know if any of you have read *The Man-Eaters of Kumaon* by Jim Corbett, but Jim Corbett was in the British Army in India before the Second World War, and was commissioned to track and kill a handful of man-eating tigers over the course of some fifteen years. These tigers were always extremely cunning and some of them had a toll of human beings running into the hundreds; more than one tiger terrorized an area of some five hundred square yards for years on end. Corbett had an unequalled knowledge of jungle lore and knew all the signs and sounds that betrayed the presence of a tiger, yet he describes several incidents when, in the absence of all perceptual clues, he still knew that a tiger was close at hand. I will quote one such passage:

> On the fourth evening when I was returning at sunset after visiting the buffalo on the ridge, as I came round a bend in the road thirty yards from the overhanging rock, I suddenly, and for the first time since my arrival at Kartkanoula, felt I was in danger, and the danger that threatened me was on the rock in front of me. For five minutes I stood perfectly still with my eyes fixed on the upper edge of the rock, watching for movement. At that short range the flicker of an eyelid would have caught my eyes, but there was not even this small movement; and after going forward ten paces, I again stood watching for several minutes. The fact that I had seen no movement did not in any way reassure me – the man-eater was on the rock, of that I was sure; and the question was, what was I going to do about it? (1944, p. 151)

Intuition is the opposite of sensation and Jung thought that if one of these was predominant, then the other was less developed. Similarly he thought that thinking and feeling were opposites. There are therefore four predominant types, and all these can fall into either being predominantly extrovert or introvert, so making eight types in all. His theory of psychological types brings him into the company of those academic psychologists who have theorized about a personality typology.

The tragedy of the schisms in psychoanalysis is that there is always truth on both sides, but followers become divided by personal loyalty. In each school important elements are lost, and we are in danger of narrow-mindedness and fanaticism. We of the Freudian school who have rejected Jung have become impoverished thereby. The truth will not be imprisoned.

DEEPER
UNDERSTANDING

21 PSYCHOSIS AND ITS SIGNIFICANCE IN THE DEVELOPMENT OF PSYCHOANALYSIS

In the next few lectures we are going to consider those psychoanalysts who were concerned to describe and understand psychosis. Freud had developed psychoanalysis as a therapeutic tool for the healing of neurotic conflicts; he did not consider that it was possible to use the same instrument when a patient was psychotic. All the analysts whom we shall be considering thought otherwise. They also recognized that in every patient there is what might be called a psychotic area of the mind, and that even in the treatment of a neurotic there would be times when the psychotic would emerge in the transference. Before going further, however, I want to try to get a clearer idea of what we mean by psychosis. In these remarks about psychosis I want to express the subjective experience. I am not concerned with an objective analysis of psychosis along classical lines.

There is one very sure sign of psychosis: that those around the psychotic are filled with anxiety. In a psychiatric unit, when a patient becomes psychotic, the doctors, nurses and other patients get into a state of acute anguish. Sometimes the reason for this anxiety is clear: the patient starts to brandish a knife and threaten those around him or her or, with the same knife, starts to lacerate himself. But sometimes his or her behaviour does not demonstrate this obvious danger: a patient may begin to declare that he is the King of England, and absurd though the assertion is, it provokes a very real anxiety in those in the vicinity.

I remember a time when I did not understand what this anxiety was about. When I was a trainee at the Institute of Psycho-Analysis a fellow trainee said to me that she was apprehensive of taking on her second training case because she feared that he might go psychotic. I remember being scornful of her temerity and saying to her, 'What are you afraid of? That he will jump out of the consulting-room window? Or that he will commit suicide?' I do not think these questions of mine were entirely futile. They may have helped to focus on where the anxiety was, but I was brash enough then to think that there was nothing to worry about as long as there were no actions as gross as my questions suggested. So what is this anxiety?

When I question myself about it I think the thing I most shun is talking to the mad person – that is, after all, what we mean by psychosis. I want to dissociate myself from the person. If I go somewhere, and I meet someone who tells me that he is the King of England, my first wish is to get away. I may want to find a member of staff and talk *about* the patient, but one thing is certain and that is that I do not want to get into communication with him. I know also that when treating a patient who suddenly goes psychotic, my first fleeting feeling is 'Oh God, why on earth did I take up this crazy profession? Why didn't I just settle for being a farmer or a solicitor?'

On the other hand, I know that the only way in which I can enter into communication with the psychotic patient is to expose the psychotic area of my own mind; I do know that it is my crazy thoughts which have to come into play. But this still does not answer the question. What is threatening about that? Why am I apprehensive and mentally looking over my shoulder to see if anyone is looking? I think there are several reasons. The first is the terrible pain that I have to share. The second is the persecuted fury from the patient that I shall inevitably experience. Lastly, to expose my crazy thoughts exposes my own disintegration and challenges my ego to become whole. I will try to give examples of all three.

You may remember the mentally handicapped but also psychotic patient whom I spoke about in my second lecture on symbolism, and the incident of the white coats. As the patient began to feel some communication and life he came in touch with a gaping emotional void which stretched down his thirty-three years of life; in the sessions he began to weep, and the tears came from deep down. I found it very difficult to be in the room with him alongside such pain; in psychosis all the emotions are enormously intensified. Quantity or intensity beyond a certain point alters quality, and in psychosis a certain threshold in intensity has been passed.

When psychosis is hidden within a neurotic system it is not seen precisely because it is so intense that it is hidden. Once a patient was telling me that he was going to Sweden for two weeks at Easter, and as he was telling me I was reminded to tell him that I was going to be away for some time a bit later. The next session he came in and told me that he was going to finish his analysis. The reasons were all very logical: he told me the problems which he had resolved, the fact that a new job was going to make it difficult and so on. I knew that something in the last session had provoked this reaction. At last I lit on my telling him that I was going to be away. Then he told me that it was not that, but the immediate coupling of my going away with his going away. In this he sensed a hint of envy on my part and this was unbearable to him, although at the time of the interaction I detected no reaction at all. The reaction came after.

Luckily in this case it was possible to trace the original stimulus, but sometimes it is not. A colleague told me of a patient whom he had been treating for some time, and whom he told one week that he would have to cancel next Monday's session. A little later in the session he interpreted that she felt abandoned by him and she said, 'After all these years do you really think that I can't manage just one day without you?' My colleague unwisely took this statement as a reasonable rebuttal of his interpretation. The following Monday, however, at precisely the time of the session, she stabbed her boss at work with a knife.

One reason why the old word 'mad' is better than psychosis is that it is more immediately linked with the idea of fury and rage and hatred, for these are always a component of madness. Intense penetrating hatred hurts, especially when the psychotic patient is so easily able to touch us where it hurts most. Every one of us has deep searching questions inside like 'Am I really able to love someone?', or 'Am I able to take responsibility for my own actions?', or 'Am I a coward?', or 'Would I put fame or career so high as to oust the crying of my child?', or 'Am I at heart self-centred and uncaring?', or 'Am I afraid to declare what I truly think about the colleague who assessed the patient I am seeing?', etc. The psychotic patient will home in on whichever area of ourselves he or she notes is most vulnerable with a devastating accuracy lacking in the neurotic. The neurotic is often so wide of the mark that I find myself being irritated by it. The psychotic, paradoxically, has more reality sense in this respect than the neurotic, not less. This is, I think, the prime reason why the psychotic patient is so anxious-making.

I said that the third reason for the anxiety was that the psychotic exposes my own disintegration and challenges my ego to become whole. As Jung emphasized, we are all of us an agglomeration of many personalities. We become more whole to the extent that these different 'complexes', as he called them, come together into a unity. Slowly they become woven into a pattern. The psychotic is in a state where these different parts have come adrift altogether in such a way that the analyst experiences projections of these bits in the transference. The analyst can only contain these bits through inner certainty and freedom, and that state comes about to the extent that the different parts in the analyst are interlinked. Any weak link will be discovered by the patient and attacked; which becomes a challenge to the analyst to do personal psychic work.

The psychotic area of the mind finds its origin in the preverbal period of infancy, and in particular in the two-person relationship between infant and mother. In psychosis the patient regresses to this stage; it is in this phase that the greatest emotional intensity exists, but also in this phase that the third party (the father) is shut out. Yet it is the anchoring in the third party that brings about consciousness and the possibility of an identification, so that the person can see something from 'the outside', as it were. In the psychotic transference the patient feels overwhelmed and almost suffocated, and cries out to the analyst to free him or her from the situation.

It is difficult to conceptualize the psychotic state without Melanie Klein's concept of part-objects. We shall describe this concept more fully when we come to her ideas in a few lectures' time, but for now perhaps I can best describe the state by telling you again about the patient who in one session would be warm and positive towards me and then in another furious and vengeful. For a long time I could not make out what prompted these different reactions, and reactions – not responses – is the right word. One talks of responding to a person but reacting is an immediate reflex stimulated by some element.

I used to think exasperatedly about the previous session: I thought I must have said something and knew that the problem would not necessarily be in the words or their meaning but their tone. Then one day it finally dawned that it was something about my appearance and as I told you, I realized that when I had a blue striped shirt with a blue tie on she was furious, but when I had brownish colours on she was warm and positive. She was homing in on a part of me; but when I say 'she' that is rather ambiguous. It was a *part* of her which reacted to part of me.

The psychotic is always identified with an omnipotent object. The ego of the psychotic is therefore enormously omnipotent, with a regression to the state of omnipotence that existed in earliest infancy, when the infant expects its needs to be met. In that state, to a large extent, they are. Indeed if the needs have been properly met (or perhaps overindulged) then the person continues to hanker after that unconditional love at later stages of development. In treatment the patient will think the analyst knows what he or she wants without expressing it in words. The patient believes that the analyst has divine knowledge. (Incidentally, it is very easy for the analyst to collude with such ideas, and think that because he has had a long training and obtained his certificate of membership he is *supposed* to know. In this way he may go along with this idea, at least to some extent.)

Recently a girl who could not maintain a love relation with a man beyond a few weeks said to me: 'In your experience you must have met other women with my problem.' I quickly replied: 'Never'. Underlying this question of hers was, apart from the phantasy of my omnipotence, a feeling that she was just the same as many others – in other words not a person. The psychotic just feels a 'part', a cog in the machine, and the analyst is the omnipotent manipulator. At least that is in one part of the personality; the other part feels omnipotent in identification and consequently enormously powerful. But such feelings of power bring with them guilt because this power does really smash up the psychotic's own awareness-feelings in various areas and also the feelings of others.

I want to make two final points. One is that combined with these factors is a merging of the psychotic with his or her primary love object, and a consequent fusing of feelings. The psychotic then finds it very difficult to discover what is him and what is the other, and one of the reasons why those around find the psychotic threatening is that they feel caught in this merged situation. The second point is that the psychotic area also has within it that area of the mind which cannot be contained within a relationship. Those areas that can find expression only in that which lies beyond, such as art and religion, belong to the psychotic area.

All the analysts whose theories we shall be considering this term, then, have been concerned to treat patients who have regressed, in treatment, to the psychotic area of the mind. Their theories are attempts to conceptualize this area.

22 FAIRBAIRN

For the whole of his professional life Fairbairn worked as a psychoanalyst on his own in Edinburgh. He had not himself been analysed; in this he was in company with many of the early analysts, but he was unique in having worked in complete isolation for a stretch of forty years. In his early professional life he taught in the Psychology Department of Edinburgh University where he met with considerable opposition and hostility from colleagues. He apparently never, however, showed any bitterness. He would also not have considered this a reason not to go on teaching, which is in marked contrast to the attitude of those who, on meeting with opposition or criticism, take flight.

Ronald Fairbairn was born in Edinburgh in 1889 and was educated at Edinburgh University, from which he graduated in 1911 with an honours degree in philosophy. Together with Freud and Bion he was one of the most rigorous thinkers within the psychoanalytic tradition. There have been many innovators within psychoanalysis whose forte has been to describe clinical phenomena accurately and reach new depths of clinical understanding, and they have done all of us a great service. But their failure to follow this through with rigorous thinking has had unfortunate consequences. It has meant that the implications of new insights have not been thought through, and this has led to muddled thinking. A more unfortunate result has been that followers have clung to a theory out of personal or group loyalty rather than robust emotional and intellectual conviction.

The great advantage of rigorous thinking is that it enables the psychoanalyst to relate the phenomena he is investigating to scientific enquiry in other fields within the human sciences. He can meet the world rather than cringe defensively. A criticism becomes a challenge to think more deeply. Bion did not take a degree in philosophy, for instance, but read philosophy and recommended it as a part of psychoanalytic education. Fairbairn followed up his degree in philosophy with a three-year period of post-graduate study in theology and Hellenistic Greek in England and Germany. He finished this just as the First World War started so he joined up and served under Allenby in Palestine.

It was during this time that he decided to become a psychotherapist. In those days this meant one had to be a doctor, so at twenty-nine he returned to Edinburgh to study medicine. After qualifying in 1923 he spent a year gaining psychiatric experience at the Royal Edinburgh Hospital, and a year later started up as a psychotherapist in private practice. He continued working steadily with a full caseload for forty years until he died a few hours before New Year's Day 1965.

Fairbairn was remarkable in that he worked all this time quite on his own and unencumbered by the power struggles and administrative hassles that sap so much creative energy in many psychoanalytic settings. He had a focused concentration on clinical work, and was awarded membership of the British Psycho-Analytical Society largely as a result of a series of impressive clinical papers. These papers appeared in book form in 1952 as *Psycho-Analytic Studies of the Personality*. Of the four or five papers he wrote subsequently the most striking is 'On the Nature and Aims of Psycho-Analytical Treatment' (1958). Fairbairn was a man of considerable independence of mind. He challenged important aspects of Freud's theory; he considerably revised the developmental views of Abraham, and took issue with Melanie Klein on several important points. It is time now to try to understand the views of this remarkable man.

What man seeks most deeply is emotional contact with his fellow human beings. This belief is at the centre of Fairbairn's theoretical structure and technical recommendations. In our clinical work I know we feel that we have succeeded at the moment that we make emotional contact with a patient, and we talk of emotional contact constantly when we speak of our work with patients, yet Fairbairn is, I think, the only theorist who places this phenomenon at the centre of all his endeavours. Two things are necessary if the emotional centre is to grow and become available and present in our interactions with others: the infant must feel loved by his mother first and foremost, then by his father and other family members close to him; and his own love must be received in a similar way. The fundamental trauma for the child is either that he or she is not loved or that his or her love is not received. If this happens the child withdraws and seeks comfort from an object inside, an object which he or she has internalized. The relationship with the internalized object is accompanied outwardly by thumb sucking, masturbation, excessive feeding or drinking, homosexuality or incest. He or she turns to the internalized object in the face of the traumatic disappointment. When emotional contact is frustrated in this way then the person turns to these frustrated actions; they are expressions of a desperateness that is a hopeless reaction to severe disappointment.

We are brought here into the middle of a big clash of views between Fairbairn and Freud. For Freud the aim of libido is pleasure, which is the subjective registration of the reduction of tension. When the organism is in a state of tension it seeks to reduce the tension through the agency of an object. In the case of hunger the state of tension in the organism is reduced through the incorporation of food into the body via the mouth. In the case of sex there is a state of tension which becomes reduced through orgasm. (Ferenczi had already pointed out that the homeostatic theory did not work very well here because in sexual foreplay the pleasure is concurrent with an increase of tension. Freud explained this by saying that foreplay was only pleasurable because its final outcome, orgasm, was already present in the mind.)

But the severe defect of this model is that it does not account for the difference between a sexual discharge achieved through masturbation or sexual intercourse, or between sexual intercourse of the one-night-stand variety and sexual intercourse between a man and woman deeply in love with each other. Freud, of course, placed considerable value on love, but what I am saying here is that his *theory* gives no place for it. Fairbairn turned the whole matter on its head and said that the aim of libido is the object; but, in addition, his conceptualization of libido is different. It is not like a quantum of physical energy generated by a physical state of the organism, but a movement that proceeds from the ego towards the object.

The English word most closely descriptive of it is *desire*, and this brings us back to Fairbairn's central focus: the desire for emotional contact. Libido does not reach its terminus at the surface erotogenic zone, whether it be mouth, anus, penis or vagina, but when it makes contact with the person in the external world in his or her emotional centre. The erotogenic zones become the pathways through which the libido can most easily pass. It is, says Fairbairn, the pathway of least resistance and here he uses an electrical analogy.

However, I think that in this he misses an important component of the erotogenic zones. They are, as he says, the pathway to the object, but they are more than that. In a sexual relationship in which there is an emotional bond the sexual-erotic zones of each person are incorporated into the emotional contact. The emotional cannot exist without the sexual-erotic, which fixes the emotional deal, as it were. The emotional receives its form from the sexual-erotic. (In an analysis the sexual-erotic form of the emotion is often present, though without a physical-sexual activity being present.) The libidinal aim, says Fairbairn, is the establishment of satisfactory relationships with objects (1952, p. 31). From his last paper I think it is clear that 'satisfactory' means a relationship in which there is emotional contact. Libido therefore issues forth from the ego. With Freud it gushes out of the id – it comes from the organism, an impersonal source. So it is consistent with Fairbairn's view that he abandoned the id and developed his own model of the inner structure.

All activity issues forth from the ego and goes forth to the object. The libido starts out from the subject and terminates in the object. In Fairbairn's model it is incorrect to think of structure and libido as two separate entities. For Fairbairn libido is structured; that is its form, just as matter and its shape are inseparable. (It is possible logically to separate the shape of a table from the wood that it is made of, but not in reality. In a similar way libido is structured between the two poles of ego and object, which are themselves also structured.) When a traumatic disappointment occurs then both the object structure and the ego structure split. The situation in the object is always paralleled in the ego.

This is the reason why a change in perception of the analyst by the patient always betokens a synthesis in the patient's ego. A patient started out with a split perception of me such that in one part of her I was marvellous, and in another I was someone not to be trusted. Then in one session she began to have the feeling not only that I had helped her a good deal, but also that I could have been more decisive and tackled some matters more firmly with her; and a general feeling that I was a bit too passive and lackadaisical. It was a feeling-judgement about me. At that moment she did not feel split in herself. Something had been healed inside her, and she felt that I could now receive her real feelings. The traumatic element (her feelings not being received) was being repaired and the split was healing.

The splitting of the ego and the (inner) object in the face of the traumatic disappointment leads to a psychological situation which Fairbairn named 'schizoid'. (I would like to emphasize that the inner object is always interpenetrated by and interpenetrates the outer object.) The schizoid person is withdrawn emotionally from those around him or her. In the presence of the schizoid person you feel emotionally ignored: the person is in the room but what you do or say is not important. Once when I felt frustrated with a girl I said to her that if she came to my door for her session one day and was met by a stranger who said, 'I am afraid Mr Symington was killed in a road accident on Monday, but I am a psychotherapist and will see you instead', she would not blink an eyelid but carry on with the stranger as if nothing had happened. It was a typical example of the exasperation that someone can feel in the face of a schizoid interaction.

Fairbairn thought that the schizoid state was a discrete diagnostic category. The schizoid person is preoccupied with himself, and his or her affective state is similar to the condition which Jung described as introversion, but Fairbairn thought that it was a pathological state rather than a character type which could be designated as healthy. The schizoid state is produced by traumatic disappointment, but no one is entirely free from these splits. Given sufficient emotional stress, any person will rend apart along these vulnerable seams.

Fairbairn held the view, shared by Melanie Klein, that we are all born with an intact ego. We are not born with a mass of discrete elements that then solidify together into an ego. However, the ego does have its weak joints, and under the stress of emotional trauma it will split in predictable places. Freud said that when a glass falls on the floor and breaks it does so along the lines of least resistance, and Fairbairn thought that the ego split in this way. An analysis, to be effective, needed to reach this deepest level, and Fairbairn believed that the centrality attributed to the experience of depression and the attainment of the 'depressive position' in Melanie Klein was a mistake. He thought that the sense of futility and hopelessness characteristic of the schizoid position was the deepest level and that defences were mobilized against the experience of this state of affairs. The sense of futility is not the same as feeling depressed. The latter is connected to guilt, which is quite different. When we come to discuss Melanie Klein's two 'positions' I shall suggest that a third position is necessary to complete her clinical model, which I have called the 'tragic position'. The most obvious manifestation of the schizoid state is in the person who drifts around, feels life has no meaning, shrugs his shoulders and says it is all right when you tell him that you do not have a vacancy. 'It is what I expected', he will tell you. If on the other hand you say that you do have a vacancy he will say, 'Well, I suppose I might as well try it; I can't think of anything else to do.' In this sort of case the schizoid state is quite overt, but sometimes there is a militant defence against it so that you might think that what confronts you is quite the opposite of anything schizoid.

I am thinking in particular of people dedicated to an ideology. A young woman came to see me once who for some years had been a dedicated Trotskyist with all the commitment that one would expect. She came, however, at a moment when her ideological certainties were beginning to totter. She wondered whether there was any point in coming for psychotherapy since life had no meaning anyway. She further described how her parents had been dedicated Stalinists, and her earliest memory was of a large photograph of Stalin over the fireplace in the living-room.

What emerged was that underneath her Trotskyism was a feeling of utter futility, and she had clung desperately to her ideology as a means of trying to save herself from this inner situation. Eventually she could sustain this ideological palliative no longer. Her own massive disappointment in infancy and early childhood was that her parents did not respond to her as a human soul-searching infant, because their eyes were mesmerized by the portrait of Stalin. When there is no feeling of inner resource the sufferer attaches him- or herself to a powerful ideology with its followers in the hope that the enthusiasm and excitement of the group will supply what he or she lacks inside.

A patient who was a Seventh Day Adventist used to say, 'When I joined it was as if I had fully wound up a clock but now it is running out.' Motivation that finds its origin in an external source usually runs out eventually. Patients of this kind often try to provoke the analyst, which gives them something to fight against. I can remember a woman who was like this, and I was duly provoked, but eventually when I managed to control myself a bit better she fell into a despairing state. It is a great temptation to the analyst in these situations to make suggestions, or give advice, to try to assuage an inner desolation. I am convinced though that nothing is to be gained by this. The analyst's task is just to stay with the patient and be with him or her with these feelings. If the depths are really entered and lived in then hope begins to emerge at the end of the long tunnel, but it is appalling for the patient and difficult for the analyst.

The ego splits in this way: the mother who does not receive the child's love becomes a painful rejecting object; and such an (inner) object, together with the part of the ego that has tried to offer its love, becomes split-off from the main body of the ego. It is not possible for the ego to sever relations altogether with the object, because the object is part of its structure, so it solves the problem by splitting part of itself off. I am reminded here of an incident in one of Lawrence Durrell's novels, of a girl, swimming underwater, whose right hand was mistakenly pinioned to the sea bed by a harpoon gun. A friend, acting rapidly, cut off the hand so that the live girl's body could float to the surface. The split in the ego is something like this: the part of the ego which is in contact with the treacherous object is split-off.

In Fairbairn's language the 'rejecting object' and the 'anti-libidinal ego' are cut off.

But the mother who does not receive the child's love or love it for itself is, strange to say, exciting. The presence of love brings with it the feeling of satisfaction: its absence is accompanied by excitement. Fairbairn tells of a patient who received little affection from mother or father. The mother showed a bit but then she died, and the child tried to make some emotional contact with her father but in vain. Then the thought suddenly occurred to her one day: 'Surely it would appeal to him if I offered to go to bed with him'. Fairbairn goes on to say that her incestuous wish represented a desperate attempt to make emotional contact with her father.

To conclude. In the absence of emotional contact there is excitement in which hatred is always an important component. So the 'exciting object' is also split-off with a part of the ego which Fairbairn names the 'libidinal ego'. The 'central ego' which remains in consciousness pretends to disown totally these two parts of the ego. The central ego is conscious while the two split-off parts are unconscious as a result of a process of repression.

23 FAIRBAIRN
Part 2

What the infant and adult seek is emotional contact with a real object. The word 'object' usually means a person, but it can mean a partial object like the breast. One of Fairbairn's complaints against Karl Abraham's scheme of libidinal development is that this is not given a central place: the mere fact that Abraham names the phases oral, anal and genital instead of breast, mother and adult partner is indicative of a false emphasis.

Fairbairn was one of the first psychoanalysts uncompromisingly to ditch Freud's homeostatic model, and he criticized Melanie Klein for not doing so. Indeed he thought that it led to an incoherence in her object relations model. In more recent years other thinkers have drawn attention to the incongruity of the homeostatic model; the analyst to study the matter in greatest detail is probably George Klein, and his arguments have been gathered together posthumously in a book entitled *Psychoanalytic Theory* (1976). But Fairbairn was the first to fire a mighty salvo against it and also put in its place another theory.

My own sense of this issue is that traditions die hard and that psychoanalytic thinking is still imbued with the homeostatic model or the 'principle of constancy', as Freud called it. Abraham's developmental schema and the principles associated with it also remain an unquestioned bulwark of psychoanalytic thinking. As we have already treated Abraham's libidinal theory in some detail I shall not go over it again here, but go straight on to look at Fairbairn's challenge.

On the basis that it is contact with a real object that man seeks Fairbairn knocked out the two anal phases and the phallic. For in these three phases there is no real contact with an object. Faeces is a symbolic object, and in the phallic stage the idealization of the object together with the rejection of the genital organs represents the sucking of an internalized but rejecting breast. It is not a real contact of the kind that exists in the oral phases and the final genital stage.

Development, for Fairbairn, is essentially the movement from infantile dependence in childhood to mature dependence in adulthood. Dependence on an object which is not differentiated from the subject constitutes infantile dependence: dependence on an object which *is* differentiated from the subject constitutes mature dependence. As Fairbairn says, this distinction is identical with the difference between narcissistic and anaclitic object choice in Freud. Infantile dependence is based upon primary identification in which the subject cathects the object on the basis of its own substance.

I think another way of understanding the phenomenon is to say that the person unquestioningly drinks in the emotional attitudes and outlook of another, while the subject's own view and understanding of the world around are totally submerged. I recently read R.D. Laing's autobiographical book *Wisdom, Madness and Folly*, in which Laing describes an occasion when he allowed himself to be hypnotized. Before being put into the trance he explained to the hypnotist that one of his favourite drinks was dry sherry. Once he was in the trance the hypnotist told him that he would find what he was about to drink disgusting, and then gave him a dry sherry. Laing found himself retching, with an abhorrent taste in his mouth. Then the hypnotist reached for a truly foul-tasting concoction and told him he would find it very enjoyable, and Laing drank it with pleasure. Here is the complete suppression of a person's individual experience and instead a total incorporation of and by the other. Primary identification means a total erasing of the individual – far greater than in any totalitarian state – and the attitudes and even such basic relations to the world as taste become those of the other. Hypnotism clearly capitalizes on the tendency in all of us to regress to a state of primary identification.

One of the most difficult clinical situations arises when a patient identifies totally with the analyst: in this state of primary identification there is an ingestion of the analyst as an idealized figure. The situation is consonant with Fairbairn's view that when the libidinal ego and the exciting object, together with the anti-libidinal ego and the rejecting object, are repressed, the central ego (which is the repository of consciousness) remains, and its relation to the object is idealized.

Further, when there is idealization it is always accompanied by a process of primary identification. The subject or ego submerges itself and assumes the cloak, outlook, vision, hearing, smell, taste and touch of the idealized object, which is also always defended with a paranoid passion. When the friend of a patient of mine said something derogatory about me my patient almost killed him with rage. The friend did not know me but was picking up the repressed hostility towards me that he felt in the patient. (It is a tell-tale sign of this state of affairs when a patient reports that friends and family are trying to denigrate the analysis.) With idealization there is always identification and omnipotence, which replace the subject's individual learning and experience. Paradoxically, humility is the bed-fellow of personal experience, and omnipotence the companion to knowledge that has come about through identification with a hero.

It is Fairbairn's contention that the earliest relationship is always based upon such an identification, but in favourable cir-

cumstances it gives way to mature dependence which 'involves
a relationship between two independent individuals, who are
completely differentiated from one another as mutual objects'
(1941, p. 42). But if traumatic disappointment takes place then
the person stays emotionally stuck in the stage of primary identification. This state of affairs is the same as what is today more
commonly called a narcissistic state.

Now Fairbairn has a different clinical approach to this problem from that of Melanie Klein. Klein stressed the need for
interpretation of the negative transference: or, put in terms of
Fairbairn's model, interpreting any signs of the split-off hostility when it emerges in the transference (and frequently it can be
very hidden). Melanie Klein also generally stressed the need to
retain the classical psychoanalytic technique and, more importantly, believed that all perceptions of the analyst on the
patient's part were manifestations of the transference. Fairbairn's approach is different, and depends on his starting-
point, which is that the state of infantile dependence is characterized by the state of identification which I have been speaking
about, and a withdrawal from emotional contact with people in
the social world. This applies particularly to primary relationships.

A patient once said to me, 'I was passionately interested in
whether America was going to support China's application to
join the United Nations, but quite uninterested when my wife
told me that our eleven-year-old son had measles.' In this state
of withdrawal the person has turned to his inner objects and
tries to find comfort in them, and is passionately antagonistic to
any real contact with a human being.

Such a patient keeps the analyst securely as an object in conformity with his or her inner world, and there is a danger that
the classical technique can become a servant of this state of
infantile dependence. By this I mean that the patient can use the
analytic anonymity to gratify his own wish that no emotional
contact with a real person should occur. In other words, such a

patient will delight in the fact that he or she does not have to take any note of the analyst, his relationships or feelings. 'I know that you do not have any feelings, but have a purely professional stance towards me', said a patient. If I had feelings or interest in her then it would put some demand on her to take notice of me, and what she wanted to stave off more than anything was another person encroaching on her inner world.

Fairbairn said that the analyst's task is to force himself into the closed world of the patient. This is achieved through the normal interpretative work, and in his paper 'On the Nature and Aims of Psycho-Analytical Treatment' Fairbairn quotes the four factors involved in psychoanalytic cure identified by M. Gitelson: insight, recall of infantile memories, catharsis, and the relationship with the analyst. Gitelson said that cure was effected not by one factor but a synthesis of the four, but Fairbairn believed that the really decisive factor was the relationship with the analyst. It was upon this relationship that the other factors mentioned by Gitelson not only depended, but they could not exist without it. It seems to me self-evident, when one realizes that it is through the relationship that the other factors come into being at all. Then Fairbairn goes on to say: 'It should be added that what I understand by "the relationship between the patient and the analyst" is not just the relationship involved in the transference, but the total relationship existing between the patient and the analyst as persons' (1958, p. 379).

He thought therefore that the actual relationship allowed the possibility of a new beginning, and that it provided an emotional contact that was not available to the person in childhood. Implied in Fairbairn's position is the importance of the right 'fit' between analyst and patient. A colleague once told me that during an initial interview with a female patient, after about half an hour had passed, the woman said to him: 'You know, I just could not be analysed by you. I just don't feel I could be understood by someone who could have such awful pictures on his wall.' The analyst felt this was quite fair. I myself remember being interviewed for analysis, but the analyst had certain characteristics in his manner that were very similar to my father's and I instinctively felt that he and I would get into some sort of mess. As it happened the man died suddenly not long after, but since that time one or two colleagues have said to me that they thought that I was right in my judgement.

This emphasis of Fairbairn's on the restorative nature of the real relationship puts him into company with Jung, and his view that the relationship itself can bring with it an emotional nurturing that the patient has lacked is in line with Ferenczi, and also with Michael Balint, whom we shall consider in Lecture 28. It is very much in opposition to what Melanie Klein practised and taught. What is distinctive about Fairbairn's theory and practice, apart from his clear-headedness, is the notion that the analyst needs to break into the closed system characteristic of the person still in a state of infantile dependence.

I will give one or two clinical examples of my own where I have followed, though unknowingly at the time, this line of thinking. I was to be host at a professional party, and a patient, having heard about this, said that she felt sorry for me as she knew how difficult I would find it and that she wished there was someone there who could help me with it. She made references to the subject a number of times over the next week or so: she knew how shy I was and she pitied me being forced to do something that I would find so uncongenial. Then one day she said something similar again and I said, 'But I function very well at parties'. She was angry with me: at my arrogance, at saying something that I was not supposed to say as an analyst, and so on; but I have no doubt that the intervention was apt. Her anger lay in the fact that the remark disrupted her inner picture of me as socially awkward, forcing her to see a real person and not a figment of her inner world.

On another occasion a patient told me – and he had said this

quite often before – that he did not want to tell me some incident because if he did so I would think him pathetic. I said to
him that I was quite free to think him pathetic, and he was very
taken aback because he had wanted to make sure that this analytic figure would think and feel as he wanted, and not as I actually did. Some analysts would not consider these interventions
of mine true psychoanalysis. Fairbairn, however, would have
thought that they were, because they successfully disrupt a
world in which the patient is nurturing his or her internalized
objects and challenge him or her to make a relation with a person in the real world.

Making a real relation has the simultaneous effect of repair-
ing the split in the ego and inner object world. This split occurred through a disappointment with the primary love objects,
and it begins to be repaired as the patient can feel safe enough to
make emotional contact again with a figure in the real world.
Fairbairn therefore thought that the essential inner process in
psychoanalytic treatment was a synthetic one whereby the split
parts came together, and that treatment aimed at facilitating this
function. For Fairbairn, then, the word 'psychoanalysis' was a
misnomer. The analysing of the bits is not the important part of
the process; the synthesis is, and this is favoured through bringing the patient up against the real person. Emotional contact
with a real person is the medicine which heals the deep splits in
the personality. The resistance is against this healing process.
Fairbairn thought it was a mistake to regard the primary cause
of this resistance as the presence of the death instinct; what was
encountered and described as the death instinct, rather, is the
patient's violent resistance to emotional closeness. It is the
absence of this closeness which has been a cause of such pain
and suffering at a forgotten period of childhood.

To return to Fairbairn's adaptation of Abraham. Fairbairn
thought that the anal and phallic phases were all part and parcel of a transitional stage between infantile and mature dependence. The anal and phallic colouring of the defensive

techniques was a mode of holding on to the stage of oral dependence: the anal and phallic bodily manner was adopted and scooped into the defensive technique. The person was not fixated at a specific erotogenic stage but was rather clinging to an inner object world – a world of bad objects – and using an anal defensive manner of doing so. In the struggle to free him or herself from the bad internalized object the patient is overwhelmed by fears of isolation and also of being engulfed by the object. The defences against these terrifying states are manifested as phobic behaviours.

This transition also manifests itself as a conflict between an urge to expel the contents of the inner world and a desire to retain them. This inner struggle is manifest and expressed in obsessional defences. In phobia, then, the conflict is between flight from and return to the object in the real world: in obsessionality it is between expulsion and retention of the inner object. The hysterical state is a manifestation of another inner conflict: that of acceptance of the object or rejection of it. The dissociative phenomena of hysterical states represents a rejection of the genitals, but ultimately of the breast, which the genitals stand for.

The paranoid state is one where there is a rejection of the external object and an acceptance of the internalized object: the paranoid person always scoops the idealized person into his or her inner world, denying real features that betray a more mundane picture. As I have suggested, Abraham explained these states by referring them to fixations at particular stages of erotogenic supremacy, whereas Fairbairn saw them as defensive techniques to deal with the struggle between infantile and mature dependence, and ultimately as defences against emotional contact with a real object.

One notices a particular difference between Fairbairn and Melanie Klein. Klein talks a great deal about unconscious phantasy whereas Fairbairn emphasizes this much less; yet I think some marriage between the two is called for. For the strange thing is that emotional contact is established between people when there is room for reverie. In fact in the reverie is the contact, and the reverie finds its source in the state of primary identification. I would want to argue that when the person matures he does not abandon his or her internalized objects altogether, but rather, as the splits heal, they become the source of a phantasy life that generates emotional contact between adult people. In love or friendship the perception and recognition of difference is essential, yet some element of deeply shared value is a necessary component. Without it no friendship can exist. I believe also that an analysis will only work when there is a deep value shared between the two people. In my second lecture, 'Insight and Emotion in Psychoanalysis', I quoted the passage from Bertrand Russell's autobiography in which Russell described his friendship with Conrad and said: 'He and I were in most of our opinions by no means in agreement, but in something very fundamental we were extraordinarily at one.' The source of that at-oneness is the stage of primary identification. No friendship, no love relation, no analysis can last without the respect for the 'other' and the at-oneness that forms a bond beween the two. Fairbairn has emphasized one element, Melanie Klein the other.

24 MELANIE KLEIN

After Freud Melanie Klein has been the most influential figure within psychoanalysis in Britain, although it is too early to assess her influence within psychoanalysis internationally. Like Freud she has attracted to her banner a troupe of devoted followers, and also like him she has had bitter opponents. Her discoveries were so startlingly revolutionary that no analyst can ignore her, and all the analysts we shall be considering in the rest of these lectures had to state their position in relation to her. They have all measured themselves against her, silhouetting their points of difference and correspondence.

Melanie Reizes was born in Vienna in 1882, the fourth and youngest child of Jewish parents who had rebelled against the religious orthodoxy of Judaism. Her grandparents had destined her father to be a rabbi, but he very much wanted to study medicine and duly became a doctor. He also cast off the wife they had forced him to marry when he was very young; he divorced and married the woman who was to be Melanie's mother. Melanie was closer to her mother than to her father, and remembered her childhood with happiness even though her favourite sister, Sidonie, died and later her beloved brother Emmanuel too. Emmanuel had taught her Latin and Greek and it was while she was at the Gymnasium in Vienna that she decided to study medicine, but this broke off when, at the age of seventeen, she became engaged to Arthur Klein, a friend of her brother's. She married in 1903 at the age of twenty-one, and for the first years of her marriage lived with her husband in various small towns in Slovakia and Silesia. But she hated being cut off from a cultural centre, and it was not a happy time for her.

Things changed, however, when she and her husband moved to Budapest, where she came across some of Freud's writings, and this led her into analysis with Ferenczi. While in analysis with him she began to develop her interest in the psychology of children, and Ferenczi encouraged her to go ahead with the analysis of children; she read her first paper to the Hungarian Psycho-Analytical Society, 'The Development of a Child', in 1919.

It is difficult for us today to realize what a big step this move into child analysis was. It had been thought that the analysis of children was not really possible, but Melanie Klein came to see that children enacted their phantasy life in their play. The play then took the place of free associations, and could be analysed. It had also been thought that because children are still dependent on their parents there could be no real transference, or that the transference, if it did develop, would seduce them away from their affection for their parents. Melanie Klein came to realize that it is the inner phantasies about the parents that constitute the transference, and that when these are interpreted the child's persecutory anxieties and projections are lessened; and in fact the child's relation with its parents improves.

At about this time she and her husband separated. The marriage had apparently been an unhappy one for some years, but there is little publicly available information about this aspect of her private life. Evidently shortly after this she had a relationship which she referred to as the most important in her life, but again little is known about it. Phyllis Grosskurth, Havelock Ellis' biographer, is currently writing Melanie Klein's biography with access to Klein's papers, and when that is published we might learn more about these aspects of her life.

At the Psycho-Analytical Congress at The Hague in 1920 she met and was deeply impressed by Karl Abraham, and it was no doubt partly this that led her to move to Berlin. Here she developed and standardized her analytic technique with children; it was much as we know it today. She also persuaded Abraham to take her into analysis with him, which he did in 1924. There were about eighteen months of analysis, but the treatment was brought to an abrupt end with his death at the end of 1925. It was also in 1925, however, that Ernest Jones invited her to come to England and give a series of lectures on child analysis to the British Psycho-Analytical Society. These were a success, and the following year she returned to London, where she remained until her death in 1960 at the age of seventy-eight.

She continued with the analysis of children in London and then also began to analyse adults and to take on candidates who were training to be psychoanalysts. Many of the best-known analysts in Britain today were analysed by her: Donald Meltzer, Herbert Rosenfeld, Elliott Jaques and Hanna Segal, to mention a few. Her views and theories and understanding were followed with respect and enthusiasm in the British Society for the first ten years of her time in London, but then hostility and opposition began, first in a small way, but ending in a great storm which culminated in the famous Controversial Discussions of the 1930s.

Although the Kleinian position was clarified through these discussions, they did nothing to repair the splits and wounds in the Society. The bitterness was made particularly poignant by the fact that Melanie Klein's own daughter, Melitta Schmideberg, also a psychoanalyst, became one of her most acrimonious opponents in the discussions. Anna Freud demanded that her own viewpoints be respected and taught to students who wanted to follow her way of thinking. Eventually a compromise was arrived at whereby Anna Freud's followers had their own training programme, and became known as the B Group or the Classical Freudians; while Melanie Klein's became known as the Kleinians. There was a large number who joined neither group and became known as the Independent or Middle Group. Over the years the passions have quietened down but the same training system obtains (on this history see Kohon, ed., 1985).

Whereas Fairbairn started with the feeling of futility and the state of withdrawal arising out of early disappointment, Melanie Klein takes as her starting-point the fear of annihilation. This fear is of something that destroys from within. This 'something' is the inner workings of the death instinct, but it is experienced phobically. By that I mean that although the feared object is an element within, it is experienced as being outside. In Melanie Klein's language it is projected out, but on to what? Like Fairbairn, Melanie Klein believed that the infant is object-related from the start; however, she elaborated clearly a distinction first made by Abraham – between a relationship to whole objects and a relationship to part-objects.

At the beginning of life the child does not have a perceptual image of 'mother'. There is a smell, the taste of milk, the feeling of the breast, tickling from the hair, the sight of the eyes. The infant does not see these as forming a pattern which we call 'mother'. Each one is a discrete entity. Each of these is a part-object, the whole object being the mother, and the most important part-object is the breast. In this way Melanie Klein, like Fairbairn, gives the central focus to the object, the breast, and not to the mouth as an erotogenic zone. She says in her paper 'The Origins of Transference': 'The analysis of very young children has taught me that there is no instinctual urge, no anxiety situation, no mental process which does not involve objects, external or internal; in other words object relations are at the *centre* of emotional life' (1952, p. 53). At the breast the baby feels satisfied and comforted, but when there is no breast he or she feels frustrated. Stimulated by frustration, the baby creates the phantasy of a bad breast through projecting the inner bad something into the phantasied breast, which then becomes not only bad but also persecuting. It is persecuting, because it is felt that the breast will attack back.

The persecuting object is always the one into which violent hostility and hatred have first been projected. Intensity of hatred is the passion that dominates this stage, which Klein named the paranoid-schizoid position. Melanie Klein started by calling this stage 'paranoid' but she incorporated Fairbairn's 'schizoid' designation, realizing that the person-infant was withdrawn from the object emotionally in this state. This cauldron of anxieties, dominated by projective mechanisms, is what constitutes the psychotic area for Klein. If there is a regression to the paranoid-schizoid position in adult life, for instance, the visual perception will be that the analyst is one person, but the emotions are part-object-related. Indeed in analysis one of the signs that the patient is functioning at this level is, quite simply, intensity.

I will give you an example from a patient I had in analysis some years ago. At the very first session she came into the room; her jaw was clenched in fury and the atmosphere was tense. She told me of an occasion when she had knifed her boyfriend, yet she also said that her bark was worse than her bite. She told me of two or three occasions when men had tried to rape her. In about the tenth session she told me in a tone of defiant rage that she had made a decision to marry. Everything was said through gritted teeth, and when I opened the door for her at the end of the session her head jinked as she passed me. Her resentment and hatred of me were palpable. I thought it possible that she might break out and attack me physically, and I took the precaution of taking any dangerous objects out of the room.

In the twelfth session I interpreted that her tone denoted that she felt me as a monster whom she hated. This released a storm of rage: I was a torturer; Hitler did not need to have ss men; all he needed was a troupe of psychoanalysts. She would let General Pinochet know of some very effective torturers whom she had lately come across. She raged on for about half an hour, ending up by saying that she would love to be a fly on the wall at a psychoanalysts' dinner party. Someone would say, 'Could you pass me the salt please?', and the analyst would reply, 'What do you mean?' The patient marched out of the room determinedly but came back the next day. (She told me a lot later that she had thought that after that I would refuse to see her any more.)

Although the tension did lessen after that first outburst, it was still very intense for at least eighteen months, and there is no doubt that she had regressed back to a very primitive state. Throughout those eighteen months the paranoid-schizoid position was dominant. I was a part-object for her – sometimes a breast, at other times a penis – and this was frequently symbolized in dreams. She was also anguished by terrible fears of being engulfed by a very menacing presence.

During this time she was also plagued by horrific nightmares. Very often she was being chased by men with long knives or guns, and the dreams were very long. I have noticed that dreams that accompany the paranoid-schizoid state are frequently very long, but it is a mistake, I think, to go through them in great detail. The mechanism was clear and confirmed for me Melanie Klein's description of what occurs in the paranoid-schizoid position: violent hostility was projected into the breast, and then the patient was in fear of her life because the torturers would come chasing after her for the crime which she had committed.

These projections were not just confined to the mental sphere. At the nonverbal level she was projecting elements of herself into people around. People were in fact terrified of her and, as I have indicated, I was afraid of her on several occasions. Apart from the specific times I have mentioned I was nearly always in a state of tension when I was seeing her over the first eighteen months. What I am getting at here is the notion that 'projecting into' people and 'damaging' them is not just an imaginary matter. The patient *was* projecting into people, and they *were* retaliating – not by chasing her with knives, but by fleeing from her. In other words, those figures chasing her with knives were parts of her attacking another part, but the attacked part was projected out into others who then retaliated.

This reality, where parts of the self are projected into others, is not accompanied by words. What the analyst encounters is an atmosphere, and he or she is powerfully affected by it. In this state the analyst is not a person but just a hated image, or a passionately idealized one. The analyst's central task when the patient has regressed to the paranoid-schizoid position is that of managing his own turmoil of emotion, anxiety and fear as well as his vanity, self-love and idealized images of himself. All this occurs at the nonverbal level. When my patient was storming me with abuse she was projecting. This does not mean to say that I had not been torturing her at all – in fact I know now that I had, but on top of that she was projecting a good deal. If I then felt frightened I was in projective identification with the frightened part of her running away from the men with knives; the object part of her personality was projected. Projective identification occurs when the outside person finds himself feeling what the ego of the patient feels. For instance, my picture of that patient could have been that she was not frightened at all; but the fact that I felt frightened told me a different story.

Another sign of the paranoid-schizoid stage was also illustrated by the same patient. It was very noticeable that on Monday she was resentfully hostile, Tuesday loosening up a little, Wednesday beginning to be a bit more trustful, Thursday there would be a sense of satisfaction in me that we had done good work together, and on Friday considerable insight and understanding would occur; then on the Monday we were back to hostility and resentment. Also, she felt absolutely devastated in the first break, although it was quite a short one. Emotionally she felt that I had simply disappeared off the planet.

One saw very well the truth of Melanie Klein's point that the hostility creating the bad breast occurred through absence. A part-object cannot be held within; it exists only while it is in the field of vision. There is then a correspondence between this feature of part-objects and Piaget's discovery that for the very young child an object that goes behind a chair has passed into non-existence. Out of sight, out of mind. When we meet someone of whom that is said then that person is probably functioning at the paranoid-schizoid level.

I would not want you to think that this manner of functioning manifests itself only in the consulting-room. People are often not conscious of it, but we are governed by atmospheres in our social interactions all the time. These atmospheres, created by projective identification, direct the source of conversations and what pathways social communication travels along. I knew a priest who had worked for some years in the East End of London. He told me one day, with a benign smile on his face, that you did not get homosexuals in the East End of London, the cockneys were all proudly masculine and homosexuals all migrated to the West End. His evidence was that although he had the confidence of many people in his parish, he had never met a homosexual.

I have no doubt how this phenomenon can be explained. He exuded a powerful atmosphere which, if it could have been put into words, would have been something like this: 'On no account shock me. I am only an innocent little child.' Again, when I was a child and in my teens I used to go and visit an uncle and aunt. My aunt was a prim though good and fair woman, but her primness came through the ether like one of the old London smogs. It would have been impossible even to think of telling a risqué story in her company.

I am sure that you can all think of numerous cases of this sort. In my experience they are always accompanied by a very powerful superego, or in Melanie Klein's language, internal persecuting objects. It is because the person is controlling others in his or her social environment that he or she is inwardly persecuted. The two always go together. With a powerful superego a large degree of projective identification is always going on.

Another important element in the paranoid-schizoid position exists, and this is again well illustrated by the female patient whom I have mentioned. In all those dreams she was running, she was frightened, she was being overwhelmed. Those projective processes coexist with a weak ego that can bear very little. Melanie Klein believed that the ego was weak, because through projective identification it has emptied itself not only of its bad objects but of the good objects, too. However, I do not accept this explanation, and agree with Fairbairn's view that it has come about because the object has not nurtured the incipient ego.

The patient told me early on in the analysis how one Christmas Eve her mother told her that she was going into town to buy some Christmas presents, but when the mother got into town she met some friends. They started drinking, and she got so drunk that she forgot all about the presents for her children. When the little girl, my patient, woke up in the morning excitedly looking for her presents all her eyes saw was a snoring, drunken mother and no sign of a present. She had never felt emotionally nurtured, and I am sure the disappointment characterized by that incident had been with her from the breast onwards.

If I was that aspect of the mother in the transference then small wonder that she abused me so. Nevertheless I think that the paranoid-schizoid state with the weak ego and projective identification is set in motion altogether by a primordial disaster such as the one described, or what Fairbairn would have called a traumatic disappointment.

Melanie Klein saw the paranoid-schizoid position as dominating the first three to four months of postnatal life. However, she preferred to call it a 'position' rather than a 'stage' in order to signal the fact that it was an internal condition, always present within the personality, as is the case with the schizoid state which Fairbairn described. There is a difference between them, however. For Fairbairn the origin of the schizoid state lies in the traumatic disappointment whereas with Melanie Klein the origin of the paranoid-schizoid position lies in the inherited quantum of death instinct. And although for Fairbairn the schizoid state was inevitable, it was not a recognizable developmental stage as it was for Melanie Klein, and it was certainly not tied down to a specific period such as the first three months of life. So, for Melanie Klein, the paranoid-schizoid position is both a stage *and* a position, a residue that remains in the personality and to which a person can revert in later life, given certain emotional triggers.

It may be helpful here if I say something about the relationship between a developmental stage and an emotional condition, and I can best illustrate it in relation to Piaget's model of intellectual development (1950, 1953). Within the 'sensorimotor phase', prior to the 'stage of invention' – terms of

Piaget's – the child has no *cognitive map*, therefore when a ball rolls behind a sofa it has vanished out of existence. At the stage of invention the baby develops the power of representing the world by mental images: he or she then has an image of the ball after it has disappeared from view. Once the stage of invention has been ushered in there can be no perceptual return to the prior stage, but the important word is *perceptually* – in contrast to emotionally. To return to the patient whom I described in the last lecture, for instance. When she walked out at the end of a session she was perceptually aware that my existence still continued, or she would not have returned for her appointment the following day, but emotionally I had vanished out of existence. Developmentally, therefore, she had passed into and beyond the stage of invention from a perceptual point of view, but not emotionally.

The paranoid-schizoid position is a similar case. From the perceptual point of view, the adult has passed out of it as a developmental stage. The patient perceives me, the analyst, as Mr Symington, a single person and a whole entity, but emotionally there is in front of her an agglomeration of separate parts that disappear as soon as the consulting-room door is closed behind her. Therefore, as a developmental stage the paranoid-schizoid phase is over by about the end of the fourth month of postnatal life, but it continues to be present in the personality as a state of affairs, a position, for life. Although this distinction is implied in what Melanie Klein writes it is not clarified.

Melanie Klein thought that the ego was called into existence at birth in order to deal with anxiety and that this was its prime role. This early ego is rudimentary and lacks coherence, its strength or weakness due to a constitutional factor, i.e., something inherited and not attributable to environmental conditioning. Here too there is a big difference between Klein and Fairbairn. Fairbairn attributed the relative strength or weakness of the ego to the behaviour of the primary love object in relation to it. For Melanie Klein the coincidence of a strong ego and moderate anxiety meant that the ego would be able to manage the anxiety, and so the baby will be able to pass into the next stage, not only perceptually but also emotionally. This next stage Klein named the 'depressive position'.

At about three to four months those separate entities or part-objects, most importantly the breast but also the hair, the smell, the face, the eyes, begin to come together to form a unified whole. It is as though in the paranoid-schizoid stage a person (baby or adult) was faced with eleven pieces of jigsaw: two eyes, two hands, two feet, hair, nose, mouth, smell and voice. And as the person looks from one to the other there seems to be no connection between them. Then suddenly one day, after staring at them for a long time, they all come together to form one pattern, a single being whom the baby eventually names 'Mamma'.

When this occurs to the three- or four-month-old, the baby has slipped into a new developmental stage which Melanie Klein called the depressive position. It is accompanied by the affect of depression. The baby feels bad and sad because an inner emotional realization dawns that its angry attacks are against not just some unfeeling object but a person with feelings and sensibilities. The stage is also associated with introjection of the object, and I need now to say something about the mechanisms of projection and introjection, which play a large part in Melanie Klein's conceptualizing of clinical experience and the early emotional development of the child.

In the paranoid-schizoid stage the infant projects outwards all unbearable feelings, mostly angry and hostile feelings but good feelings also. When it feels frightened by the inner workings of the death instinct which threaten it with annihilation, it projects these unbearable feelings out too – but into what? The bad breast. The bad breast is a dual-faceted phenomenon. It is the actual breast of the mother, but also the experience of not having a comforting feed when the baby wants it. Therefore there is a connaturality between the inner experience of the death instinct and the outer 'non-feed experience', and this allows a projection of the inner into the outer to occur. This very primitive form of projection is of a special type and Melanie Klein called it, as we've seen, 'projective identification'; she saw it as the dominant mechanism in the paranoid-schizoid position.

I might give an example. I used to see a man early in the afternoon, and must candidly confess to a tendency to sleep in the early afternoon – I am by nature in sympathy with the Spaniards' habit of closing their places of work after lunch and retiring to sleep. I found with this patient that more than once I was overcome with sleep. Now the tendency in me existed quite independently of my patient, but it is also true that at that time he was the only patient who could regularly send me off happily into the arms of Morpheus. He remained awake, his free associations singing a peaceful lullaby in my mind. Projective identification was happening, I think, in the following way. His inner feeling of death was projected into an emotionally switched-off analyst, and it became a re-enactment of his experience, as a baby, of almost dying because of an emotionally switched-off mother. It was true that he had nearly died of starvation as a baby. When I went to sleep I was experiencing something of the near-death state of his early childhood.

In the example I have given I have put a particular emphasis on the coincidence of inner and outer happenings, of their occurring in unison, if projective identification is to take place. I think that in Melanie Klein's own writings this conjunction of the inner and the outer is implied though not clinically emphasized. My own emphasis is different from that of those who believe that projective identification can take place without any co-operation, conscious or unconscious, on the part of the analyst; I think this denies the extent to which the analyst is affected by the projection.

Projection of a less primitive kind, where the analyst is misperceived by the patient, belongs to the depressive position. Here the whole object is perceived, but tinged with an emotional bias which alters perception. In this case the introjected object – an internal cognitive/perceptual imago – is contaminated with unbearable aspects of the self. With projective identification, on the other hand, there is no introjected object but only a hated part-object experience into which unbearable inner experiences are projected. If this projective mechanism is too intense then good feelings also are evacuated from the self, and the infant feels empty and hopeless. What Fairbairn attributes to a non-responsive mother, Melanie Klein ascribes to powerful projective mechanisms fuelled by envy which is largely inherited.

The predominant mechanism of the depressive stage is introjection. As well as feeling bad and sad about having damaged the mother, and now perceiving her as a feeling person, the baby introjects her as a whole object. If the caring and feeding situation is a good one, the infant will introject this, meaning that it takes in a good sense of things from outside. It has inside it a good feeling-sense of the object. At the paranoid-schizoid stage the infant had already taken in the good breast but also the bad breast, and in order to defend itself against the bad breast the good became idealized. Idealization and denigration were the two poles on the emotional spectrum through which the infant saw the world. In the depressive position, however, there is an opportunity to introject a good experience, which then acts as an adjustment to the biased bipolar view of the paranoid-schizoid position.

Melanie Klein held the view that the splitting which is characteristic of the paranoid-schizoid stage is essential, and in particular that good and bad should be separated from each other so as to enable an introjection of the good. In the depressive position, however, the mother as a whole is perceived, and the good and bad aspects of her are taken in as an integral pattern. When a good caring and feeding mother is introjected the infant absorbs, as it were, the idealized bit of the good which had been internalized in the paranoid-schizoid stage, and similarly absorbs the denigrated bit of the bad.

It was Bion who formulated the notion of the mother as a container, absorbing these violent passions and so modifying them, a development adumbrated by Melanie Klein, but not clarified by her. I mention it now, however, as it makes sense of the depressive stage as one where the introjected good mother acts primarily as a modifier of the 'exaggerated' aspects of the perceptions arising through the projections of the paranoid-schizoid stage. If, on the other hand, there is no introjection of a good mother, this usually follows on upon an already more-distorted-than-normal paranoid-schizoid stage, so the badly established depressive stage just compounds an already serious situation.

The depression is the affect generated by the guilt at having damaged the primary love object who is loved. There is no conscious guilt when hatred and love are split from each other and projected outwards towards different part-objects which are not seen as being connected; guilt emerges when it is 'realized' that the hatred is projected into the same person who is loved, and also because the hate and love are felt as proceeding from the same ego. Guilt is the affect accompanying projection of the unwanted part into the object.

I may have told you of the obsessional patient I was seeing who mentioned twice one week that she was relieved after seeing me because she could dump all her tension and so she felt better, but she also said that in every other way she hated coming. So there was hatred of me, but the only relief for her was that she could dump the bad feeling into me like shit into the toilet. I let two references to this pass by without interpreting, though noting them, but without at the time quite being able to formulate to myself their significance. Now at that time there was a Dimplex heater in the waiting-room outside my consulting-room, and I used to turn it on before my patients came and off again after the last one had left in the evening. In the same week as my obsessional patient was talking about dumping her tension into me I found one day, as I walked back into the house from the waiting-room at the end of the day, that I was not sure whether I had turned the heater off. 'Have I turned it off or haven't I?', I asked myself, so I returned irritated to the waiting-room to find that it was indeed turned off.

Three days later exactly the same thing occurred, and I thought to myself, 'This is strange, it is not like me, something odd and unusual is happening', but I still did not think directly of my obsessional patient, though I might have done, because every day of her life she had to check and re-check whether she had turned off the gas taps on the kitchen stove, whether the bottle she had dropped into the dustbin hadn't broken so that the dustman would cut himself, whether by not reporting a parcel she had seen beside the road she would indirectly be responsible for innocent passers-by being blown up by an IRA bomb, and so on.

Then the night of my second instance of obsessional behaviour I had a dream, in which it was quite clear that my patient had well and truly dumped some of her obsessional violent shit into me and my behaviour was evidence of it. I determined then to interpret the matter before my incipient neurosis developed any further. My patient was crucified by a savage superego; hence she was being punished for projecting in this way into me but also into others of her environment. An inner tyrannical god punishes unmercifully the person who is operating, albeit unconsciously, through projecting unwanted shitty parts of themselves into others; and it is clinically useless to interpret to such patients in such a way that they get the impression that the analyst is saying that they are merely 'having phantasies' of attacking, but implying that they are not 'really'.

In the paranoid-schizoid phase the guilt is entirely unconscious, but in the depressive stage it begins to creep into consciousness. The female patient I referred to in the last lecture

and then again in passing in this one – for whom I vanished
when she walked out of the door – entered, after about eighteen
months, into a depressive phase. This was marked by the following differences. She began to feel badly about herself.
Whereas until then she had spoken of her boss at work and of
many other people with a bitter hatred, complaining of their
utterly uncaring attitude towards people who were more
unfortunate than they, she now began to see that she was just
like those people of whom she had complained so bitterly, and
she became depressed with herself.

Her dreams changed. Whereas before they had been nightmares in which people were chasing her with knives or guns,
now she would be damaging people with arrogant noncha-
lance. She dreamed one night that she was driving a Land-
Rover, and she ran over two people on the ground. Blood
spurted out of their bodies, and they cried out, but she just
drove on. She felt terrible about this dream and others.
Whereas before she had spoken of how dreadfully her mother
had treated her, she now remembered her mother saying to her,
'If looks could kill then I would be dead'.

In other words she began to sense other people as feeling
objects, and got some insight into her immense violence
towards them. She apologized to me at this time for her vicious-
ness towards me in the early phases of the analysis. So, in the
depressive position, there is a dual sense: of the object as a
whole person with feelings on the one hand, and of the subject's
own responsibility on the other. The sense of his or her own
responsibility comes, likewise, with an awareness of him- or
herself as a whole person from whom the violence issues forth.
Then, slowly, the person works through the depressive position – but to what? I shall return to this point in a critique of
Klein's theory at the end of the lecture, but I want to finish this
section by talking about Melanie Klein's last important work:
Envy and Gratitude (1957). The focus here is on the envy, but
the gratitude, which is its opposite, is the goal of the analytic
process.

Melanie Klein started her career as a psychoanalyst with enormous enthusiasm and with a dream that Utopia would be here when all mankind had been psychoanalysed. She was not so stupid as to think that every person could be directly analysed, but that the analytic attitude of emotional understanding could come through to each and every person via parents, teachers, lecturers and all those in society responsible for the upbringing and training of others. However, by the end of her life she was much more pessimistic. She had come up against the depth of people's resistances and began to feel that here was a constitutional – an instinctual – factor at work. This factor was envy. But Melanie Klein meant by it unconscious envy. If I say to a friend: 'I do envy you your ability to learn languages so easily', then here is something conscious and manageable which can even be a spur to me to emulate him. However, if I say bitterly of this same friend something like: 'John only pretends he can speak many languages', then I am expressing unconscious envy.

I went to a conference, one where someone gave a very good paper on a therapeutic subject from a cross-cultural angle. An excellent paper, it was derived from the lecturer's own experience of working within a particular working class culture; I had never heard a better paper on the subject. As I came out of the lecture hall I found myself brushing shoulders with someone who fancied himself in the same field as the lecturer. 'Excellent paper, wasn't it?', I said to him, and my interlocutor replied with barely concealed contempt: 'I suppose he'd read a lot'. I am sure that the lecturer had indeed read quite widely, but the source of the paper was in his own experience, daring and creativity. It was this which my acquaintance could not bear.

The patient for whom I vanished at the end of a session was overawed by me at the beginning of the analysis, and said several times that I was obviously able to analyse her because I had read so many books (there was a large bookcase in the consulting-room). She also made references to the fact that I had had

the opportunity to be educated whereas she had not, and there
was truth in this; but later in the analysis, when she was in the
depressive phase, the realization came to her one day that my
capacity to analyse lay in something inside myself. This was
what she envied so deeply.

Melanie Klein said that the infant's envy is ultimately
directed against the bountiful feeding breast. I have said that it
is the internalization of the good breast that, in Melanie Klein's
view, lays down the foundation-stone of mental health. Powerful envy attacks this good breast so that introjection of it does
not occur. I had a patient once who used to behave in this way;
when I made an interpretation that hit the mark and clearly
affected her, she would greedily want to grab the breast that
gave the interpretation. She could not bear the fact that I had
such capacity, and although she wanted very much to get better
it was more tolerable to her to stay ill than that I should sit back
and apparently glory in my capacity creatively to help her.

Unfortunately I cannot treat in detail all the aspects of envy
discussed by Melanie Klein in her very lucid book. But there is
one defence against knowing about envy that I do want to make
reference to, because I have frequently found it of great use in
my clinical work. An envious person will defend himself or
herself against the knowledge of his or her unconscious envy by
stirring up envy of him- or herself in others; and will therefore
be enormously anxious about the analyst's envy. I have often
come across patients in whom it is quite clear that they have not
tapped their own talents to anything like the degree to which
they could, and it is because they are terrified of others'
destructive envy. Ultimately, however, it is the powerful envy
in themselves which is projected into others but is then experienced as existing in others around them. Very often such a
patient is also terrified of developing a talent because he or she
fears the analyst's wrath. The patient frequently fears that the
analyst is going to moralize and condemn, and here lies the significance of Melanie Klein's reference to 'stirring up' envy.

To illustrate what I mean I will tell you of a patient who many times managed to stir this up in me, but – are you surprised? – the occasion I remember best is when I managed to resist being stirred up. She had been complaining bitterly that I had helped her to communicate better with me in the sessions, but I had not helped her at all to communicate with others in the world outside. The following session she came in and was silent for some ten minutes; then she said in a superior voice tinged with reprimand: 'Yesterday I went to see Dr X. [about a gynaecological problem]. Now *he* is really sympathetic to women. *He* is really understanding of women's problems. I could speak to *him* very easily.'

I felt my blood rising at these innuendoes and wanted to point out her contempt of me and her desire to put down my own attempts at understanding her, but I didn't. I just knew that an interpretation that came out of me when my blood was boiling or even gently simmering would always be destructive. I waited until the tension had ebbed away. Then the point came to me, so I said: 'You are letting me know that you have resolved something and taken a step forward since yesterday's session and that now you *are* able to communicate well with someone outside.'

I knew that this was right, and she knew it, too, and desisted from trying to stir me up any more in that session. If I had said what I wanted to say in the heat of the moment she would have succeeded in stirring up my envy and jealousy, rather than experience *her* envy of me. Once I had calmed down inwardly it was clear that it was her envy that was being communicated. Her envy of the fact that I *had* helped her to communicate outside the consulting-room. But I also believe that it would have been a mistake to have pointed this out to her. I was saying to her, in effect, 'You are letting me know that my good breast *did* give you a good feed yesterday' (in other words, 'My breast has withstood your envious attack'), but that is already implied in what I said. If I had said to her, 'You see how your own envy of the good work I did in the session yesterday is contained in your comment', she would have felt me to be saying, 'I'm the King of the Castle, you're the dirty rascal'. In other words, her envious attack *would* have stirred something triumphant in me. This happens to be a rather vivid illustration of the way in which a patient can stir envy in the analyst, but I have experienced it on many other occasions too. Melanie Klein is right: this sort of envy is diabolically destructive and undermining, and it calls for a lot of painstaking work and self-examination to make any headway with it. There follows now a critique of Melanie Klein's theory.

1. The quality of the object is not considered sufficiently. I want to start by drawing your attention to the quality of Klein's language:

> If the undisturbed enjoyment in being fed is frequently experienced, the introjection of the good breast comes about with relative security.

Cast in that language this sentence does not have emotional meaning for me but in the following form it does:

> If the undisturbed enjoyment in being fed is frequently experienced, the child takes in the mother's love for him, and he feels secure in his possession of it.

I ask myself, why does Melanie Klein's language so often have this impersonality and jargonized ring about it? I can only think that it reflects an underemphasis of the interpersonal encounter, a problem which is sometimes then reflected in Kleinian technique, through which the patient may experience the analyst as a part-object which tends to reinforce the paranoid-schizoid position.

2. Mechanisms are emphasized to the exclusion of the object. The emotional quality of the object is understressed, and the mechanisms of projection and introjection are correspondingly overstressed. I shall say more about the quality of the object under my sixth heading.

3. There are noxious emotional states other than anxiety. Anxiety is central in Melanie Klein's work, and it stands as the foundation-stone of all her work, but there are emotional states that block development just as much which I think cannot rightly be called anxiety directly. I think that any writer of novels would describe the sort of state that a person dominated by the paranoid-schizoid position is in as anxious or anguished, but I do not think this fits well with the emotions corresponding to the depressive position. In that state a person might be described as grieving, as sad, as feeling bad or self-reproachful, but not as anxious. Also, some patients come into analysis because of the absence of a vital experience. The person feels a vacuum, but I would not describe it as anxiety.

4. There is, I think, a contradiction in the argument. Melanie Klein says that in the depressive position the infant (or adult patient) feels guilty about the violent attacks it made when in the paranoid-schizoid position. But how can this be so unless there was some dim realization of the existence of an object all along, so that the paranoid-schizoid position is a defence against feeling the object as a whole object? This would presuppose that the patient or baby had once experienced the object as whole but had reverted *from* this state into the paranoid-schizoid one. Such a sequence would argue in favour of Fairbairn's view that the schizoid state results from a traumatic disappointment at an early developmental stage.

5. Melanie Klein does not say much about what comes after the depressive position. She talks of working through the depressive position, but towards what? As I said, in connection with Fairbairn, I believe that there is a further stage, which I call the 'tragic position'. The angry female patient whom I told you about started in the paranoid-schizoid position and then moved into the depressive position, but then into a further position which I shall now try to describe. A deep realization came that the deficiency in her early caring could not be attributed to her mother's or father's fault alone and that she was not responsible for it altogether, either. There had been other factors beyond

the control of mother or father: an economic crisis in the country they lived in meant that her father had to go abroad for employment. This caused many of the difficulties suffered by father, mother and all the family, including my patient. It was this realization that brought my patient in touch with the tragic: an integral part of *la condition humaine* and extremely difficult to bear. I believe that the depressive and paranoid-schizoid positions are a defence against this deeper abyss of non-meaning.

6. Objects are two-dimensional. I do not have the sense in reading Melanie Klein that the object world she describes quite has the feeling-quality of objects as real people. Some of Melanie Klein's followers did stress this deficiency. Paula Heimann wrote a classic paper on countertransference (1950) which, quite simply, invited analysts to use their own feelings in clinical work. Esther Bick (Personal communication) differentiated between two-dimensionality and three-dimensionality: two-dimensionality means that objects are emotionally perceived as part-objects; three-dimensionality means people as whole objects. Herbert Rosenfeld (Personal communication) stressed that a resistance or panic state or depression in a patient are often ushered in through emotional insensitivity on the part of the analyst, and by no means exclusively through envy or obstinacy on the part of the patient.

7. Responsibility for change lies too much on the side of the ego of the patient. For Melanie Klein the original source of the trouble, as it were, lies in the patient – the anxiety brought about through the presence of the death instinct within the infant. I think this can lead to persecutory interpretations. The trouble, if you can tolerate me putting it that way, lies in the nature of the real object in relation to this particular baby. There is a sort of joint responsibility here, just as there is between analyst and patient, if any positive development is to take place.

26 LEARNING FROM EXPERIENCE AND FREEDOM IN BION'S THINKING

Instead of starting this lecture with a biographical synopsis I want to give some anecdotes, hoping thereby to convey something of the character of the man. The first two come from an article entitled 'Gosling on Bion' that appeared in *The Tavistock Gazette* several years ago:

> [The example comes] from a group relations conference in the United States at which he was a member of the staff, a conference in the tradition of the Leicester Conferences [regular events at which group analytic experiences are conducted] here. At such events a good deal of confusion and stark experience inevitably emerge as the exploration of groups proceeds. One of the exercises at such a conference has the aim of studying relatedness between groups as it comes about and it usually involves the whole conference at some point falling into a good deal of disarray. On one such occasion the staff had just been evicted from their room, two members were having a fierce argument that looked as if it might escalate into violence at any moment, a whole group of people on the stairs were undecided about whether to go up further or come down again, and several bewildered individuals were drifting round the place as if they were sleep-

walking. The noise and the turmoil were considerable. In the midst of all this one distraught member came up to Bion in some urgency and said, 'Oh, for God's sake, Dr Bion, what do you think?' It is reported that Bion's reply was, 'I do not find the circumstances right for thought.' (Gosling, 1980, pp. 22–25)

I think this illustrates well a particular quality of Bion's: his belief that a thought has to emerge and cannot be forced into consciousness through artificial induction; and his capacity to wait until it does so.

The second example, again from Robert Gosling's article, is of a conversation Bion is said to have had with a patient. 'With great puzzlement and a furrowed brow he said, "I don't understand why you are so angry with me. I wasn't trying to help you"' (p. 23). This well illustrates Bion's own freedom to do his own emotional task with no hint of guilt about what he should be doing.

The next example is from the second volume of Bion's *Brazilian Lectures*. It is an excerpt from his account of an analysis, and I have done the unpardonable thing of cutting it short.

> I was asked to see a young man of twenty-one who was said to be very intelligent; not much the matter with him and probably a suitable case for psychoanalysis . . .

Bion then tells how the psychiatrist, the mother, the father and the sister all got in touch with him to give him information about the patient, but all their statements were contradictory, in fact in complete opposition to each other. Bion goes on:

> By this time I was beginning to wonder who was talking about what. I summed up the situation to myself as being one in which, to use the English expression, they were all 'off their heads', but I had no idea which head belonged to whom. So I settled down to listen to the patient's story.

It seemed coherent; he occasionally showed a lot of animation, but said nothing particularly witty or funny. He said that his sister was hostile to him and disapproved of him because he liked the smell of faeces. As the analysis proceeded he used more and more vulgar words and expressions which are not usually used in polite conversation. I asked him whether he spoke like this to everybody, or only to a person like a psychoanalyst. He said he saw nothing wrong with that language and he *liked* the smell of faeces . . . I pointed out that we did not know why he came to see me, and he said, 'I thought you knew. My difficulty is that I blush terribly. I thought you would have noticed by this time.' In fact he was always pale; I never saw any colour in his face . . .

Somewhere towards the end of the first year . . . he started mentioning that he had been drinking at the fountain. It seemed a strange expression, but I put it down to his being by way of a poet and a writer. From time to time he repeated that he had been drinking at the fountain until, to confirm my suspicions, I asked him, 'What do you use for a fountain?' He replied, 'Of course an ordinary wine glass'. It emerged after a time, bit by bit, one part of a sentence one week, another part of the sentence a week later, another part another week that what he was doing every time he said he was drinking at the fountain was drinking his urine. At this point I wondered what kind of desirable, witty, intelligent, co-operative patient I had . . .

At the time the patient lived in his room behind drawn curtains, and had so arranged things that nobody ever called him on the telephone, because it disturbed him that people could come right into his room through the telephone and interrupt the peacefulness of his life. That was the way he liked to live; he liked faeces; he liked urine; he liked living out of reach of anybody in this dark room. He explained that he could not bear being called on the telephone because he always became so terrified that it must be bad news.

I would have liked to say, 'If you arrange that nobody should call you on the telephone naturally you would think it was very bad news if they did; naturally you would be frightened if the telephone bell rang . . .' But I said, 'I think you are able to hear my interpretations but I don't think they mean anything.' 'Yes, that's right, that's right. You're quite right,' he said, 'they don't . . .'

I thought, 'How satisfying it would be if I were a good analyst and if I could be right; but I don't think I'm right; I don't think that this patient needs to be fed on psycho-analysis – not by me.' . . .

Another occasion: the telephone rings. 'Are you Dr Bion? Do you know Mr X.?' 'Yes.' 'This is the police. We have this gentleman locked up in our cell. Will you come and fetch him?' In this way I was prevented from thinking about other patients, because I was always expecting the telephone to ring with a fresh bit of news about Mr X. Of course, I could cut off the telephone and darken the room, not see anything or hear anything, so that I could devote myself to him. Who was analysing whom? Was I curing him, or was he curing me? I do not tell you the answer, but leave it for you as an exercise in conjecture – you may have such an experience in your practice. Perhaps your friends or relations will say you are such a good analyst – they have just the right patient for you: young, witty, twenty-one, intelligent, just your 'cup of tea'. Such is fame – for psychoanalysts. I used to wonder if I had chosen the wrong job; if I might not have been better off as an ordinary doctor. But ordinary doctors have the same kind of patient. Ordinary fathers and mothers have the same kind of children. Ordinary sisters have brothers like that. Ordinary brothers have sisters like his sister . . .

I was able to draw the patient's attention to the feeling that if he became important enough, if he became a famous patient, then at last he would feel that it was worth killing himself if enough people knew about it. I could imagine the patient saying, 'But I *like* murder; I would like to murder myself; I would like to be there and see the funeral.' One day I received a message: the patient had left his room and had been found dead in the fields some twenty miles from London. I cannot say that I felt I had done well. On the other hand, I cannot say that I even felt sure what the mistakes were that I had made. But I certainly could not believe that anybody would regard that as a satisfactory analysis of a witty, intelligent, clever, co-operative and friendly young man. (1974, pp. 105–113)

After Bion's tenth lecture in the same series to the same audience a questioner asked him:

Referring to the patient you talked about in Lecture 7: you interviewed the father, the sister, had a letter from a friend and a recommendation, I suppose from a colleague, maybe a psychiatrist, to attend this patient. Was any of this information of any use? The sister lied, the father told the story of the girlfriend which the young man denied. In what sense was this information used? Did it help you to take this patient into treatment? Did he come alone? What care and attention did he have? (p. 165)

And Bion replied:

The thing that helped me to take that patient more than anything else was sheer ignorance and unjustified daring. My qualifications for seeing that patient were precisely nothing. After seeing that patient and realizing what I had agreed to, I think I was a wiser man. I did not want another one of those. There was not a single one of those persons whose statements could be relied upon. The only thing that could be said about analysing such a person was that the analyst who did it was extremely ignorant and foolhardy. (p. 166)

The last example comes from something Bion said to me when I introduced to him the details about a psychotic patient in a supervision session. I told him about this patient's hallucinations, and in particular her feeling and experience of herself as merged with her mother, and her vicious attacks on her boyfriend, and was just about to start presenting a session when he stopped me and said: 'And this patient had the idea that you would be able to help her?' Embarrassedly I said, 'Yes, I think she did have that idea.' I realized that he was talking of my phantasy that I would be able to help her. As the years have gone on I have come to know that the psychotic patient has a deep phantasy that the analyst's power is divine. I think that the central focus of such an analysis therefore is on the omnipotent phantasy which I was colluding with in my belief that I could help her. Bion trusted what he himself could see and experience in the consulting-room, whereas Winnicott, as we shall see, was prepared on occasions to let the patient be treated by family members. Whereas Bion was distrustful of the family's therapeutic resources, Winnicott had considerable faith in them. For Bion the focus was on the analyst's experience with the patient, and the narrative about the man who committed suicide had in it Bion's implied conclusion that information from family members was to be distrusted.

I had a patient who would frequently ask me what I thought about something. In the early stages I sometimes answered but I noticed after some time that if I threw the ball back to her she would say something like this: 'I don't know . . . well, a very far-fetched possibility occurs to me', and then she would tell me her thoughts; on every occasion she came to a conclusion which seemed to me to be correct. But she hated it when I threw the ball back into her court. She would say, 'Do I have to?' or she would sigh. Bion said that individuals and groups hate learning from experience.

A person prefers to pick a ready-made item off the shelf rather than make one him- or herself, and I wonder if this tendency is not indulged even further in this age of commercialized entertainment. In a psychiatric prison once it had been decided with my agreement that I would take a group. The psychiatrist asked me to begin with whether I would like to see the files of the group members, but I decided not to. In the first session the group members were all convinced that I had read their records and that therefore my mind was prejudiced against them. They asked me if I had read the files, but I did not answer. In about the sixth session, however, I told them that I had not read their files, and they were furious. Obviously I was not serious, I was not doing the job properly and did not want to know them. I was able to interpret that they hated a situation where my only means of coming to know them was through my experience of them in the group.

The conclusion one comes to from thinking about this central preoccupation of Bion's is simply this: I fight a hard battle against coming to know what I think and feel. There are powerful forces which prevent me from coming to know what *I* think and what *I* feel, there is a strong pull against doing that. I may replace it with a substitute. I slip cannily into the shadow of another and speak his thoughts, his ideas or express his feelings about life and the world. Or I may take up the opposite posture and be determinedly against someone, his idea and thoughts. You probably all know of people who have started their career in loyal devotion to a particular hero and then, with a sudden volte-face, be passionately against him. I think Dostoevsky had some such swing from political left to political right ideologically. In such cases there is a powerful evacuation of feelings.

How do I become my own subjective self? This is the question which Bion addresses. Bion understands that the difficulty is particularly great in the face of powerful projective mechanisms, and I spoke about the effect of projective identification in the first lecture on Melanie Klein. Bion understood that this existed within the whole human community, that it was not just confined to the consulting-room, and that one of the tasks of the analyst is to be free of such pressures. He realized that people put enormous pressure on one another; the patient puts a crushing weight against the analyst, so much so that it can immobilize his thinking, his imagination, his feelings or his memory.

I had a man in treatment who demonstrated some hysterical mechanisms. One week in particular there was an important forward move in the Monday and Tuesday sessions, and then the Wednesday was missed for valid reasons. On the Thursday I interpreted away and said some things that probably would have passed muster at a clinical presentation, but at the end of the session I realized that the whole session had been completely isolated and that I had forgotten all about the Monday and Tuesday sessions. What is more I was dimly aware that no mention had been made of the missed Wednesday session; I further realized that I had quite forgotten the content of the Monday and Tuesday sessions. I did know that an important developmental step had occurred in them, but I could not remember an iota more than that.

On the Friday I pointed out how Thursday had been a 'trough' session, and he noted that neither he nor I had mentioned the Wednesday session. I then said (still not remembering the content of the two sessions) that he had made an important move forward over the weekend and in the Monday and Tuesday sessions. He said, 'You know, I've completely blanked out Monday and Tuesday – I cannot remember a thing about them.' He had also managed to blank out my memory as well, but luckily there was just a coded fragment left: I had the categorized knowledge that something important had happened.

I can think of an obsessional patient who effectively erased my own personal feelings for many years. It is in the face of these powerful forces that the individual is faced with the task of becoming his own subjective self. How can this come about? Bion hypothesized the presence in the personality of an alpha function through which an emotional experience is transformed into dream thoughts. At a foundation level in the personality there are happenings made up of sense impressions and emotions, and through alpha function they are transformed into dream thoughts. They are turned into personal possessions as opposed to 'facts' which just 'are'. I will try to explain the difference.

Many years ago I went to a lecture on the sociology of religion given by a sociologist. In the course of it he said that Luther had been harking back to the scholastics and, in particular, Thomas Aquinas and producing a rational system of religion against the irrational piety of his time. The lecturer was challenged by someone in the audience who said that Luther had been in revolt against the rationality of the scholastics, and that his had been an emotional *cri de coeur* against the logic and systematization of Aquinas. The lecturer then said that he had heard Archbishop Anthony Bloom make the point about Luther harking back to the scholastics three days before but had not understood it himself. In other words, the lecturer had just imported something and regurgitated it undigested; it had not been processed through his ego. It just sat in his personality as an object. It was not something which he actually thought and felt. For Bion this means that alpha function is not working.

For me the central aspect of Bion's idea of alpha function is really this: that in the absence of alpha function sense impressions, emotional happenings, inner and outer stimuli just sit in the personality. (Bion called these beta elements.) If you will forgive me, I will give you an example of a transformation from my own experience. I was reading an illustrated book on Venetian art and came across a reference to a Mannerist painting, and there was a reproduction of Bassano's *Beheading of John the Baptist*. I was reading it in bed before going to sleep, and thought I must fetch the *Oxford Dictionary of Art* and look up Mannerism; but the turgid language of the dictionary acted as an effective sleeping tablet, and I dropped off to sleep after I had read only about two paragraphs.

Some time in the night I had some kind of hypnagogic experience which might have been a dream or a phantasy, but in that phenomenon the picture came back to me before my eyes, and I just instinctively understood what was meant by Mannerism. Some transformation had occurred so that *I* had an intuitive understanding, whereas previously the picture just stood there in front of me, and I tried to take in the art critic's explanation. I think that in my hypnagogic experience there was both a rejection of the 'expert', and a transformation of the static picture into a personal living experience through which I understood what Mannerism was. This moment was a combination of an emotional and cognitive understanding – alpha function came into being. I think it was significant that I had abandoned the attempt to understand via reading of the 'expert' and allowed myself to relax and go to sleep.

Some emotional space favoured by time, relaxation and reverie are favourable to the operation of alpha function. Bertrand Russell had this method of tackling a subject about which he was going to write a book: he would read up about the subject, and then he would put it out of his mind and tackle some other subject, or write a book on another topic. When that was over he would come back to the first one. By then he found that he had digested it and made it his own, in such a way that he was able to write about it in a personal way. I will say it now in passing – but return to it in the last lecture – that only those interpretations which result from the operation of alpha function are effective. It is only these that make contact with the patient.

In a seminar Bion was asked what value he placed on supervision. He said that there was a lot of weight against it because it favoured the trainee's parroting of the supervisor but that, on balance, he was just in favour. However, his own manner of supervising was unusual. He did not say what the trainee or therapist should do – as in the example I gave from my own experience. He made remarks which, if they fell on fertile ground, might lead to emotional development and insight. In another of his Brazilian lectures Bion said:

> John Rickman described to me a patient who covered himself completely with the blanket, with the exception of one eye – that was all that Rickman had to interpret. It is no good trying to look that up in analytic books; it is no good asking anybody else what the interpretation is. You have to go there; you have to have a patient who behaves like that, and you have to be able to stand it long enough for something to emerge. (1974, p. 71)

What accounts for the presence of alpha function in one person and its absence in another? Bion believed that it could be destroyed through powerful envy. He thought that it became consolidated if the mother of the young infant was able to contain the anxiety and projections of the child. Then the infant was able to introject the good container; he would have a processing function intact within, and this too Bion called alpha function. An analysis can restore damaged alpha function if the analyst is capable of reverie and is able to contain his fear.

27 BION'S THEORY OF THINKING

Thinking and the solving of problems hold a central place in Bion's preoccupations. The originality of this work is striking: like a Copernicus he overturned all previous theories of thinking. In Bion there first comes a development of thoughts and this then calls forth an apparatus to deal with them: thinking. Thoughts come before the thinking. Or: it is the thoughts that need an apparatus to think them. Having said that, I want to start with Bion's statement that 'first there comes a development of thoughts' and try to understand it better.

Bion distinguishes between verbal thought, and thinking with imagery or ideographs. The latter kind of thinking has already developed at the paranoid-schizoid stage. Perception is interpenetrated with cognition. The size of an object is not 'seen' according to the size of the projection of that object on the retina; we will 'see' a plane as larger than its projection on the retina. Hence in the seeing there is already a thinking. The process is already so built-in that we frequently do not realize that we do so. If, however, you take up painting in midlife, one of your first difficulties as a novice is to see shape and colour as they fall on the retina and not as they have been corrected by a cognitive process. For instance, if we are standing near a pillar-box at the side of the road a car will look bigger from thirty

yards away than the pillar-box, but the artist has to banish the
cognitive in order to get a faithful painting. So when the Impre-
ssionists painted shadow as blue it was because they recorded
the blue that was there. Perception is actively selective, in particular of movement and change, and this is so even in animals.
The retina of the frog's eye has a special receptor for reacting to
small crawling creatures. We have cognitive templates so that
we actively 'shape' the environment that we see. I am trying to
emphasize that in the perceptual activity of everyday life thinking is going on, but the thinking is with images, as is the case in
dreams.

This sort of thinking is not normally conscious. It becomes
conscious in the painter, but it is not normally so. In a psychotic state the patient will revert to thinking with images, the only
thinking present in such a state. I once had a rather striking
example of it with a patient who would communicate in this
way:

My cat bit my ear and blood dripped on the carpet.

I went for a walk in a meadow and discovered a dead squirrel
in the grass.

My father came in and gave me a special soldier suit on my
fifth birthday.

My sister hugged me when I heard my uncle had died.

He spoke in a dreamy way, and as he went round and round
these images kept coming back. They were memory-pictures,
representing intense emotional experiences which kept droning
on through his mind. They were also his thinking about a
traumatic experience which he was trying to master, and these
memory-pictures were his way of communicating it. It was also
clear to me that he was not aware of what he was thinking about
deep down: the trauma remained hidden. But he was thinking.
He was trying to solve a problem. It is these images which Bion

called ideographs. The image, be it a memory or a current perception, is grasped and taken in because it is the realization of an existing preconception.

I will try to describe what is meant by this. For a thought to emerge a preconception – a state of emotional seeking – has to be wedded to a realization. When the infant is seeking for the breast and finds it, there is no thought. There is an experience of satisfaction. Then when there is no breast there is a confused frantic searching. Then a moment of clarity and a picture of the breast which satisfies: the moment when the picture comes signifies the emergence of the thought. Hence Bion's point that a thought only emerges in the absence of the object, and hence that a realization always connotes a frustration.

Let me relate this to what I said in the last lecture about beta elements and alpha elements and the point that dream thoughts derive from alpha elements. Bion says that subsequent upon dream thoughts comes the preconception, followed by a thought or conception, and then one higher up on the scale comes a concept. The difference between a conception or thought, and a concept is that the latter is verbal and can be communicated to another in language. Then one higher up on the scale is a scientific-deductive system and lastly algebraic calculus. You will see that as we move up the scale the phenomena become more and more shorn of sensory elements until we reach the last category, H., in which this is completely the case. Within each category there is notation, attention, enquiry and action. The sequence I have described is Bion's 'Grid', which he prints at the beginning and end of some of his books – Second Thoughts, for example, is one.

A theory is at the concept level – F. This is not the mental attitude required of the analyst; an analyst works with reverie, at level C. Reverie is in the area of dreams and myths, just one above alpha function. Bion thought that the mother's capacity for reverie was an essential maternal prerequisite; if she had this capacity then she became a good container of the baby's anxieties. Out of fear of annihilation the baby projects dread and fear of death into the mother, but if the mother is able to contain these then they become modified, and the baby receives them back in a digestible form.

But what does it really mean when we say that the mother is able to contain these projections? Negatively it means that she does not herself become so depressed that she is unable to respond to her baby, or that she fears the baby, or that she is disgusted by the baby or envious of the baby. I am reminded here of Winnicott's classic paper 'Hate in the Counter-Transference' (1947), which lists fifteen good reasons for a mother to hate the arrival of her baby. Now if the baby gets such a negative response, he feels that he is too much for his mother and himself internalizes a bad sense of himself. Positively, on the other hand, the presence of reverie in the mother enables her to 'tune in' to her baby so that when he makes gestures, looks at her, gurgles to her she is in turn able to respond with gestures which meet his, with looks which meet his, or gurgling sounds which meet his. The baby then feels comforted and satisfied. This is what we mean roughly, as far as we know, when we say that the baby's anxieties are contained and returned to him in a modified form.

How does the notion of containment apply in the analytic situation? It means that the analyst's proper stance in relation to the patient is one of reverie. Negatively it means that he or she does not have a theory in his or her mind with which he or she tries to make sense of the patient's communications. For the possession of a theory with which to meet the patient screens the analyst from what the patient is projecting outwards. If the analyst possesses a theory, a key, with which to understand the patient, then how can there ever be new thought, and thus new theory? Therefore the state of reverie essentially means that the analyst is prepared to be changed by his patient. Sometimes a patient has said to me that he or she feels hopeless, up against a brick wall; if so, it is usually engendered by the feeling that nothing that he or she says or does will change me or get beyond a particular attitude of mine.

I will tell you of a patient with whom this was the case. The patient, a woman, criticized me mercilessly for a long time. When I made an interpretation that seemed to hit the mark and lead to some development, she would quickly castigate me for doing so little. If there was a session in which emotional understanding clearly developed, she would in the next session remind me of one, perhaps a year before, in which I had been insensitive. I formulated the situation to myself along Kleinian lines: that there was fierce envy of the penis. That when the penis penetrated, it filled her with hatred, but that the hatred of the penis was itself transferred from a hatred of the breast so that she was functioning at a part-object level. I therefore constantly showed her these castrating attacks and pointed out how destructive she was being to any good work that was being done.

One day she came in to her session and announced that she had been back to the provinces to see the lady counsellor who had first referred her to me: she was so upset about the way her therapy was going that she had gone back to the lady to ask her advice about it. Then she was silent. After a while I asked her what the lady had said. She said her reply had been,

> It sounds as if he cannot hear the screams of a distressed baby.

I was about to say something when I was gripped at the very centre of myself by a dawning realization of the truth of what she had just said. Until that moment I had for months been interpreting her destructiveness, envy and attacks on good development, but suddenly when she reported this statement of the lady counsellor's, I heard the deeper distress of a distraught child who had been crying out to me for months. All the attacking was for my not hearing. I had heard the words of the song but not the deep musical rhythm. As this realization

hit me I was deeply moved and it took a few moments to gather
my composure, and then I said to her,

   I think what you have just said is quite correct,

and she burst into tears. I sensed a child who had been hammer-
ing and screaming with helpless rage, trying to get through her
mother's impermeable wall and communicate her intense pain.
At that moment I caught an emotional glimpse of the intensity
of her suffering. At that moment I admired her for her
undaunted determination to get through to me. She had gone
on month after month, year after year, trying to get through.
Eventually she had even gone out to the provinces to talk to her
first counsellor in an attempt to get through the wall. I had held
on to the theory to protect myself from the horrific screams of
a suffering child. It is central to Bion's thinking that the analyst
needs to be open to the patient's pain and suffering. When I was
interpreting according to theory I was not in reverie, but I think
that at the moment when she told me the lady counsellor's
words she reached the area of my reverie. Then I could hear.

   Bion, therefore, did not agree with the often-stated dictum
within psychoanalytic communities that clinicians need a
theory as a sort of platform from which to observe and codify
the communications of the patient. Bion developed the Grid to
try to help analysts relate to the different levels of communication between analyst and patient, and so cut across any superficial theory structure. The analyst needs to be emotionally at
C. or D., at the level of dream or more probably preconception, so that his or her emotional state can be ready to mate with
a similar level of the patient's communication and so produce a
thought which emerges as insight. Insight is the baby of the
intercourse between patient and analyst, and it leads to new
understanding and growth in both analyst and patient.

   Bion did, however, realize that we do cling to theories to
protect ourselves from threatening situations. A conscious
state of not-knowing underpinned by a preconception stance

seems to be what Bion recommends. Through the analyst's being a container in the way I have tried to indicate it is possible for a transformation to occur in the patient, from a means of communicating through projective identification to one where there are dream thoughts. This explains the paradox that when the patient has a dream, a phantasy or a thought about a particular thing it means that the thing is already within manageable proportions and can be so dreamed, phantasied or thought about. What had been got rid of through projective identification has now been reintrojected in a modified form, so can be dreamed about.

I want to dwell a little further on ideographs. In a regression to the paranoid-schizoid position the patient is in a state where he is overwhelmed by intense emotional experiences which he tries to think about. But he has no words to do this with, because words are not suitable vehicles for highly charged emotional states. By their very nature they are removed from the centre of emotionality to an area which is best described, paradoxically, as the more spiritual area of man. So the psychotic patient is trying to find images that will express the emotional experience. In his classic paper 'Differentiation of the Psychotic from the Non-Psychotic Personalities' (1957, pp.56–59), Bion instances a patient who said, 'My head is splitting; maybe my dark glasses', and remarks that some five months earlier he, Bion, had worn dark glasses. Bion says that the psychotic personality has to wait for the occurrence of an apt event before it feels it is in possession of an ideograph suitable for use in communication with itself or others. In this case the dark glasses contained a hint of the baby's bottle. They resembled the breast, and they were dark because the breast was frowning and angry; they were of glass to pay him back for trying to see through them, the breasts, when they were breasts; they were dark because he needed darkness to spy on the parents in intercourse; they were dark because he had taken the bottle not to get milk but to see what the parents did; they were dark because he had swallowed them, and not simply the milk they had contained; and they were dark because the clear good objects had been made black and smelly inside them.

Now Bion attributes this thinking to the non-psychotic part of the personality on the basis that where there is thinking, then projective identification and psychosis are absent. As an analyst it is very unnerving to find that a psychotic patient has suddenly brought back an image that appeared in the treatment a long time ago and is using it to think with. But Bion emphasizes that in image or ideographic thinking there is no awareness, because awareness is inextricably bound up with verbal thought.

Bion distinguishes between verbal thought and thought with images. Ideographic thought is bound up with a merged state of affairs, although it proceeds from the individuated aspect of the personality, and does not differentiate between inner and outer, patient and analyst. The person dominated by the psychotic part of the personality is not able to bring the ideographic thought out of the chrysalis into the sunlight of verbal thought. This is because words are removed from the perceptual or more primitive level, and are therefore consonant with (conscious) psychic reality. Bion says that there is a connaturality between the awareness of psychic reality and words – that is, awareness and words are of the same nature. For this to be true it is necessary to reiterate that (conscious) psychic reality is essentially divested of the perceptual. Awareness of psychic reality or consciousness can only be achieved through verbal thought. Through thinking with words someone is able to be aware of his own internal experiences.

Bion stresses, though, that words can become the objects of projective identification, and when this occurs they are enveloped just as other objects are. In a psychotic state the patient splits the area of awareness into minute bits and some of these bits then get projected into objects in the room. When an object is thus enveloped it swells up and becomes invested with animate qualities. So, the patient will feel that he is being listened to by the gramophone or watched by it, depending on whether the part projected is part of the auditory or visual apparatus. In a similar way a word can be enveloped and it can become a persecuting presence to the person. Bion thought that this phenomenon was much more widespread than it would seem from a few overtly psychotic people in the consulting-room.

In this wider sense the psychotic is that which dominates the personality and prevents psychological development. In his later years Bion became more and more preoccupied with the division between those who become someone else and those who struggle to be themselves, and he came to place the decisive happenings in the womb. In his earlier writings he seems to imply that the infant has the capacity to make a decision: either to evade frustration or to modify it, but he does not say how this decision occurs. From my reading of it he seems to recognize the existence of some mysterious quality that can lead one person in general to modify, whereas the other evades. There is indeed no doubt that in an analysis a patient frequently has to make decisions: when an awful thought is borne in upon him or her it can be pushed away or faced, and it seems that at some very primitive level this process starts very early in life.

Bion was addressing the existence of the patient. He tried to resist the powerful pressures to be, say or do something that was not him, Bion. He said in another of his Brazilian lectures that his goal in analysis was to introduce the patient to himself. The problem is: how do you do that if there does not seem to be a person there?

28 THE WORK OF
MICHAEL BALINT

Michael Balint was Hungarian and was analysed by Sandor Ferenczi. He worked in his early years as an analyst in Hungary but came over to England in the late Thirties, and became a prominent member of the British Psycho-Analytical Society. When, subsequent to the Controversial Discussions, there emerged three groupings in the British Society, Michael Balint, along with Donald Winnicott, became one of the most important clinicians and theoreticians of the Independent or Middle group. In this context he was very critical of the technique adopted by the Classical Freudians and the Kleinians in their analytic method with patients manifesting a psychotic area.

Balint's book *The Basic Fault* (1968) is about this primitive area of the personality. Various terms have been used for it: psychotic, primitive, pre-Oedipal, pregenital, and so on. Balint prefers to use a term of his own: the area of the basic fault. His concern is with – and this he describes vividly – the way in which a patient may have been coming for some time and taking in interpretations and being co-operative, and then there is a change. The patient is no longer co-operative, feels the analyst as a hostile presence, and develops a sour, resentful attitude. He or she feels that the analyst 'owes' something to him or her, that the analyst is malevolent. Balint notes, though, that in these patients there is no despair or sense of hopelessness but instead a determination to see it through. This determination makes such patients very attractive to an analyst, and he can very easily be seduced.

When in this state these patients also have an uncanny ability to see into the private life of the analyst with great accuracy. I have myself experienced this on many occasions, and have also supervised people who have treated patients where this is true. Yet, though this accuracy is so great, it is disproportionate and exaggerated and therefore not true in an overall sense. It is like the zoom lens of a television camera, which focuses in on one particular spot but precisely because of this the surrounding, contextual environment is obliterated. The area which is focused upon with such deadly accuracy is perceived in a paranoid way.

The intensity of emotion generated is such that we know, in Kleinian terminology, that the patient is relating to the analyst in a part-object way. The patient's intense hatred of the analyst is directed at this one quality, and it blots out all other qualities that the analyst has. Of course, this is a state which we all know in ordinary life in a less extreme form. Swapping some gossip one person says to another of a third, 'Oh, I can't bear him, he's so complacent and self-satisfied', or 'She's so ambitious and deceitful that I loathe her', and so on. In all these cases the particular characteristic assumes great importance, and the rest of the personality becomes submerged under the one undesirable trait.

Balint says that when this shift occurs clinically it is very difficult to manage. He criticizes those who are encapsulated within a Classical technique, and also those who use a Kleinian technique, for the following reasons. Rather cynically, he says of the Classical Freudians that when this area emerges, they find the patient 'too disturbed' and quickly terminate the analysis. Balint believed that the Classical technique, particularly in America, was too rigidly bound to the Oedipal level of functioning and to words, in that in the area of the basic fault the patient often cannot appreciate that an interpretation is an interpretation. If so then the Classical technique clearly cannot be used. But Balint repudiated the conclusion that the patient is therefore too disturbed to continue analysis. A different technical approach needed to be adopted, one which could reach the many patients who could not be reached where they needed to be reached. Balint had also noted that there was an increasing number of patients who came, not because of a precise symptom, but because they felt a meaninglessness: it was particularly these patients who were likely to enter the area of the basic fault in their analysis. In other words, to adhere to the Classical technique could relegate psychoanalysis to a treatment backwater, for failing to confront the most prominent maladies of our age.

Balint's criticism of Kleinian technique was rather different. He recognized that Kleinians had addressed themselves to the area with which he himself was concerned, but he said that they interpreted too much and did not allow the patient enough emotional space or place in which to grow. When a patient is in this state, to be hammered by interpretations increases the sense of the analyst's omnipotence in the patient's eyes. In the end, he says, the patient resignedly submits and drinks in the jargon language in which these interpretations are often couched. Externally he or she becomes an obedient disciple but is inwardly resentful that his or her own individuality has not been encouraged to grow.

I have certainly heard some presentations which would well earn Balint's description. I remember thinking during one presentation, 'Can't you leave the poor bloody patient in peace for a couple of minutes?' In less extreme cases there seems to be a tendency to dot every 'i' and cross every 't', but little cultivation of the *mot juste*. Though common, this tendency is true only of certain Kleinians: this whole style, for example, was quite foreign to Bion.

Having criticized these two approaches Balint goes on to give his own. In order to arrive at this, I will outline first his understanding of the 'basic fault'. This also gives meaning to the technique which he favours.

Balint says that he uses the term 'basic fault' to describe what most other analysts have referred to as the psychotic area, because this is how patients themselves refer to it. Such a patient complains of feeling that there is a fault in him or her. It means a fault, Balint says, in the sense that a geologist will talk of a fault in a mineral seam. A person simply feels that there is something wrong with him or her. I can think, for instance, of a patient who used to say that she knew there was something wrong with her, but she was not sure what it was. His notion is quite simply this; there is nothing complicated about it.

How has this fault come about? He says that it arises at a very early stage of development when the infant is being nurtured by its mother. What has gone wrong to cause this fault? There is a 'misfit' between mother and her child. I do not think I can do better here than quote Balint's own words:

> In my view the origin of the basic fault may be traced back to a considerable discrepancy in the early formative phases of the individual between his bio-psychological needs and the material and psychological care, attention, and affection available during the relevant times. This creates a state of deficiency whose consequences and after-effects appear to be only partly reversible. The cause of this early discrepancy may be congenital, i.e., the infant's bio-psychological needs may be too exacting (there are non-viable infants and progressive congenital conditions, like Friedreich's ataxia or cystic kidneys), or may be environmental, such as care that is insufficient, deficient, haphazard, over-anxious, over-protective, harsh, rigid, grossly inconsistent, incorrectly timed, over-stimulating, or merely un-understanding or indifferent.

As may be seen from my description, I put the emphasis on
the lack of 'fit' between the child and *the people* who represent his environment. (1968, p. 22)

Balint says in this passage that the problem is only partly rever-
sible. When the patient slips into the changed state in analysis
that he describes, it is because the area of the basic fault has been
reached and the patient, in the transference, feels that the
analyst is hostile and antipathetic to him. To use Balint's
favourite phrase, the patient feels that the analyst is not 'in tune'
with him or her. Now Balint thinks that the best procedure,
when the patient gets into this state, is for the analyst to provide
an environment where the patient can express all this, that to
allow the patient to enter this experience is therapeutic for him
or her.

This is difficult for an analyst; as I said in the lectures on
transference and on the significance of psychosis for psychoanalysis, it is very hard psychologically to bear a powerful
transference. I know from my own experience that I find it
so, but from supervising others I know that this is not confined
to myself. I will give you an example. I had a patient who used
to idealize me in a particular kind of way. She 'knew' that I did
not have the slightest personal feeling for her. My interest was
purely professional. She saw a film once in which a psychiatrist
got annoyed with his patient and she was very worried by it –
precisely because here was an instance of a patient arousing the
personal feelings of the psychiatrist. Week in week out, she
used to say she knew I was perfectly detached and was not the
slightest bit affected by what happened to her. I did interpret,
simply, from time to time, that it was very important for her to
feel absolutely safe with me. This she accepted all right but
from time to time I interpreted that she was anxious that she
had aroused me or would arouse me. Then she would fly into a
panicked kind of rage, would say that I knew that was impossible, so why on earth did I say something so stupid?

I did it again and again, and every time there would be the same reaction. If I pressed it, further questioned her 'knowing', she would panic even further, and the session would get into a state of disarray. Every time this happened I knew that I had done something wrong, that I had pressed a point against a better judgement that lay in me somewhere but did not seem able to emerge.

The point was a very simple one – that in the transference I was a figure quite out of the sphere of other men, I was not moved by the emotions and passions of others. That is what I found so intolerable. When at last the light had dawned I said that it seemed clear that she held me in a totally different category from other men, so that when I made a comment that brought me into the same category as others it created a panic in her.

My interpretation was accepted and the session changed in mood, and she became quieter and more reflective. Then she said something which indicated a powerful resentment of me and I pointed this out. She said she now realized that she hated me very deeply, and ended the session by calling me a 'fucking bastard'. This was a big shift from her normal stance of consummate politeness. But it was clear that I had resisted the expression of this hatred for a long while. Then for some time there was a sustained experience of her hatred and resentment.

I did not need to say very much but only to 'allow' her the experience. Here I was following the sort of technique that Balint recommends. On this issue Balint (and Winnicott, for that matter) differ considerably in technique from some Kleinians, in that they believe that it is possible for the patient to have an experience that in some measure genuinely makes up for a deficiency in infancy. When the patient is in this state the analyst understands what it is an expression of and just allows it. When a patient says 'I hate you' or 'I love you' there is no interpretation to be made. It is certainly a great mistake for the analyst to say at that point: 'You are expressing towards me how you used to feel as a child towards your mother'. The patient is feeling something directly towards the analyst, and the analyst 'allows' it, and this is healing for the patient.

I want to interpose a point here that Balint speaks about only by implication. Sometimes a patient regresses to what I can only call a 'feeling of quiet harmony' in which very little is said by either patient or analyst. It is a gross mistake, when the patient is in that state, to make interpretations or even interventions that disrupt the mood. I am reminded of a time when I was working in a psychiatric unit, and a patient put her arm through a window and cut herself. A psychiatrist was called, but purely to do the medical work of dressing the wound on her arm. The patient was now sad, quiet and near to tears. At this point the psychiatrist said to her, 'Did you see the cricket match on television today?'

In the area of the basic fault the psychoanalyst's task is to be in tune with the patient. It is so simple a point that it would be obvious to any person of sensitive feeling, but two factors make it difficult and therefore worth emphasizing: the resistance in both analyst and patient to the emergence of this mood, and the ethos of our training. I think when we first start to listen to a patient we tend to say to ourselves, 'Now I must interpret something. A quarter of an hour has passed and I have not interpreted anything.' A sort of guilt connected to the idea of the Protestant work ethic gets hold of us: 'I am paid to make interpretations just as a barber is paid to cut hair, so I must make some in every session, or I may be accused of professional sloth.' If 'being in tune with' comes naturally to you, then thank God that you are paid for an inborn gift. Balint says that this is the analyst's prime task when the patient is in the area of the basic fault: the work of interpretation comes later or is at least secondary. This is the big division between Balint's recommendation and that of most Kleinians, for whom interpretations and words have a central importance. You may remember the quotation from Hanna Segal on the necessary connection between interpretation and change, that I gave in Lecture 2, which I think illustrates the point.

The analyst's role, for Balint, is to be *with* the patient as a sort of friendly equal. The patient needs to feel that the analyst is really *with* him or her and not 'up there'. If the patient can really feel this then there is a chance of a new beginning. Balint gives a very charming illustration of this from his own practice. He had been treating a very lively, vivacious and slightly flirtatious girl in her late twenties for two years. She had been unable to achieve anything either professionally or in her personal emotional life. Then Balint gave her an interpretation in which he said that it seemed the most important thing for her was to keep her head safely up with both feet planted firmly on the ground. In response she mentioned that she had never been able to do a somersault as a child, although at various periods both then and since she had tried to do one.

Balint then said to her: 'What about it now?' – whereupon she got up from the couch and did a perfect somersault with no difficulty, much to her amazement. He goes on to say that this was a breakthrough and led to other favourable developments. She passed a difficult post-graduate exam, then married, and over the next few years had to bear some severe hardships, including German occupation of her country, but she managed all this. Balint says that a *new beginning* occurs because the patient feels in the presence of a safe object, in no sense is she in the presence of a superego figure. Balint puts it in these words: '. . . at the crucial moment the analyst was not felt as a stimulating, exciting, or forbidding adult object, in whose presence no proper young lady would think of doing somersaults, but as a safe object in whose presence a patient could and might indulge in childish pleasures' (1968, p. 134).

Regression for Balint, paradoxically, does not mean re-experiencing something. Here was an experience of something for the first time and hence it is a *new beginning*, which phrase Balint puts in italics. I said earlier that this view is not held by the majority of Kleinians, but there are prominent exceptions. In private communications and seminars I have frequently heard Dr Herbert Rosenfeld, for instance, make the same point as Balint. Moreover, the idea of a new beginning is closely linked to a point which I made in the lecture on transference: that in the initial interview the patient will nearly always tell the analyst how he is to treat him or her in some specific respect. This nearly always means that he or she was not so treated in childhood. A patient said to me in an initial interview that she had to stop seeing her previous therapist because 'he thought I was just complaining', letting me know thereby that there was a something that was real, and that if I was going to dismiss it as *just* complaining then it would be no good. She needed me to understand that and act upon it if she was to have a *new beginning*.

There are two sorts of defences against getting into the area of the basic fault. Balint called them 'philobatic' and 'ocnophilic'. These terms are elaborated in detail in his book *Thrills and Regressions* (1959), and Balint sees the two tendencies as deep character traits. The philobat escapes from his objects out into open spaces. His objects are dangerous and he keeps a safe distance from them. These characters like mountain climbing, sailing on their own in a yacht across the Atlantic, getting away from the crowd. For example, a woman recently described her husband to me as a man who in his personal life was exaggeratedly private. Although well known professionally, he lived with her most of his leisure time in a remote cottage and developed his own private interests.

The ocnophil clings to his objects in fear. The sort of person who hangs on every word that another says, and tends to have heroes in whose shadow he lives. A patient whom I used to see here in the Tavistock never walked across the courtyard to the front door but walked hurriedly along the two walls to the front door as if wanting the cover and protection of the building.

If there is a successful negotiation of the area of the basic fault then a new relation to the person's objects is established and there is a modified restructuring of these defences. Both defences are generated by the basic fault area and mobilized against objects, and the two are often present in the same person, though Balint would hold that one or the other mode would be predominant. The ocnophilic mode is somewhat similar to what Esther Bick has called 'adhesive identification' (Personal communication), by which she means a clinging relationship in which there is no space.

To end the lecture, I will just give you an example of how a fear of objects gave way and modified in the course of treatment. I told you earlier in the series of a patient who had a terror of water: in that she shrank away from it and clung to the shore, this was an ocnophilic defence. At the seaside she had never gone into the water and consequently had never learned to swim. In treatment the patient entered very early into the area of the basic fault, and a lot of work was done in her analysis. When she became a little more at ease with me she told me one day that on a camping holiday she had managed to paddle in the water, did not feel afraid of it any longer, and now wanted to swim. As I said when discussing Jung, water represented the unknown depths of the unconscious, inhabited by dreadful monsters – the objects of which she was terrified. She had to stop the analysis prematurely for external reasons, so I never knew how her aquatic achievements developed. But I think this would be a case of a defence dissolving as a more balanced relation with her objects was achieved.

I want to introduce Donald Winnicott by quoting you a passage from an article in which Harry Guntrip records some of his experiences when he was in analysis with Winnicott. Guntrip first had an analysis with Fairbairn which lasted several years, and later one with Winnicott over a few years but in which there were comparatively few sessions. The article is in part a comparison of the two analyses. Guntrip was living and working in Leeds and came to London once a month, and on each occasion he had two or three sessions with Winnicott. It was a surprise to learn, he says, that despite Fairbairn's stress on the personal relationship with the analyst being the crucial therapeutic factor, he interpreted on quite Classical lines. Guntrip also says that Fairbairn was freer of Freud intellectually, but that Winnicott in his clinical practice had departed from him further.

One particular section of the article gives a good flavour of the kind of analysis which Guntrip had with Winnicott. To put it in context, however, I should explain that Guntrip had had a younger brother, Percy, who died when Guntrip was three and a half. His mother later told him that he had walked into a room in their home and seen Percy lying naked and dead on her lap. He rushed up and grabbed him and said, 'Don't let him go.

You'll never get him back', but this event and the years before it were sealed off in his mind and he could remember nothing of them.

From 1962 to 1968 I had 150 sessions and their value was out of all proportion to their number. Winnicott was surprised that so much could be worked through in such widely spaced sessions, due I think in the first place to all the preliminary clearing that had been done by Fairbairn and to the fact that I could keep the analysis alive between visits; but most of all to *Winnicott's profound intuitive insights into the very infancy period I so needed to get down to.* He enabled me to reach extraordinarily clear evidence that my mother had almost certainly had an initial period of natural maternalism with me as her first baby, for perhaps a couple of months, before her personality problems robbed me of that 'good mother'. . . My amnesia for that early trauma [which had not been broken with Fairbairn] was not broken through with Winnicott either. Only recently have I realized that in fact, unwittingly, he altered the whole nature of the problem by enabling me to reach right back to *an ultimate good mother, and to find her recreated in him in the transference.* I discovered later that he had put me in a position to face what was a double trauma of both Percy's death and mother's failing me.

As I re-read my records I am astonished at the rapidity with which he went to the heart of the matter. At the first session I mentioned the amnesia for the trauma of Percy's death, and felt I had had a radical analysis with Fairbairn of the 'internalized bad-object defences' I had built up against that, but we had not got down to what I felt was my basic problem, not the actively bad-object mother of later childhood, *but the earlier mother who failed to relate at all.* Near the end of the session he said: 'I've nothing particular to say yet, but if I don't say something, you may begin to feel I'm not here.' At the second session he said:

'You know about me but I'm not a person to you yet. You may go away feeling alone and that I'm not real. You must have had an earlier illness before Percy was born, and felt mother left you to look after yourself. You accepted Percy as your infant self that needed looking after. When he died, you had nothing and collapsed.'

That was a perfect object relations interpretation, but from Winnicott, not Fairbairn. Much later I said that I occasionally felt a 'static, unchanging, lifeless state somewhere deep in me, feeling I can't move'. Winnicott said:

'If 100% of you felt like that, you probably couldn't move and someone would have to wake you. After Percy died, you collapsed bewildered, but managed to salvage enough of yourself to go on living, very energetically, and put the rest in a cocoon, repressed, unconscious.'

I wish there were more time to illustrate his penetrating insight in more detail, but I must give another example. I said that people often commented on my ceaseless activity and energy, and that in sessions I did not like gaps of silence and at times talked hard. Fairbairn interpreted that I was trying to take the analysis out of his hands and do his job; steal father's penis, Oedipal rivalry. Winnicott threw a dramatic new light on this talking hard. He said:

'Your problem is that that illness of collapse was never resolved. You had to keep yourself alive in spite of it. You can't take your ongoing being for granted. You have to work hard to keep yourself in existence. You're afraid to stop acting, talking or keeping awake. You feel you might die in a gap like Percy, because if you stop acting mother can't do anything. She couldn't save Percy or you. You're bound to fear I can't keep you alive, so you link up monthly sessions for me by your records. No gaps. You can't feel that you are a going concern to me, because mother couldn't save you. You know about "being active" but not about "just grow-

ing, just breathing" while you sleep, without your having to
do anything about it.'

I began to be able to allow for some silences, and once, feeling a bit anxious, I was relieved to hear Winnicott move. I
said nothing, but with uncanny intuition he said:

'You began to feel afraid I'd abandoned you. You feel silence
is abandonment. The gap is not you forgetting mother, but
mother forgetting you, and now you've relived it with me.
You're finding an earlier trauma which you might never
recover without the help of the Percy trauma repeating it.
You have to remember mother abandoning you by transference on to me.'

I can hardly convey the powerful impression it made on me
to find Winnicott coming right into the emptiness of my 'object relations situation' in infancy with a non-relating
mother.

Right at the end of my analysis I had a sudden return of hard
talking in session. This time he made a different and extraordinary statement. He said:

'It's like you giving birth to a baby with my help. You gave
me half an hour of concentrated talk, rich in content. I felt
strained in listening and holding the situation for you. You
had to know that I could stand your talking hard at me and
my not being destroyed. I had to stand it while you were in
labour being creative, not destructive, producing something
rich in content. You are talking about "object relating",
"using the object" and finding you don't destroy it. I
couldn't have made that interpretation five years ago.'

Later he gave his paper on 'The Use of an Object and Relating through Identifications' (in Winnicott, 1971) in America
and met, not surprisingly, I think, with much criticism.
Only an exceptional man could have reached that kind of

insight. He became a good breast mother to my infant self in my deep unconscious, at the point where my actual mother had lost her maternalism and could not stand me as a live baby any more. It was not then apparent, as it later became to me, that he had transformed my whole understanding of the trauma of Percy's death, particularly when he added:

'You too have a good breast. You've always been able to give more than take. I'm good for you but you're good for me. Doing your analysis is almost the most reassuring thing that happens to me. The chap before you makes me feel I'm no good at all. You don't have to be good for me. I don't need it and can cope without it, but in fact you are good for me.'

Here at last I had a mother who could value her child so I could cope with what was to come. (1975, pp. 152–153)

It is very difficult to summarize the thinking and theory of Winnicott because he did not propose them as a coherent body of doctrine as did Fairbairn or Melanie Klein. In no way did he wish to found a school. He was a truly independent thinker and enormously flexible in his approach to patients, something which is very clearly illustrated in his paper 'Symptom Tolerance in Paediatrics' (1953). While at private boarding school an eight-year-old boy, Philip, began to steal and thereby started an epidemic of stealing; the headmaster wrote to his parents asking them to remove Philip from the school. However, the headmaster recognized that the boy was ill and so did not take any punitive measures; it was very lucky, Winnicott says, that Philip was referred for treatment before a moralizing attitude towards his delinquency had become organized.

From the history which the parents gave Winnicott he realized that Philip had missed out in mothering as a baby. Winnicott also saw that psychoanalysis for the boy was out of the question because the family lived in the country a long way from London. Winnicott mentions that the mother had a dislike of psychology and claimed to know nothing about it, but that this fact was valuable in his management of the case because he was able to rely on her feelings and intuitive understanding of human nature. I think this aspect of the case gives some insight into Winnicott's ability to see the positive side of situations, even those which to other eyes might look very unpromising prognostically.

Winnicott therefore proposed that the boy return home for a year, become a baby again, and that the mother give him the nurturing which he had missed out on at an early age. Philip regressed and became iller and iller and stayed much of the time in bed. The mother and the family recognized that he was ill and adapted to him, as is the natural course of things with a young baby, and with guidance from Winnicott the family was able to cope with his needs. During the regression, for instance, he wet the bed and the mother attended to him each night; Winnicott believed that enuresis could not usually be successfully treated unless the regressive needs behind it were recognized. Winnicott also mentions that Philip possessed a greyhound which turned out to be very important and played a vital part in his cure. The boy got some bodily comfort from his pet when he was at his worst. Then after several months he wanted to get up, and this marked the beginning of his recovery. At the beginning of the next academic year the boy returned to his school and was and remained a healthy and moral schoolboy.

You can see from this case how Winnicott mobilized all the resources in the family and founded his therapy on a repaired family setting which he realized that even a weekly visit to London for therapy would disrupt. He had an unusual capacity to look at a clinical situation, find where its strengths were, and use them to their full potential.

I said when talking about Melanie Klein that she overemphasized mechanisms and understressed the nature of the object. With Winnicott the situation is the reverse. The nature of the object is central and mechanisms are always in second place, so it is not surprising that the notions of the True Self and the False Self hold a central place in his understanding. Winnicott says that if the mother has not responded to her baby appropriately then it puts up a screen to protect its own individual self, which Winnicott called the 'True Self'. The pregenital fears of invasion, annihilation or breaking in pieces are felt by this individual self. When Melanie Klein spoke of these pre-Oedipal anxieties she referred to them as being felt by the ego; Winnicott gives a better description of the entity by referring to it as the True Self.

When the analyst encounters pre-Oedipal anxieties in the patient it is the patient's individual selfhood that is felt to be endangered. I can think of a patient who, when he came into analysis, was terrified that I would plonk down on top of him a lot of Freudian doctrine. It was not that he was particularly antipathetic to Freud but rather had a terror of an individual core of himself being swamped by any group ideology, a great fear of the individual in him being submerged within a group uniformity.

The point I am trying to make is that the subject of these fears is the central core of individuality, which Winnicott names the 'True Self'. Whereas Melanie Klein says that the threat to this part of the personality comes from the inner workings of the death instinct, Winnicott says that the threat lies in maternal failure, from which the True Self retreats and protects itself; it is the mother's sin of omission that leads to trouble. If the mother omits to respond in the crucial way then the baby slips into a compliance and identifies with the negative functioning of the mother.

Thus in the transference the analyst meets with a hostile reception when he or she tries to get near to the patient in a sympathetic way. This is because the analyst is meeting the defensive False Self. When I spoke to a patient about holding her, rocking her in my arms or looking after her she hated it and violently tried to repudiate me. The patient, over a long life, has developed a habit of protecting her True Self and is terrified that if she exposes it the analyst will reject it, which will mean catastrophe. Now I want to try to explain what it is that the mother must positively do if she is to nurture and 'feed' the True Self.

From time to time, says Winnicott, the baby gives expression to a spontaneous gesture and this issues forth from the True Self. The mother needs to meet this gesture with an affirming gesture of her own, coming from her own True Self. The True Self does not become a living reality, is not affirmed, unless the mother repeatedly meets the spontaneous gestures of the child with a gesture of her own, but one that meets the child's. It is of the essence that no principles can be laid down about what this spontaneous response will be. The mother may get up and dance in front of her child, or pick up the child and rock it and sing, or lie him down and stroke him, or give him a feed.

The mother's capacity to do this is closely linked to what Winnicott named 'primary maternal preoccupation'. His assumption is that when a woman becomes pregnant she gradually achieves a high degree of identification with her infant. The identification develops during pregnancy, is at its height at the time of birth, and slowly ebbs away after some months. This essential maternal function enables the mother to know about her infant's earliest expectations and needs, and makes her personally satisfied in so far as the infant is at ease.

Through it the mother knows how to hold her infant, and the baby can then start existing and not purely reacting. The True Self is its own source of action, a notion which is closely linked to the philosophical theory of the Transcendental Ego. This is the radically anti-deterministic view that the person has within him or her a source which cannot be explained by its antecedents alone. Freedom then is the capacity to act from this source. Winnicott's theory is that the mother, through her spontaneous responses, is able to bring this source of creative activity to birth; and that some analogous attitude needs to be present in the analyst in regard to his or her patient.

In this particular matter Bion and Winnicott are very close in their thinking. Just as a mother cannot find out what to do from books or from anyone else when her baby spontaneously reaches out towards her in gesture and action, so also the analyst ultimately has no mentor or book to turn to, especially at certain moments. Of course a mother can be taught a lot: she can be shown how to hold the baby, how to feed the baby, how to wind the baby, how to bath the baby and so on, but only she can know how to respond when the baby gives her that strange look, makes that peculiar noise, suddenly throws his hand in the air or starts to look intently at some object in the room. So also the analyst can be taught the general lines of how to conduct a session, and certain general principles can be set out; but there are moments when only the analyst himself can act. The patient will demand that something comes from the analyst.

This demand may come verbally, or the emotional intensity of the situation generated may place a responsibility on the analyst to act. The action may be to remain silent or to speak, but whatever it may be, the patient is wanting a gestural response that comes out of the analyst's True Self, which by definition has no antecedent. At that moment it is the analyst and the analyst alone from whom the response must come. This is particularly the case with a psychotic or suicidal patient: here the analyst needs to fall back on the resource of his or her True Self and that alone, and is the ultimate authority in these cases. (It is for this reason that I have not had medical cover for my patients for some years.) Winnicott said that there could be a False Self made up of psychoanalytic techniques, and he believed that psychoanalysis was going up a false trail when technical matters became predominant.

Winnicott worked for some forty years as a paediatrician at Paddington Green Children's Hospital in London, where he did over 20,000 consultations with the mother-and-child couple. I doubt whether there has ever been an analyst who knew as much about the interaction between mother and child as Winnicott. In particular, he understood how illness or character disorder in the mother affected the child, because they blocked her capacity to respond from her True Self and also to identify with her baby. Two processes occur when there is such a disorder in the mother. Firstly the child misses out on an essential psychological experience, and secondly he or she becomes terrified at a deep level: in the absence of a responsive mother the child feels filled with terror.

In order to deal with this gaping abyss the baby internalizes the bad False Self mother functioning. The False Self is therefore composed of the hated non-responsive aspects of the mother, and one finds in the patient the very attitudes that he or she abhors. A patient whose mother had possessively wanted to hold him to herself, and keep him within her own orbit, hated this deeply and had managed to break free (or so he thought and in fact had managed to in certain respects), but acted towards the analyst in exactly the same way. Now I am not quite sure why this happens, but I think it is the baby's way of creating a feeling-closeness to the mother, to compensate for mother's distance. Clinically I also know that when the analyst is caught up in this kind of feeling-closeness with the patient a very marked feeling-change occurs in both if the analyst manages to break the collusion. The patient feels very lonely, and the analyst feels a quality of adultness in the relationship.

I will give you an example of this. A female patient in a long analysis with me had an ambivalent relationship with her mother, but most essentially felt deeply that her mother was very possessive and did not want her to succeed. She painted a picture of a mother who envied her and wanted to keep her to herself. I had a warm feeling towards this girl and felt a certain loyalty from her towards me, which was rather pleasing. Her analysis ended, and she was now very much better than she had been at the beginning.

Some three years later her mother died and she rang me. I knew that this was an extremely important event for her and consequently she returned for psychotherapy. I felt a devotion towards me that I was not happy about and, as a result of some things which she said to me, I asked her if she would like to see someone else instead of me. She was terribly shocked, and I felt I was giving up on her. I also felt cruel when I said it. However, ultimately she felt cared for because she realized that I was more concerned that she get well than that she continue with her loyal devotion to me. After this, however, she felt very lonely and abandoned, and I also felt a loss, which I can best describe as having lost the warm satisfying kind of feeling that arises from a child's trusting its parent and being proud of him. I had become her mother in the transference, and the feelings that existed between her mother and her were all there between her and me. My reconstruction is that the identification with mother which I have described served to mitigate the dreadful feeling of being in a lonely abyss. But it was noticeable that at the same moment as the rupture between us in the transference, she began to be more open with potential boyfriends and she said to me, 'It is the first time that I felt David cared for me'.

Winnicott believed that in the early months the baby felt itself and its mother to be one substance. The baby then slowly separated itself out from mother. One of the mother's tasks was to 'disillusion' her baby, so that the baby begins, painfully, to realize that he is not Lord and Master of a world there to serve his every need. He begins to separate himself from the substance of his mother, and in this early stage mother needs to adapt to her baby. If she does not, the baby feels impinged upon and filled with persecutory feelings. You will notice that Winnicott attributes the inborn feelings of Melanie Klein's paranoid-schizoid position to failures in the mother – failure to adapt to the baby, failure to hold the baby both physically and psychologically.

For Winnicott, development is also a question of the baby's separating himself out from the mother through father's help. He interpreted in this way and therefore did not stress the libidinal attachment to mother, but rather the baby's struggle to become free. For instance, some of the interpretations from Guntrip's analysis with him which I quoted at the beginning of the lecture show that Winnicott comes right in to the centre of Guntrip's inner feelings: his state of feeling with his switched-off mother, and his survival defences against so awful an inner world. There is great depth of feeling in Winnicott's emotional contact with his patient. He is on the side of the pain and the life-striving of the patient.

As differentiation between the infant and his or her mother occurs, so there develops the capacity to form symbols; but, for Winnicott, there is a stage in between these two when the tactile relation to the mother has not given way to the internalized one. At this time the infant holds something material – such as a rag doll or a piece of blanket – that represents the mother, or more properly the mother's breast, and this he called the 'transitional object'. The attachment to the mother is through sight, smell and touch and the baby invests the object with maternal qualities at this level. In this phase the baby is neither one with the mother nor separate; the transitional object is thus neither in nor out. It is this area in which illusion occurs, where the individual creates the object world but in a particular way. The sharing of an illusion by a group accounts for the way in which reality is created and always some element of experience is left out. The subjective understanding of facts is through the medium of illusion.

I want to make one final point. The functioning of illusion is dependent for Winnicott on the mother's responsiveness to her baby; for Bion reverie, which is closely allied to illusion, is dependent upon alpha function, which in turn needs a mother who can contain. But it would be wrong to assume that Winnicott and Bion have the same theoretical model of early experience. Bion, following Klein, supposes that from birth the infant experiences the mother or the breast as separate; Winnicott says that the infant thinks that the breast is his, is part of

him or her. It follows, for Winnicott, that for the baby there is
no interchange at this stage of development.

   In this lecture I have given only the most cursory review of
Winnicott and have not done justice to his wide ranging imagination and understanding of the mother-and-child couple and
of human development, or to his sensitive empathy with his
patients. I hope, however, that what I have said may stimulate
you to read Winnicott for yourselves.

30   THE LAST LECTURE

In this last lecture I want to speak about those aspects of psychoanalysis which for me are central. I do not believe that any lecturer can hide his or her own personal attitudes or bias any more than a psychoanalyst can do so from his or her patient. But what I want to do, in this last lecture, is to make explicit what has been implicit. This has a clarifying function for me, and for you; for when my attitudes stand out clearly it gives you a better opportunity to compare your own with mine and to find where you agree and where you disagree.

I have stressed that the psychotic patient will burrow away until he finds out what is in the analyst's heart. What does the analyst really think and feel? This is what will concern him. I have found, for instance, that all the mentally handicapped patients who have been referred to me have wanted to discover whether at heart I really want their existence on this planet or, if honest, would I prefer that they drop off the edge of the world and disappear from my sight for ever. No amount of supervision or technical improvement will alter the situation one bit.

I have said that this is also true of psychotic patients, but I follow Melanie Klein in believing that in all neurotic patients there is an underlay of psychosis, and therefore the analyst's attitude is of importance to the therapeutic outcome in all our patients. I once had a patient who frequently went into a droning tone of voice that made him inaccessible. For years I could get no understanding of this; then one day I commented that he had passed over, in an aside, his involvement in a series of lectures opposing apartheid. I knew that inside him he felt passionately about the issue, and I said that he wanted to hide it from me, because he was afraid that I would rob him of his passion. I added for good measure, 'In other words, you fear that I will castrate you'.

Then I noticed that he went into his droning tone, and felt convinced that this was connected to my comment about castration. I kicked myself. Why the hell had I not been satisfied with what I had said about robbing him of his passion? Why did I have to go on to make the remark about castration? I think somewhere I was lured into thinking that a good follower of Freud would make sure he spoke about the penis and castration. And after all, surely I wanted to be a good potent analyst? Still kicking myself, I said to him that I had noticed that since my last remark he had gone into his droning voice. He said that when I had added that last phrase about castration he thought I was just dishing out analytic talk, and he just slipped into a tone of futility. Of course what he rightly perceived was that at that moment I had lost interest in him and in making contact with him, and instead was concerned to wave my penis around and say, 'See what a potent analyst am I'.

Each new patient therefore challenges the analyst to further his emotional development. We all flee from emotional contact, especially in those areas where we are not in good emotional contact with ourselves. It is for this reason that I have stressed that the most difficult matter for the analyst is to 'take' a transference. The interpretation of it is relatively easy, but taking a transference has a special difficulty which I shall explain, for the transference is a distorted truth about the analyst.

The analyst is misperceived in some particular way, and very often this is uncongenial to him. It will be uncongenial only if the analyst has not come to terms with that particular element in his own personality. I gave you the example of the psychotherapist whose patient said she was like Mrs Thatcher, and I can think of another therapist whose patient called him a rigid Freudian. He could not bear it, and yet it is necessary to bear it for the following reason.

When the analyst manages to make contact with the healthy developing side of the personality it will always be the case that the infantile side will rise up against the fertilizing analyst. The infantile side will feel the good intercourse between the analyst and patient to be a threat to its existence, as indeed it is, and it will feel the analyst to be authoritarian, or persecuting, or feeble, or cowardly, or uncaring, or 'just like my mother always was', and so on.

Now there is no doubt that if I look into myself I *am* authoritarian, am persecuting, am feeble, cowardly and uncaring. I am not saying that I am like this all the time, but given certain stimuli then these elements will come out. If I cannot come to terms with my cowardice then I will not be able to take it when my patient calls me a coward. That is the type of transference that I will not be able to bear, and demonstrates the meaning of Harold Searles' statement (1975) that in every transference there is some grain (or more than a grain) of truth.

What I am saying is very closely connected to another truth, summed up in the epithet, 'The analyst cannot make an interpretation when he is too anxious about the topic'. If an analyst is very anxious about sexual feelings which he or she is having with a particular patient, he will have difficulty in interpreting the patient's own sexual feelings towards the analyst. I remember that when I was in charge of a small psychotherapy unit a psychiatrist rang me, with some urgency in his voice, to ask if I could see a patient who had been in a group of his for some time. He mentioned that she had been in another group before that, but neither he nor the other psychiatrist had been able to get her settled in the group; he felt she would do much better with individual treatment.

I explained the procedure to be followed by those who wanted psychotherapy at the unit. He said to me, 'But she is a special patient. Could you not see her without going through all those formalities?' I told him that she would have to. The patient duly sent in a letter and a form, and I sent her an appointment, but before she came for it, the psychiatrist was on the telephone again, wondering why I had not seen her. The anxiety in him was palpable and I began to wonder what sort of patient would walk through my door next Tuesday at midday.

It was not a surprise when an attractive and vibrantly sexual girl came into my consulting-room. An hour passed during which she told me many things, but with definite reluctance I said to her, 'I wonder how confident you feel about yourself as a sexual woman?' And there poured out of her a great torrent about her intense feelings of inferiority and low self-esteem as a sexual woman. The apparent sexual vibrancy was the False Self, behind which was a frightened girl who was quite unsure of herself.

I said that I put my question to her with reluctance. I could feel the sexual vibes, and it worried me enough to mean that I had to take an inward gulp before I could put my question to her. I came to believe that the problem with the two psychiatrists had been that they had felt aroused sexually, felt anxious or guilty about it, and then found they could not say anything about the most manifest symptom. This is a rather straightforward example of what I mean when I say that the analyst cannot make an interpretation on a topic about which he is too anxious; there are many which come up every week in analytic work which are more subtle than this. It may take a long time before the analyst can overcome his difficulty, if he ever manages to.

Once an analyst has become aware of his envy in a certain respect, for instance, he can see how he is being stimulated and

he has this material available for interpretation; but what is he
to do *before* he becomes conscious of it? The answer is of
course that he cannot, by definition, do anything about something of which he is not aware. In whom then does the patient
(and the analyst too) put his or her trust?

A female patient said to me once, 'How do I know that you
do not envy my femininity and so block me subtly?' She could
not be certain and I could not be certain. What I was able to
interpret, however, was her phantasy that I did know and then
later her notion that I had power over the process of knowledge. If I wanted to know then I could know, just by a conscious act of will. It was a disappointment to her when she
realized that I, just as much as she did, had to wait for
enlightenment. She then became aware that a process was going
on in the two of us, and that we could not hurry it faster than it
would go. So: there is the patient and the analyst in the consulting-room, but there is also a process. This is the third term in
which trust is ultimately placed. The process of analysis is the
master of both analyst and patient.

What will help the patient (and the analyst) to develop is
emotional understanding. The analyst's job, then, is to make
emotional contact with the patient: it is when an analysis is a
rich emotional experience for both parties that it enables the
patient to grow. Emotional contact, together with understanding, nurtures man's soul and then he can grow and develop to
full capacity. Intellectual understanding alone cannot nurture –
what the patient requires is intersubjective emotional understanding.

I think I can best illustrate this idea from the psychotherapy
of a patient who was mentally handicapped. According to his
records he had an IQ of 59. For many months he was in a great
state of anxiety, and used to pace up and down and around the
consulting-room. I did not feel at ease just sitting down in my
normal chair and watching him, so I used to stand and walk
around the room as well. He pounded me with questions which

I would not answer, but a stage was reached where he began to ask for my picture of him. How did I think of him? He was frantic to know, and shouted to such an extent that on a couple of occasions people knocked at the door, enquiring whether everything was all right, which it obviously wasn't.

During all this time there were two forms of speech: one the direct speech to me and the other, words that slobbered out of the side of his mouth that I was not supposed to hear. In his frantic way of talking he said in the direct speech,

> Well, if you're not going to give me a picture what are you going to give me?

Then there slobbered out of the side of his mouth these words,

> And thirty-three years? Is that all nothing?

I had often heard this particular slobber before, and in a flash I understood that he felt his whole life to be an empty waste so I said to him,

> You want me to give you a picture and I think it is like this. Imagine that you are sitting in a railway carriage and you find yourself facing a man whose face is torn and bleeding and terrible to look at – this is you with thirty-three years of empty waste. You ask me for a picture because with this you can cover up this awful sight.

And he said,

> Well, if you aren't going to give me a picture then what are you here for?

At that point I came and stood beside him and I held his shoulders and said,

> If you've got me here beside you, looking with you, it just might be possible for you to look at this awful thing.

Then there was a sigh followed by a pregnant silence. Then he went over to the chair and collaped into it . . .

   That is what I mean by emotional contact accompanied by understanding. With this patient that moment led to observable change: he no longer pounded me with questions; he usually sat in the chair opposite me like my other patients; his conversation was 'normal', which it had not been before; and his anxiety quotient dropped dramatically. It is these moments of emotional understanding which heal and facilitate real integration.

   I will give you one other example. I was treating a man who hated the long summer break, hated it when I moved house and pressurized me into accepting his view of the world. One day I had a flash of understanding and I said to him,

> You feel me as your baby and you are mother to me and you want to hold me close to you and not let me go. When I go away for the summer break you feel as if I-your-baby have been ripped away from you.

After a long pause he said,

> I get a picture of myself talking to Sarah and pleading with her to stay with me.

I said,

> This is your way of patterning the feeling and understanding it.

He said,

> I have a feeling that Mary's hatred of the analysis has something to do with this.

I said,

> Mary was your baby and you protected her, which she hated, but which she also wanted. When you turned to me and took me as your baby instead she could not bear it.

There was a powerful emotional atmosphere in the room, and it was released through the image of me as his baby and him as my mother. It was a striking realization for him – but for me also. The emotional experience of being a baby with a possessive mother was extremely uncongenial to me, and I have no doubt that it was this which accounted for the long years it took me to see what I have just recounted.

Closely connected to what I have just said is the idea that the analyst must desire his own emotional development. As I have said several times in this series, patients will challenge the analyst to grow emotionally. If the analyst does not want this, or if he reaches middle age and thinks to himself that he will gently settle down, then analysis is at an end for him. Emotional development does not happen smoothly, but by great upheavals that are extremely disturbing; Bion said that during one of these upheavals you do not know whether you are breaking up or breaking down. However, there is no possibility of being a satisfactory analyst if you do not desire your own emotional development; and patients for whom analysis is the appropriate treatment are those who want a revision of their emotional lives. Psychoanalysis is not for the person who has had a breakdown and just wants to start functioning again, because as the analysis proceeds he may have to revise his whole life and alter it radically. I think that psychoanalysis is for those who have a curiosity about life, but also a wish to live it inwardly.

I believe that the only interpretations which really work are those that proceed from the analyst's ego. There is a very powerful group superego operative within the psychoanalytic community and this forms a mythology; I would like to mention a number of these myths. The first is that the patient knows nothing about his analyst; whereas in fact the patient makes quite an accurate assessment of the analyst at the very first interview. This assessment, it is true, is often covered over with illusory elements which partly make up the transference, but the fact remains that the patient learns a lot about the analyst in that first meeting.

Actually there is no doubt that the patient knows the analyst better than his social acquaintances and even friends do. The patient may know fewer biographical facts about the analyst, but these are not the facts that illuminate a person's character. So if this is the case, then is it really necessary to hide oneself so carefully? To be over-careful about not revealing things about oneself limits the richness of analytic possibility. For psychological realities are extremely difficult to describe and convey, and the analyst needs every bit of personal experience available for use.

I once had a patient who was very frightened of violent emotion, but the reason for it was that she did not feel held. At home we used to have one of those rather noisy coffee grinders, and if we put it on and our two-year-old boy was in the kitchen he burst into tears, but if either my wife or I picked him up and held him while the infernal machine was doing its worst he felt all right and did not cry. This was the best analogy I could think of to explain my patient's fear. She could bear violent emotion when she was being held but not when she was not, so I told her about my son and how she was similar in this way.

Similarly, I once wanted to speak about a primitive form of communication with a patient, and the only way I could describe it was to tell him of an incident that George Orwell relates in *Homage to Catalonia*. If I had held back because I thought I should not let him know that I had read this book, then I would not have been able to put into words what I wanted to express. I believe the communication would have been impoverished thereby. Transference is such a powerful emotional phenomenon that I do not think some acknowledgement of personal attitudes interferes with its operation.

It is an ideal within analysis that the patient should tell the analyst everything, but this goal is never fully attained. Every patient keeps his secrets, and even consciously does not reveal everything to his analyst. Further, in every analysis there will be unanalysed areas, even some important areas. This is inevitable, given the limitations of character in the two people. Related to this is the fact that it is not possible for any analyst to hold a neutral stance in relation to his patients, or even in relation to particular aspects of a patient's character as they are manifested in the consulting-room. I think nowhere does this show itself more than in attitudes to pleasure.

The last myth that I want to explode is that the patient needs the analyst, but not the other way round. The analyst does need his patients, and I have not found this more clearly stated than in the paper by John Klauber entitled 'Elements of the Psychoanalytic Relationship and Their Therapeutic Implications':

> Patient and analyst need one another. The patient comes to the analyst because of internal conflicts that prevent him from enjoying life, and he begins to use the analyst not only to resolve them, but increasingly as a receptacle for his pent-up feelings. But the analyst also needs the patient in order to crystallize and communicate his own thoughts, including some of his inmost thoughts on intimate human problems which can only grow organically in the context of this relationship. They cannot be shared and experienced in the same immediate way with a colleague, or even with a husband or wife. (1976, p. 46)

It is only to a patient that an analyst can say certain things, and it is often crucial for his own development that he does say them. Closely related to this point is the fact that the patient also acts as therapist to the analyst. I want to quote here the first paragraph of Harold Searles' article 'The Patient as Therapist to His Analyst':

> This paper is devoted to the hypothesis that innate among man's most powerful strivings towards his fellow men, beginning in the earliest years and even earliest months of life, is an essentially psychotherapeutic striving. The tiny

percentage of human beings who devote their professional careers to the practice of psychoanalysis or psychotherapy are only giving explicit expression to a therapeutic devotion which all human beings share. As for the appreciably larger percentage of human beings who become patients in psychoanalysis or psychotherapy, I am suggesting here not merely that the patient wants to give therapy to, as well as receive therapy from, his doctor; my hypothesis has to do with something far more fundamental than that. I am hypothesizing that the patient *is ill because, and to the degree that,* his own psychotherapeutic strivings have been subjected to such vicissitudes that they have been rendered inordinately intense, frustrated of fulfilment or even acknowledgement, admixed therefore with unduly intense components of hate, envy and competitiveness; and subjected, therefore, to repression. In transference terms, the patient's illness expresses his unconscious attempt to cure the doctor. (1975, p. 103)

I have been cured of deficiencies of character by patients. It has also been clear to me that when I have allowed a patient to heal some character defect of mine, the experience has been enormously enhancing to the patient's ego. The patient definitely gains in ego strength. In particular I have found that this process happens towards the end of an analysis. The patient needs to cure the analyst of a character defect so that the analyst can analyse some element that has eluded effective interpretation until that time; and so that the patient can have the experience of giving something of real value to the analyst. This then becomes an act of gratitude on the patient's part.

The quality which every patient needs of his analyst is self-knowledge. No one knows himself entirely, because every human being is in a constant state of development. What the patient wants to find in his analyst is a process of self-knowledge that accompanies his, the analyst's, development. In the absence of this it is difficult to believe that an analyst can analyse effectively. In the absence of self-knowledge an identification with an ego ideal is substituted, which shrouds the person from self-knowledge. Lacan, for instance, was violently anti-authoritarian and declaimed against the International Psycho-Analytical Association, yet when he was in authority over his own society he was enormously authoritarian, seemingly without knowing it. There are blind spots in all of us, sometimes in areas of importance; but when the blind spot is as gross as in the example just quoted it is difficult to have any confidence that such a person could be a good mediator of the psychoanalytic process.

Lastly, I want to return to the theme with which I opened these lectures: the central importance of truth. Ultimately the mind is healed by truth. This comes before all technique or theoretical approaches, and I have always found that when things have gone seriously wrong it is the baseline to return to and I have never found it to fail. Truth is not the same as honesty; the latter can be in the service of sadism, but truth is servant to no person or thing. It is closely wedded to love and to goodness, which is the *wholeness* of the human person. Psychoanalysis is a servant in that human struggle after goodness. Psychoanalysis is subordinate to truth; it does not possess the truth but has its place in relation to truth along with the natural sciences, human sciences, art, literature, philosophy and religion.

The truths we seek to express are very deep and yet startlingly simple. At the end of a long analysis a patient said to me that he had not heard me say anything which he could not have heard from his mates in the local pub. When I heard this I thought perhaps I had at last begun to become an analyst. There is nothing that I have said in this last lecture that is not extremely obvious; but as I said at the beginning of the series, in the last few years I have come to the conclusion that it is very well worth while stating the obvious.

ADDENDA

Bibliography

Place of publication is London unless otherwise indicated. *SE* denotes James Strachey, ed., *The Standard Edition of the Complete Psychological Works of Sigmund Freud*, 24 vols, Hogarth, 1953-73.

Abraham, Karl (1921) 'Contributions to the Theory of the Anal Character', in Abraham (1949), pp. 370-392.

Abraham, Karl (1924) 'A Short Study of the Development of the Libido, Viewed in the Light of Mental Disorders', in Abraham (1949), pp. 418-501.

Abraham, Karl (1949) *Selected Papers of Karl Abraham*. Hogarth.

Augustine of Hippo (397-8) *Confessions*. Harmondsworth: Penguin, 1961.

Balint, Michael (1959) *Thrills and Regressions*. Hogarth.

Balint, Michael (1968) *The Basic Fault*. London and New York: Tavistock.

Beckett, Samuel (1973) *Not I*. Faber.

Bettelheim, Bruno (1982) 'Freud and the Soul', *New Yorker*, 1 March 1982.

Bettelheim, Bruno (1983) *Freud and Man's Soul*. Chatto & Windus and Hogarth.

Bion, W.R. (1957) 'Differentiation of the Psychotic from the Non-Psychotic Personalities', in Bion (1967), pp. 43-64.

Bion, W.R. (1967) *Second Thoughts*. Heinemann Medical.

Bion, W.R. (1974) *Bion's Brazilian Lectures*, vol. 2. Rio de Janeiro: Imago Editora Ltda.

Bion, W.R. (1979) 'Making the Best of a Bad Job', Unpublished lecture to the British Psycho-Analytical Society.

Brome, Vincent (1980) *Jung*. Granada.

Carotenuto, Aldo (1984) *A Secret Symmetry: Sabina Spielrein between Jung and Freud*. Routledge.

Corbett, Jim (1944) *The Man-Eaters of Kumaon*. Harmondsworth: Penguin, 1964.

Darwin, Charles (1859) *On the Origin of Species*. Harmondsworth: Penguin, 1968.

Eliot, George (1871-2) *Middlemarch*. Harmondsworth:Penguin, 1965.

Ellenberger, H.F. (1970) *The Discovery of the Unconscious*. Allen Lane.

Ellis, Havelock (1900) 'The Analysis of the Sexual Impulse', *The Alienist and Neurologist* 21: 247-262, quoted in Sulloway (1979), p. 309.

Fairbairn, W.R.D. (1941) 'A Revised Psychopathology of the Psychoses and Psychoneuroses', in Fairbairn (1952), pp. 28-58.

Fairbairn, W.R.D. (1952) *Psycho-Analytic Studies of the Personality*. Routledge.

Fairbairn, W.R.D. (1958) 'On the Nature and Aims of Psycho-Analytical Treatment', *Int. J. Psycho-Anal.* 39: 374-385.

Ferenczi, Sandor (1927) 'The Problem of the Termination of the Analysis', in Ferenczi (1955), pp. 77-86.

Ferenczi, Sandor (1928) 'The Elasticity of Psycho-Analytic Technique', in Ferenczi (1955), pp. 87-101.

Ferenczi, Sandor (1930) 'The Principles of Relaxation and Neocatharsis', in Ferenczi (1955), pp. 108-125.

Ferenczi, Sandor (1931) 'Child Analysis in the Analysis of Adults', in Ferenczi (1955), pp. 126-142.

Ferenczi, Sandor (1933) 'Confusion of Tongues between Adults and the Child', in Ferenczi (1955), pp. 156-167.

Ferenczi, Sandor (1955) *Final Contributions to the Problems and Methods of Psycho-Analysis*. Hogarth.

Ferenczi, Sandor, and Rank, Otto (1923) *The Development of Psycho-Analysis*. New York and Washington: Nervous & Mental Disease Publishing Co.

Freud, Sigmund (1888) 'Preface to the Translation of Bernheim's *Suggestion*'. *SE* 1, pp. 71-88.

Freud, Sigmund (1893) 'Charcot'. *SE* 3, pp. 7-24.

Freud, Sigmund (1895) 'Project for a Scientific Psychology'. *SE* 1, pp. 281-397.

Freud, Sigmund (1900) *The Interpretation of Dreams*. *SE* 4-5.

Freud, Sigmund (1905) *Three Essays on the Theory of Sexuality*. *SE* 7, pp. 123-243.

Freud, Sigmund (1913a) 'On Beginning the Treatment'. *SE* 12, pp. 121-144.

Freud, Sigmund (1913b) 'The Disposition to Obsessional Neurosis'. *SE* 12, pp. 311-326.

Freud, Sigmund (1914) 'On Narcissism'. *SE* 14, pp. 67-104.

Freud, Sigmund (1915a) 'Observations on Transference Love'. *SE* 12, pp. 157-171.

Freud, Sigmund (1915b) 'The Unconscious'. *SE* 14, pp. 159-204.

Freud, Sigmund (1915c) 'Instincts and their Vicissitudes'. *SE* 14, pp. 109-140.

Freud, Sigmund (1915d) 'Thoughts for the Times on War and Death'. *SE* 14, pp. 273-300.

Freud, Sigmund (1916a) 'On Transience'. *SE* 14, pp. 303-308.

Freud, Sigmund (1916b) 'Difficulties and First Approaches'. Lecture 5, *Introductory Lectures on Psycho-Analysis*. *SE* 15, pp. 83-99.

Freud, Sigmund (1917) 'Mourning and Melancholia'. *SE* 14, pp. 237-258.

Freud, Sigmund (1919) 'Lines of Advance in Psycho-Analytic Therapy'. *SE* 17, pp. 157-168.

Freud, Sigmund (1920) *Beyond the Pleasure Principle*. *SE* 18, pp. 1-64.

Freud, Sigmund (1921) *Group Psychology and the Analysis of the Ego*. *SE* 18, pp. 65-143.

Freud, Sigmund (1923) *The Ego and the Id*. *SE* 19, pp. 1-59.

Freud, Sigmund (1925) *An Autobiographical Study*. *SE* 20, pp. 1-74.

Freud, Sigmund (1927a) 'Postscript to *The Question of Lay Analysis*'. *SE* 20, pp. 251-258.

Freud, Sigmund (1927b) *The Future of an Illusion*. *SE* 21, pp. 1-56.

Freud, Sigmund (1930) *Civilization and Its Discontents*. *SE* 21, pp. 57-146.

Freud, Sigmund (1933) 'The Dissection of the Psychical Personality'. Lecture 31, *New Introductory Lectures*. *SE* 22, pp. 57-80.

Gallup, Gordon G. (1970) 'Chimpanzees: Self-Recognition', *Science* 167:86-87.

Gosling, Robert (1980) 'Gosling on Bion',*The Tavistock Gazette*, Diamond Jubilee Issue, pp. 22-23.

Greene, Graham (1943) *The Ministry of Fear*. Harmondsworth: Penguin, 1963.

Groddeck, Georg (1922) 'The Compulsion to use Symbols', in Groddeck (1977), pp. 158-171.

Groddeck, Georg (1951). *The Unknown Self*. Vision.

Groddeck, Georg (1977) *The Meaning of Illness*. Hogarth.

Guntrip, Harry (1975) 'My Experience of Analysis with Fairbairn and Winnicott', *Int. Rev. Psycho-Anal.* 2: 145-156.

Heimann, Paula (1950) 'On Counter-Transference', *Int. J. Psycho-Anal.* 31:81-84.

Jahoda, Marie (1977) *Freud and the Dilemmas of Psychology*. Hogarth.

Jones, Ernest (1916) 'The Theory of Symbolism', in Jones (1948), pp. 87-144.

Jones, Ernest (1948) *Papers on Psycho-Analysis*. Baillière, Tindall & Cox.

Jones, Ernest (1953) *Sigmund Freud: Life and Work*, vol. 1. Hogarth.

Jones, Richard M. (1970) *The New Psychology of Dreaming*. Harmondsworth: Penguin, 1978.

Jung, C.G. (1935) *The Tavistock Lectures*, in H. Read, M. Fordham, and G. Adler, eds, *The Collected Works of C.G. Jung*, vol. 18. Routledge.

Jung, C.G. (1963) *Memories, Dreams, Reflections*. Collins and Routledge.

Kafka, Franz (1925) *The Trial*. Harmondsworth: Penguin, 1953.

Kern, Stephen (1973) 'Freud and the Discovery of Child Sexuality', *History of Childhood Quarterly* 1:117-141, quoted in Sulloway (1979), p. 279.

Klauber, John (1966) 'A Particular Form of Transference in Neurotic Depression', in Klauber (1981), pp. 91-108.

Klauber, John (1971) 'The Relationship of Transference and Interpretation', in Klauber (1981), pp. 25-44.

Klauber, John (1976) 'Elements of the Psychoanalytic Relationship and Their Therapeutic Implications', in Klauber (1981), pp 45-62.

Klauber, John (1979) 'Formulating Interpretations in Clinical Psychoanalysis', in Klauber (1981), pp. 109-120.

Klauber, John (1981) *Difficulties in the Analytic Encounter*. New York and London: Jason Aronson.

Klein, George S. (1976) *Psychoanalytic Theory*. New York: Int. Univs Press.

Klein, Melanie (1952) 'The Origins of Transference', in Klein (1975), pp. 48-56.

Klein, Melanie (1957) *Envy and Gratitude*, in Klein (1975), pp. 176-235.

Klein, Melanie (1975) *The Writings of Melanie Klein*, vol. 3. Hogarth.

Kohon, Gregorio, ed. (1985) *The British School of Psychoanalysis: The Independent Tradition*. Free Association Books.

Kris, Ernst (1954) *The Origins of Psycho-Analysis*. Imago.

Laing, R.D. (1985) *Wisdom, Madness and Folly: The Making of a Psychiatrist*. Macmillan.

Maugham, W. Somerset (1938) *The Summing Up*. Pan, 1976.

Maugham, W. Somerset (1951) 'Mr Harrington's Washing', *Collected Short Stories*, vol.3. Pan, 1976, pp. 178-215.

Mead, G.H. (1936) *Movements of Thought in the Nineteenth Century*. Chicago and London: Univ. Chicago Press.

Meltzer, Donald (1983) *Dream-Life*. Strath Tay: Clunie.

Otto, Rudolph (1923) *The Idea of the Holy*. Oxford: Oxford Univ. Press.

Parsons, Talcott (1964) 'The Superego and the Theory of Social Systems', *Social Structure and Personality*. Free Press, pp. 17-33.

Piaget, Jean (1950) *The Psychology of Intelligence*. Routledge.

Piaget, Jean (1953) *The Origin of Intelligence in the Child*. Routledge.

Popham, E.J. (1941) *Proceedings of the Zoological Society of London*, quoted in Sir Alister Hardy, *Darwin and the Spirit of Man*. Collins, 1984, p. 115.

Rank, Otto, and Sachs, Hanns (1913) *Die Bedeutung der Psychoanalyse für die Geisteswissenschaften*. Wiesbaden.

Reich, Wilhelm (1933) *Character Analysis*. Vision, 1950.

Roazen, Paul (1976) *Freud and his Followers*. Allen Lane.

Russell, Bertrand (1967) *The Autobiography of Bertrand Russell*, vol. 1. Allen & Unwin.

Searles, Harold (1975) 'The Patient as Therapist to His Analyst', in

Robert Langs, ed. *Classics in Psycho-Analytic Technique.* New York and London: Jason Aronson, 1981, pp. 103-134.

Segal, Hanna (1957) 'Notes on Symbol Formation', in Segal (1981), pp. 49-65.

Segal, Hanna (1962) 'The Curative Factors in Psycho-Analysis', in Segal (1981), pp. 69-80.

Segal, Hanna (1981) *The Work of Hanna Segal.* New York and London: Jason Aronson.

Sharpe, E.F. (1937) *Dream Analysis.* Hogarth.

Sulloway, F.J. (1979) *Freud, Biologist of the Mind.* Burnett.

Symington, Neville (1983) 'The Analyst's Act of Freedom as Agent of Therapeutic Change', *Int. Rev. Psycho-Anal.* 10: 283-291.

Teilhard de Chardin, Pierre (1957) *Le Milieu Divin.* Fontana.

Van Ophuijsen, J.H.W. (1920) 'On the Origins of the Feeling of Persecution', *Int. J. Psycho-Anal.* 1:235-239.

Whitehead, A.N. (1925) *Science and the Modern World.* New York: Mentor, 1948.

Winnicott, D.W. (1941) 'The Observation of Infants in a Set Situation', in Winnicott (1958), pp. 52-69.

Winnicott, D.W. (1947) 'Hate in the Counter-Transference', in Winnicott (1958), pp. 194-203.

Winnicott, D.W. (1953) 'Symptom Tolerance in Paediatrics', in Winnicott (1958), pp. 101-117.

Winnicott, D.W. (1956) 'Primary Maternal Preoccupation', in Winnicott (1958), pp. 300-305.

Winnicott, D.W. (1958) *Collected Papers: Through Paediatrics to Psychoanalysis.* Tavistock.

Winnicott, D.W.(1969) 'The Use of an Object and Relating through Identifications', in Winnicott (1971), pp. 86-94.

Winnicott, D.W. (1971) *Playing and Reality.* Tavistock.

INDEX

This edition of *The Analytic Experience*
was printed in July 1986.

It was phototypeset in 10/12½ pt Garamond
by a CRTronic 300, the copy having been keyed
on a BBC Micro and transferred via a Discovery 5.
The printing was done on a Harris cold-set web offset press
onto Publishers' Antique Wove 80g/m², vol. 18.

The book was commissioned by Robert M. Young,
edited and word processed by Ann Scott with the
technical assistance of Tony Solomonides, indexed by
Albert Dickson, designed by Carlos Sapochnik
and produced by Free Association Books.